中国国家汉办赠送
Donated by Hanban, China

经典的回声·ECHO OF CLASSICS

雷 雨
THUNDERSTORM

曹禺 著
王佐良 巴恩斯 译

Written by Cao Yu
Translated by Wang Zuoliang and Barnes

外文出版社
FOREIGN LANGUAGES PRESS

图书在版编目（CIP）数据

雷雨：汉英对照 / 曹禺 著；王佐良 巴恩斯 译.
－北京：外文出版社，2001
(经典的回声)
ISBN 7-119-02775-1
I. 雷… II. ①曹… ②王… ③巴… III. 英语－对照读物，话剧－汉、英
IV. H319.4：I
中国版本图书馆 CIP 数据核字（2000）第 78567 号

外文出版社网址：
　http://www.flp.com.cn
外文出版社电子信箱：
　info@flp.com.cn
　sales@flp.com.cn

经典的回声（汉英对照）

雷　雨

作　　者	曹　禺
译　　者	王佐良　巴恩斯
责任编辑	刘春英　胡开敏
封面设计	陈　军
印刷监制	张国祥
出版发行	外文出版社
社　　址	北京市百万庄大街 24 号　　邮政编码　100037
电　　话	（010）68320579（总编室）
	（010）68329514 / 68327211（推广发行部）
印　　刷	北京市铁成印刷厂
经　　销	新华书店 / 外文书店
开　　本	大 32 开　　　　　　　　字　数　250 千字
印　　张	13.25
版　　次	2006 年 3 月第 1 版第 3 次印刷
装　　别	平装
书　　号	ISBN 7-119-02775–1 / I · 174（外）
定　　价	20.00 元

版权所有　侵权必究

出 版 前 言

  本社专事外文图书的编辑出版，几十年来用英文翻译出版了大量的中国文学作品和文化典籍，上自先秦，下迄现当代，力求全面而准确地反映中国文学及中国文化的基本面貌和灿烂成就。这些英译图书均取自相关领域著名的、权威的作品，英译则出自国内外译界名家。每本图书的编选、翻译过程均极其审慎严肃，精雕细琢，中文作品及相应的英译版本均堪称经典。

  我们意识到，这些英译精品，不单有对外译介的意义，而且对国内英文学习者、爱好者及英译工作者，也是极有价值的读本。为此，我们对这些英译精品做了认真的遴选，编排成汉英对照的形式，陆续推出，以飨读者。

外文出版社

Publisher's Note

Foreign Languages Press is dedicated to the editing, translating and publishing of books in foreign languages. Over the past several decades it has published, in English, a great number of China's classics and records as well as literary works from the Qin down to modern times, in the aim to fully display the best part of the Chinese culture and its achievements. These books in the original are famous and authoritative in their respective fields, and their English translations are masterworks produced by notable translators both at home and abroad. Each book is carefully compiled and translated with minute precision. Consequently, the English versions as well as their Chinese originals may both be rated as classics.

It is generally considered that these English translations are not only significant for introducing China to the outside world but also useful reading materials for domestic English learners and translators. For this reason, we have carefully selected some of these books, and will publish them successively in Chinese-English bilingual form.

Foreign Languages Press

目　　录
CONTENTS

登场人物　时间和地点	2
第一幕	4
第二幕	120
第三幕	230
第四幕	318

THE CHARACTERS	3
ACT ONE	5
ACT TWO	121
ACT THREE	231
ACT FOUR	319

曹禺像
The picture of Cao Yu

登场人物

周朴园(朴)——某煤矿公司董事长,五十五岁。
周繁漪(繁)——其妻,三十五岁。
周　萍(萍)——其前妻生子,年二十八。
周　冲(冲)——繁漪生子,年十七。
鲁　贵(贵)——周宅仆人,年四十八。
鲁侍萍(鲁)——其妻,某校女佣,年四十七。
鲁大海(大)——侍萍前夫之子,煤矿工人,年二十七。
鲁四凤(四)——鲁贵与侍萍之女,年十八,周宅使女。
周宅仆人等:仆人甲,仆人乙……老仆。

时间和地点

第一幕　夏天,郁热的早晨。
　　　　——周公馆的客厅内。

第二幕　当天的下午。
　　　　——景同第一幕。

第三幕　当天夜晚十时许。
　　　　——在鲁家一个小套间。

第四幕　当天半夜后。
　　　　——景同第一幕。

THE CHARACTERS

ZHOU PUYUAN, *55, chairman of the board of directors of a coal-mining company*
ZHOU FANYI, *35, his wife*
ZHOU PING, *28, his son by a former marriage*
ZHOU CHONG, *17, his younger son by his present wife*
LU GUI, *48, his servant*
LU SHIPING or LU MA, *47, Lu Gui's wife, employed as a servant in a school*
LU DAHAI, *27, her son by a former marriage, a miner*
LU SIFENG, *18, her daughter by her present husband, a maid at the Zhous'*
Various other servants in the house

*

ACT ONE — *In the Zhous' drawing-room.*
    TIME — *a sultry summer morning.*

ACT TWO — *The same.*
    TIME — *the afternoon of the same day.*

ACT THREE — *In a little inner room at the Lus'.*
    TIME — *ten o'clock that evening.*

ACT FOUR — *The same as Act One.*
    TIME — *after midnight that night.*

第一幕

一个夏天的上午,在周宅的客厅里。左右侧各有一门,一通饭厅,一通书房,中间的门开着,隔一层铁纱门,从纱门望出去,花园的树木绿荫荫的,听得见蝉叫声。右边一座大衣柜,铺着一张黄桌布,上面放着许多摆设。触目的是一张旧相片,很不调和地和这些精致东西放在一起。右边壁炉上有一只钟,墙上挂一幅油画。炉前有两把圈椅。中间靠左的玻璃柜里放满了古玩。柜前有一张小矮凳,左角摆一张长沙发,上面放着三四个缎制的厚垫子。沙发前的矮几上放着烟具等物,台中偏右两个小沙发同圆桌,桌上放着吕宋烟盒和扇子。

所有的帷幔都是崭新的,家具非常洁净,有金属的地方都放着光彩。

郁热逼人。屋中很气闷,外面没有阳光,

Act One

It is a summer morning in the drawing-room at the Zhous'. A door on the left leads to the dining-room and one on the right to the study. A third door stands open in the middle, and through the wire-gauze screen in front of it the shady green of the trees in the garden can be seen and the shrilling of cicadas can be heard. An old-fashioned bureau stands against the wall to the right of the door, covered with a yellow runner. A number of objets d'art are arranged on it and also, conspicuously out of place, an old photograph. On the right-hand wall is the fireplace, with a clock on the mantelpiece, and on the wall above hangs an oil painting. In front of the fireplace are two armchairs. To the left of the centre door is a glass case full of curios, with a stool in front of it. The lefthand corner is occupied by a sofa with several plump, satin-covered cushions on it, in front of this stands a low table with a cigarette-box and ash-trays on it. In the centre of the stage and slightly to the right are two small sofas with a round table between them, and on this table are a cigar-box and a fan.

The curtains are new, the furniture is spotless, and all the metal fittings are gleaming.

It is close and oppressive, and the room is stuffy. Outside is a grey, overcast sky. A thunderstorm

天空灰暗,是将要落暴雨的气氛。

　　开幕时,四凤在靠中墙的长方桌旁,背着观众滤药,她不时地揩着脸上的汗。鲁贵——她的父亲——在沙发旁擦着矮几上的银烟具。

　　四凤约有十七八岁,脸上红润,是个健康的少女。她整个的身体都很发育,手很白很大,走起路来,过于发育的乳房很显明地在衣服底下颤动着。她穿一件旧的纺绸的裤子,一双略旧的布鞋。她全身都非常整洁,举动活泼。经过两年在周家的训练,她说话很大方,爽快,却很有分寸。她的一双大而有长睫毛的水凌凌的眼睛能够很灵敏地转动,也能敛一敛眉头,很庄严地注视着。她有大的嘴,嘴唇自然红艳艳的,很宽,很厚,当着她笑的时候,牙齿整齐地露出来,嘴旁也显着一对笑涡。然而她面部整个轮廓是很庄重地显露着诚恳。她的面色不十分白,天气热,鼻尖微微有点汗,她时时用手绢揩着。她很爱笑,她知道自己是好看的,但是她现在皱着眉头。

　　她的父亲——鲁贵——约莫四十多岁的样子,神气萎缩,最令人注目的是粗而乱的眉

seems imminent.

When the curtain rises, Lu Sifeng is standing at a table against the centre wall with her back to the audience, filtering medicine and wiping her perspiring face every now and then. Her father, Lu Gui, is polishing the silver cigarette-box on the low table in front of the sofa.

Sifeng is a healthy, rosy-cheeked girl of eighteen with a well-developee figure and large white hands. When she walks, the movement of her over-developed breasts is plainly visible under her clothes. Her silk slacks and cloth slippers are old and slightly worn, yet she is neatly dressed and brisk in her movements. Her two years' service with the Zhous has taught her poise and ease of manner, but this does not mean that she does not know her place. Her big, limpid eyes with their long lashes will dance with animation or, when she frowns, stare gravely. Her mouth is large, with full lips that are naturally and deliciously red. When she smiles, we see that her teeth are good, and a dimple appears on each corner of her mouth, yet her face as a whole retains its expression of dignity and sincerity. Her complexion is not particularly fair. The beat has brought a faint perspiration to her nose, and she dabs it from time to time with a handkerchief. She is aware of her good looks and usually enhances them with a smile — though just at the moment she is frowning.

Her father, Lu Gui, is a mean-faced man in his forties, whose most conspicuous features are his thick, bushy eyebrows and his swollen eyelids. His

毛同肿眼皮。他的嘴唇，松弛地垂下来，和他眼下凹进去的黑圈，都表示着极端的肉欲放纵。他的身体较胖，面上的肌肉宽弛地不大动，但也能很卑贱地谄笑着。和许多大家的仆人一样，他很懂事，尤其是很懂礼节。他的背略有点伛偻，似乎永远欠着身子向他的主人答应着"是"。他的眼睛锐利，常常贪婪地窥视着，如一只狼。他很能计算的。他穿的虽然华丽，但是不整齐。现在他用一条抹布擦着东西，脚下是他刚刷好的黄皮鞋。时而，他用自己的衣襟揩脸上的油汗。

贵：四凤！

　　四凤装做不听见，依然滤她的汤药。

贵：四凤！

四：（看了她父亲一眼）喝，真热。（走向右边的柜旁，寻一把芭蕉扇扇着。）

贵：（望着她，停下工作）四凤，你听见了没有？

四：（冷冷地）干什么？爸。

贵：我问你听见我刚才说的话了么？

四：都知道了。

loose, pendulous lips and the dark hollows under his eyes tell a tale of unbridled sensual indulgence. He is rather fat, and his flabby face remains expressionless most of the time, though he will put on a cringing, obsequious smile when occasion demands. Like most servants in big houses, he is shrewd and has faultless manners. He has a slight stoop, which gives him the appearance of being for ever on the point of saying "Very good, sir," but the look of greed and slyness never leaves his sharp, wolfish eyes. He is astute and calculating. His clothes are showy but untidy. At the moment he is rubbing the silver cigarette-box over with a duster. On the floor at his feet is a pair of brown shoes which he has just polished. Every now and then he wipes his perspiring face with the loose skirts of his long gown.

LU GUI: Sifeng!

(*She pretends not to hear, but goes on filtering the medicine.*)

LU: Sifeng!

SIFENG (*with a glance at her father*): Whew isn't it hot! (*She walks over to the bureau, picks up a palm-leaf fan and begins to fan herself with it.*)

LU (*stopping what he is doing and looking across at her*): Did you heas what I said, sifeng?

FENG (*unconcernedly*): Why, what is it now, Dad?

LU: I mean did you hear what I was telling you a moment ago?

FENG: Yes, every word of it.

贵：(一向是这样被女儿看待的，只好抗议似地)妈的，这孩子！

四：(回过头来)您少说闲话吧！(挥扇，嘘出一口气)天气这样闷热，回头多半下雨。(忽然)老爷出门穿的皮鞋，您擦好了没有？(到鲁贵面前，拿起一只皮鞋，不经意地)这是您擦的！这么随随便便抹了两下——老爷的脾气您可知道。

贵：(一把抢过鞋)我的事用不着你管。四凤，你听着，我再跟你说一遍，回头见着你妈，别忘了把新衣服都拿出来给她瞧瞧。

四：(不耐烦)听见了。

贵：叫她想想，还是你爸爸混事有眼力，还是她有眼力。

四：(轻蔑地)自然您有眼力啊！

贵：你还别忘了告诉你妈，你在这儿周公馆吃的好，喝的好，就是白天侍候太太少爷，晚上还是听她的话，回家睡觉。

四：那倒不用告诉，妈自然会问的。

贵：(得意)还有啦，钱，(贪婪地笑着)你手下也有不少钱啦！

LU (*who is used to being treated like this by his daughter and so can do nothing more than make a feeble protest*): Oh, what's the use of talking to you?

FENG (*looking round at him*): You talk too much! (*Fanning herself vigorously.*) Whew! With the weather as close as this, ten to one it'll rain presently. (*Suddenly.*) Have you cleaned the master's shoes that he'll be wearing to go out? (*She goes across, picks up one of the shoes and glances contemptuously at it.*) You call this cleaned? Just a couple of wipes with a duster! You just wait till the master sees them, and then you'll be for it!

LU (*snatching the shoe from her*): I'll thank you to mind your own business! — Now listen, Sifeng, while I tell you again: when you see your mother presently, don't forget to get all your new clothes out and show them to her.

FENG (*impatiently*): I heard you the first time.

LU: Let her see who knows what's best for you, she or your dad!

FENG (*contemptuously*): Why, you, of course!

LU: And don't forget to tell her how well you're treated here — good food, light work, just waiting on the mistress and the young gentlemen in the daytime and going straight home in the evening just as she told you to do.

FENG: There's no need for me to tell her that, because she's sure to ask anyway.

LU (*gloatingly*): And then, the money! (*Laughing avariciously.*) You must have quite a bit put by!

11

四:钱!?

贵:这两年的工钱,赏钱,(意有所指地)还有那零零碎碎的,他们……

四:(不愿意听他要说的话)那您不是一块两块都要走了么?喝了,赌了。

贵:你看,你看,你又急了,急什么?我不跟你要钱。喂,我说,我说的是——(低声)他——不是也不断地塞给你钱花么?

四:(惊讶)他?谁呀?

贵:(索性说出来)大少爷。

四:(红了脸)谁说大少爷给我钱?爸爸,您别又穷疯了,胡说乱道的。

贵:好,好,好,没有,没有。反正这两年你不是存点钱么?我不是跟你要钱,你放心。我说啊,等你妈来,把这些钱也给她瞧瞧,叫她也开开眼。

四:哼,妈不像您,见钱就忘了命。(回到中间茶桌滤药。)

贵:(坐在长沙发上,得意地)钱不钱,你没有你爸爸成么?要不到这儿周家大公馆帮主儿,这两年尽听你妈的话,你能每天吃着喝着,

FENG: Money?

LU: Yes, two years' pay, and tips, and — (*meaningfully*) and the odd little sums every now and then, which they —

FENG (*cutting him short*): Yes, and you've relieved me of every penny of it, a dollar or two at a time! And it's all gone on drinking and gambling!

LU: There you go again! Getting worked up over nothing! Don't worry, I'm not after your money. No, what I mean is — (*lowering his voice*) he — er — hasn't he been giving you money?

FENG (*taken aback*): He? Who?

LU (*bluntly*): Master Ping.

FENG (*crimsoning*): What on earth do you mean? Master Ping giving me money indeed! You must be off your head, Dad, talking such nonsense!

LU: All right, all right, so he hasn't, then. But in any case you must have saved quite a bit these last two years. — Don't worry, I'm not after your money. All I meant was you can show it to your mother when she comes. That'll be an eye-opener for her!

FENG: Humph! Mother isn't like you — show you a handful of coppers and you'll break your neck to get at it! (*She goes back to the table to attend to the medicine.*)

LU (*sitting down on the sofa with a smirk*): Money or no money, where do you think you'd be without your old dad? If you'd taken your mother's advice over the last two years instead of coming to work in a big house like this, you surely don't

大热天还穿得上小纺绸么?

四:哼,妈是个本分人,念过书的,讲脸,舍不得把自己的女儿叫人家使唤。

贵:什么脸不脸?又是你妈的那一套!你是谁家的小姐?——妈的,底下人的女儿,帮了人就失了身分啦?

四:(厌恶地)爸,您看您那一脸的油!——您把那皮鞋再擦擦吧。

贵:讲脸呢,又学你妈那点穷骨头,你看她,她要脸!跑他妈的八百里外女学堂里当老妈。为着一月八块钱,两年才回一趟家。这叫本分,还念过书呢!简直是没出息。

四:(忍气)您留几句回家说吧,这是人家周公馆。

贵:咦,周公馆也挡不住我跟我女儿谈家务啊,我跟你说,你的妈……

四:(突然)我跟您先说下,妈可是好容易才回一趟家。这次,也是看哥哥跟我来的,您要是

imagine you'd be living as comfortably as you are now! And you wouldn't be wearing nice, cool silk clothes in the middle of summer, either!

FENG: Yes, but mother has her principles. She's educated, and she can't bear to see her own daughter at someone else's beck and call. She's got her pride, you know.

LU: Pride be damned! If that isn't just like her! What do you think you are, an heiress? Pooh! A servant's daughter, and it's beneath her dignity to go into service!

FENG (*disgustedly*): Look at your face, Dad. You might at least wipe it! — And you'd better have another go at those shoes, too.

LU: Pride indeed! If you insist on giving yourself airs you'll end up a poor, miserable creature like her. Pride? Just look at her! She travels three hundred miles to be a skivvy in this girls' school of hers, and all for the sake of eight dollars a month and the privilege of coming home once every two years! That's where her "principles" have got her! So much for her "education"! A lot of good that's done her!

FENG (*restraining herself*): You'd better keep that until we get home. Remember you're at the Zhous' now, not in your own house.

LU: Why should that stop me discussing my family affairs with my own daughter? Now, listen here: Your mother —

FENG (*suddenly*): Just a minute! I've got something to tell you first. It isn't every day that mother can get home, and when she does it's only to see Da-

再给她一个不痛快,我就把您这两年做的事都告诉哥哥。

贵:我,我,我做了什么事啦?(觉得在女儿面前失了面子)喝点、赌点、玩点,这三样,我快五十的人啦,还怕他么?

四:他才懒得管您这些事呢!——可是他每月从矿上寄给妈用的钱,您偷偷地花了,他知道了,就不会答应您!

贵:那他敢怎么样?(高声地)他妈嫁给我,我就是他爸爸。

四:小声点!这有什么喊头。

贵:哼!(滔滔地)我跟你说,我娶你妈,我还抱老大的委屈呢。你看我这么个机灵人,这周家上上下下几十口子,哪一个不说我鲁贵聒聒叫。来这里不到两个月,我的女儿就在这公馆找上事,就说你哥哥,没有我,能在周家的矿上当工人么?叫你妈说,她成么?——这样,你哥哥同你妈还是一个劲儿地不赞成

hai and me. If you so much as say a word to upset her, I'll tell Dahai just what you've been up to these last two years.

LU: Me? And what have I done, pray? (*Feeling that his paternal dignity is at stake*.) If you mean I've had a little drink and a flutter now and then, and a bit of fun with the girls, well, what of it? After all, I'm nearly fifty. What's it to him, anyway?

FENG: Oh, he couldn't care less about that sort of thing! But what's happened to the money he sends home from the mine every month for mother? You've spent every penny of it on the sly, and if he found out about it he wouldn't let you get away with it!

LU: What could he do about it? (*Raising his voice*.) His mother's married to me, so I'm his father!

FENG: Ssh! No need to shout.

LU: Humph! (*With sudden eloquence*.) Now just you listen to me. I've never stopped blaming myself for marrying your mother. To think that a smart chap like me should go and do a thing like that! Now is there a single person in all this big house who doesn't think I'm one of the best? I hadn't been here two months when I got my own daughter a nice job in the house, and even your brother — he'd never have got that job in the Zhous' mine if I hadn't put in a word for him. Could your mother ever have done as much for the two of you? And what thanks do I get for it? Your mother and your brother are still ganged up against me as much as ever! If she still tries to

17

我。这次回来,你妈要还是那副寡妇脸子,我就当你哥哥的面上不认她,说不定就离了她,别看她替我养个女儿,外带来你这个倒楣蛋的哥哥——

四:爸爸。您——

贵:哼,谁知道是哪个王八蛋养的儿子。

四:哥哥哪点对不起您,您这样骂他干什么?

贵:他哪一点对得起我?当大兵,拉包月车,干机器匠,念书上学,哪一行他是好好地干过!好容易我荐他到了周家的矿上去,他又跟工头闹起来,把人家打啦。

四:(小心地)我听说,不是我们老爷先叫矿上的警察开了枪,工人们才动的手么?

贵:反正这孩子混蛋,吃人家的钱粮,就得受人家的管。好好的,要罢工,现在又得靠我这老面子跟老爷求情啦!

四:你听错了吧。哥哥说他自己要见老爷,不是找您求情来的。

贵:(得意)可谁教我是他爸爸呢,我不能不管

put on airs and come the great lady over me this time, I'll disown her, and in front of your brother, too! I may even divorce her, even if she has given me a daughter — and brought along that come-by-chance of hers into the bargain!

FENG: Dad! How can —

LU: God knows what bastard fathered him!

FENG: What right have you to say such things about Dahai? What's he ever done to upset you?

LU: What's he ever done to make me feel proud of him, I'd like to know? He's tried his hand at being a soldier, a rickshaw boy, a mechanic, a student — he's been a Jack of all trades, but hasn't stuck to any of them for long. After all the trouble I had getting him this job in the mine, he has to go and spoil everything by picking a quarrel with his foreman and beating him up!

FENG (*cautiously*): But from what I heard, the men didn't do anything until the master told the police at the mine to open fire on them.

LU: Whatever happened, the boy's a bloody fool. He should have had enough sense to realize that if somebody's paying your wages you've got to take orders from them. But no: he has to down tools, and then come and try and get round his poor old dad to smooth things out with the master for him.

FENG: You've got it all wrong, I'm afraid. He's not asking you to do anything of the sort. He said he's coming to see the master himself.

LU (*smugly*): Well, after all, I am his father, and I can't very well just stand aside and let him get on

四:(轻蔑地看着她的父亲,叹了一口气)好,您歇歇吧,我要上楼给太太送药去了。(端起药碗向左边饭厅走。)

贵:你先等一会儿,我再说一句话。

四:(打岔)开午饭了,普洱茶先泡好了没有?

贵:那用不着我,他们小当差早侍候到了。

四:哦,那我走了。

贵:(拦住她)四凤,你别忙,我跟你商量点事。

四:什么?

贵:你听啊,昨天不是老爷的生日么?大少爷也赏给我四块钱。

四:好极了,(口快地)我要是大少爷,我一个子儿也不给您。

贵:(鄙笑)这话有理!四块钱,够干什么的,还了点账就干了。

四:(伶俐地)那回头您跟哥哥要吧。

贵:四凤,别——你爸爸什么时候借钱不还账?现在你手下方便,随便匀给我七块八块的好么?

四:我没有钱。(停一下)您真是还账了么?

with it on his own, now, can I?

FENG (*eyeing him contemptuously and heaving a sigh*): Well, if you'll excuse me I'll take this medicine up to the mistress. (*She picks up the little bowl and goes towards the dining-room door.*)

LU: Just a minute. I've got something else to tell you —

FENG (*in an effort to change the subject*): It's nearly lunchtime. Have you made the Yunnan tea yet?

LU: That's no concern of mine. The girls will have seen to that.

FENG: Mm, well, I'd better be off.

LU (*standing in her way*): What's the hurry, Sifeng? There's something I'd like to talk over with you.

FENG: What?

LU: You know yesterday was the master's birthday? Well, Master Ping gave me a tip — four dollars.

FENG: Very nice too. (*Letting her tongue run away with her.*) — Though I wouldn't give you a penny if I were him!

LU (*laughing coarsely*): There's something in that, too! What can you do with four dollars, anyway? I paid off a debt or two and now I'm broke again.

FENG (*adroitly*): You'd better touch Dahai for a few dollars, then, when he comes.

LU: Don't be like that, Sifeng. When did I ever borrow money and not pay it back? Now, what about a little loan of seven or eight dollars, now that you're in the money?

FENG: I haven't got any money. (*She pauses a moment.*) Did you really use that money to pay off

贵：真的！（赌咒）我跟我的亲生女儿说瞎话是王八蛋！——说起来这不怪我。昨天那几个零钱，还大账不够，小账剩点零，所以我就耍了两把，也许赢了钱，不都还了么？谁知运气不好，连喝带输，还倒欠了十来块。

四凤望着鲁贵。

贵：这可一句瞎话也没有。

四：那我实实在在地告诉您，我也没有钱！（说完就要拿起药碗。）

贵：(着急)凤儿，你这孩子是什么心思？你可是我的亲生孩子。

四：亲生的女儿也不能见天见地替您老人家还赌账啊！

贵：(严重地)孩子，你可放明白点，你妈疼你，只在嘴上，我可是把你的什么要紧的事情，都放在心上。

四：(明白他有所指)您又要说什么？

贵：(四面望了一望，逼近四凤)我说，大少爷常跟我提过你，大少爷，他说——

your debts?

LU: Of course! (*With an air of injured innocence.*) You don't think I'd sink so low as to tell lies to my own daughter! — Though it isn't really my fault that I'm in debt now. The measly little tip I got yesterday wasn't enough to pay off the big debts, though there was some left over after I'd paid off the small ones, so I had a couple of games of cards with the rest — you see, I hoped I'd win enough to get out of debt once and for all. How was I to know I was going to have a run of bad luck? Anyway, what with the losses and a few drinks, I'm now in debt to the tune of ten dollars. (*Sifeng stares hard at her father.*) And that's the truth, every word of it.

FENG: Then let me tell you something that's just as true: I haven't got any money, either! (*She goes to pick up the bowl of medicine again.*)

LU (*becoming agitated*): Now, Sifeng. What's the matter? You're my own daughter, aren't you?

FENG: Yes, but even your own daughter can't be expected to pay your gambling debts for ever!

LU (*solemnly*): Now, my dear girl, be reasonable. Your mother only talks about loving you, whereas I take a real interest in everything that concerns you.

FENG (*realizing that he is hinting at something*): What else is worrying you?

LU (*after a swift glance all round he moves closer to her*): Listen. Master Ping often talks to me about you. Well, he says —

四：(管不住自己)大少爷！大少爷！你疯了！——我走了，太太就要叫我呢。

贵：别走，我问你，前天我看见大少爷买衣料——

四：(沉下脸)怎么样？

贵：(上下打量)嗯——(盯住四凤的手)这戒指，(笑着)不也是他送给你的么？

四：(厌恶地)您看您说话的神气！

贵：你不必这样假门假事，你是我的女儿。(忽然贪婪地笑着)一个当差的女儿，收人家点东西，用人家一点钱，没有什么说不过去的。这不要紧，我都明白。

四：您就直说吧，究竟要多少钱用？

贵：不多，三十块钱就成了。

四：哦，那您就跟您那大少爷要去吧。

贵：(恼羞)好孩子，你以为我真装糊涂，不知道你同那混账大少爷做的事么？

四：(压住怒气)您是父亲么？父亲有跟女儿这样说话的么？

FENG (*unable to contain herself*): Master Ping, Master Ping all the time! You're off your head! — Well, I'm going. The mistress will be asking for me in a minute.

LU: No, don't go. Just let me ask you one thing. The other day I saw Master Ping buying material for a dress —

FENG (*darkly*): Well, what of it?

LU (*looking her up and down*): Well — (*his eyes now rest on her hand*) this ring — (*laughing*) didn't he give you this, too?

FENG (*with disgust*): The nasty-minded way you talk about everything!

LU: You don't have to put on an act with me. After all, you are my daughter. (*With a sudden avaricious laugh.*) Don't worry, there's nothing wrong in a servant's daughter accepting gifts or money from people. Nothing wrong at all. I quite understand.

FENG: Don't beat about the bush. Exactly how much do you want?

LU: Not much. Thirty dollars would do.

FENG: I see. Well, you'd better try and touch your Master Ping for it.

LU (*mortified and angered*): Now look here, my girl, you don't really think I'm such a fool that I don't know what's going on between you and that young scoundrel?

FENG (*suppressing her anger*): Call yourself a father? That's a fine way to talk to your own daughter, I must say!

贵：我是你的爸爸，我就要管你。我问你，前天晚上——

四：前天晚上？

贵：我不在家，你半夜才回来，你干什么来着？

四：(掩饰)我替太太找东西呢。

贵：为什么那么晚才回家？

四：(轻蔑地)您这样的父亲没有资格来问我。

贵：好文明词！你就说不上你上哪儿去了。

四：那有什么说不上！

贵：那你说！

四：那是太太听说老爷刚回来，又要我捡老爷的衣服。

贵：哦，(低声，恐吓地)可是半夜送你回家的那位是谁？坐着汽车，醉醺醺，直对你说胡话的那位是谁呀？(得意地微笑。)

四：那，那——

贵：(大笑)你不用说了，那是我们鲁家的阔女婿！——哼，我们两间半破瓦房居然来了坐汽车的男朋友，找我这当差的女儿啦！(严厉)我问你，他是谁？你说。

LU: It's just because I am your father that I have to keep an eye on you. Now, tell me, the night before last —

FENG: The night before last?

LU: Yes, the night when I wasn't at home. You didn't turn up till midnight. What had you been doing all that time?

FENG (*inventing an excuse*): I had to hunt out some things for the mistress.

LU: And what kept you out so late?

FENG (*contemptuously*): A father like you has no right to ask such questions.

LU: Ho, getting superior, aren't we! You still can't tell me where you were, though.

FENG: Who says I can't?

LU: Come on, then, let's hear it.

FENG: Well, as a matter of fact, the mistress heard that the master had just got back, and she wanted me to get his clothes out ready for him.

LU: I see. (*In a menacing undertone.*) And who was the gentleman who brought you home in a car at midnight that night! — The one who'd had a drop too much and kept talking a lot of nonsense to you? (*He smiles triumphantly.*)

FENG: Well — er —

LU (*with a roar of laughter*): No, you needn't tell me: it was our rich son-in-law, of course! To think that our rickety little hovel should be honoured by a visit from a gentleman in a car, running round after a servant's daughter! (*Suddenly stern.*) Now, tell me, who was it?

雷雨

四凤愣住。

鲁大海——四凤的哥哥，鲁贵的半子——进，他身体魁伟，眉毛粗而黑，两颊微微地向内凹，方方的下巴和锐利的眼睛，都表现他的性格的倔强。他有一张薄薄的嘴唇，正和他的妹妹带着南方的热情的，厚而红的嘴唇形成强烈的对照。他说话微微有点口吃似的，但是在他的感情激昂的时候，词锋是锐利的。现在他刚从六百里外的煤矿回来。矿里罢了工，他是煽动者之一。几月来的精神的紧张，使他现在露出有点疲乏的神色，胡须乱蓬蓬的，看去几乎老得像鲁贵的弟弟。只有逼近地观察他，才觉出他的眼神同声音，还正是和他的妹妹一样年轻，一样地热，都是像火山要爆发，满蓄着精力的白热的人物。他穿了一件工人的蓝布褂子，油渍的草帽拿在手里，一双黑皮鞋，有一根鞋带早不知落在哪里。进门的时候，他略微有点不自在。

他说话很简短，表面是冷冷的。

大：凤儿！

四：哥哥！

贵：(向四凤)你说呀！装什么哑巴。

四：(看大海)哥哥！

(*Sifeng is speechless.*)

(*At this moment. Lu Dahai — Sifeng's half-brother and Lu Gui's stepson — comes in. He is tall and powerfully built, with bushy black eyebrows and slightly hollow cheeks. His stubborn character shows in his square jaw and his piercing eyes. His lips are thin, in striking contrast to his sister's, which are the full, red lips of a passionate southerner. He speaks with a slight stutter, but when he gets excited his tongue can have a sharp edge to it. At the moment he has just arrived from the coal-mine two hundred miles away where he has helped to organize a strike. The strain of the past few months has told on him and aged him. Weary and unshaven, he lookes old enough to be Lu Gui's brother, and only the closest observation reveals that his eyes and his voice are just as youthful and ardent as his sister's. Like her, he is inwardly consumed by the white-hot passions of youth and has the latent energy of a simmering volcano. He wears a miner's short jacket of coarse blue cotton and in his hand is a greasy straw hat. One of his shoes has lost its lace. As he comes in, he seems rather ill at ease. His speech is terse, which makes him appear cold and aloof.*)

DAHAI: Sifeng!

FENG: Dahai!

LU (*to Sifeng*): Now, come on! Don't pretend you're dumb.

FENG (*appealing to her brother*): Dahai!

贵：(不顾)你哥哥来也得说呀。

大：怎么回事？

贵：你先别管。

四：哥哥，没什么要紧的事。(向鲁贵)好吧，爸，我们回头商量。

贵：回头商量？(再盯四凤一眼)好，就这样办。(向大海，傲慢地)咦，你怎么随随便便跑进来啦？

大：(简单地)我在门房等了半天了。

贵：大海，到底你是矿上打粗的，连一点大公馆的规矩也不懂。

四：人家不是周家的底下人。

贵：你在矿上吃的也是周家的饭哪。

大：(冷冷地)他在哪儿？

贵：(故意地)他，谁是他？

大：董事长。

贵：老爷就是老爷，什么董事长，上我们这儿就得叫老爷。

大：你给我问他一声，说矿上的工人代表来了。

贵：我看，你先回家去。(有把握地)矿上的事有你爸爸在这儿替你张罗。回头跟你妈，妹妹

LU (*ignoring this*): It makes no difference with your brother here. I still want to know.
HAI: What's the matter?
LU: None of your business.
FENG: It's nothing important, Dahai. (*To her father.*) It's all right, Dad, we can talk it over later on.
LU: Later on? (*He gives her a significant glance.*) All right, then, we'll leave it. (*To Dahai, haughtily.*) Now then, what do you mean by just barging in like this! Where's your manners?
HAI (*simply*): I got fed up with waiting in the porter's lodge.
LU: That's just like you, Dahai, a ham-fisted miner without the least idea how to behave in a big house.
FENG: He's not a servant here, you know.
LU: His wages still come out of the Zhous' pocket, though.
HAI (*coldly*): Where is he?
LU (*pretending not to understand*): "He?" Who's "he"?
HAI: The company chairman.
LU: If you mean the master, then say so. Whatever he's called at the mine, he's "the master" to you while you're in this house.
HAI: Tell him the miners' representative has come to see him.
LU: I think you'd better go home first. (*Confidently.*) You needn't worry about your job at the mine; leave it to your old dad to straighten every-

聚两天。等你妈走,你回到矿上,事由还是有你的。

大:我们的事你不懂,就别再操心了。

四:(希望鲁贵走)爸,你还是看看老爷的客走了没有,再领着哥哥见老爷。

贵:(摇头)哼,我怕他不会见你吧。

大:(理直气壮)你告诉他,工人代表鲁大海要见他。他把我们约来的,就前天,已经在这儿的公司见过他啦。

贵:(犹疑地)那我先给你问问去。

四:你去吧。

贵:(走到书房门口,转过来)他要是见你,你可少说粗话,听见了没有?(很老练地走着,自以为是阔当差的步伐,进了书房门。)

大:(目送鲁贵进了书房,摇摇头)哼,他忘了他还是个人。

四:(有些责备地)哥哥!(胆怯地望着哥哥)哥哥你说话小声点,老爷就在里边呢!

大:(望望她)好。妈也快回来了,我看你把周家

thing out for you. Have a couple of days at home with your mother and your sister, and when your mother's gone you can go back to the mine, and you'll find your job still waiting for your there.

HAI: You don't understand what it's all about. You needn't bother.

FENG (*anxious that her father should go and leave them alone together*): Why don't you go and see if the visitors have gone, Dad? If they have, you could take Dahai in to see the master.

LU (*shaking his head*): I doubt very much if he'll see you.

HAI (*with the confidence of a man convinced of the rightness of his cause*): Tell him that Lu Dahai, the miners' representative, wants to see him. He asked us to come, and we saw him in the office only the day before yesterday.

LU (*hesitantly*): Well, in that case I'd better find out if you can see him.

FENG: Yes, go on, Dad.

LU (*turning round as he reaches the door of the study*): If he does agree to see you, you'd better watch your tongue, see? (*He disappears into the study with the confident tread of a senior servant with years of lucrative service behing him.*)

HAI (*watching Lu Gui out of sight and shaking his head*): Ugh! He forgets he's a man!

FENG (*rather reproachfully*): Dahai! (*Looking timidly at him.*) I shouldn't speak so loud if I were you. Remember the master's through there.

HAI (*looking at her*): All right. Mother will be back

的活儿辞了,好好回家。

四:(诧异)为什么?

大:这不是你待的地方。

四:为什么?

大:(仇恨地)周家的人不是好东西。这两年我在矿上看够了他们做的事。(缓缓地)我恨他们。

四:你看见什么?

大:凤儿,你不要看这样威武的房子,哼,这都是矿上压死的苦工人给换来的!

四:你别胡说,这屋子听说直闹鬼呢。

大:(忽然)刚才我看见一个年轻人,在花园里躺着,脸色发白,闭着眼睛,像是要死的样子,听说这就是周家的大少爷,我们董事长的儿子。啊,报应,报应。

四:(气)你,——(忽然)他待人顶好,你知道么?

大:他父亲做尽了坏事弄钱,他会是个好东西?!

四:(望大海)两年没见你,你跟从前不一样了。

大:这两年——(走了两步,又回身向四凤,望着她)我倒觉得你变了。

鲁贵由书房门上。

soon. I think you'd best pack up this job here and go back home.

FENG (*surprised*): But why?

HAI: This is no place for you.

FENG: Why not?

HAI (*bitterly*): The Zhous are rotten through and through. I've seen enough of their doings at the mine these last two years. (*Deliberately.*) I hate them.

FENG: And what are these things you've seen?

HAI: Take this house, Sifeng. A "stately home," you might say. Tcha! Built with the blood of miners crushed at the coal-face!

FENG: Don't you start: they say this room's haunted as it is.

HAI (*with sudden scorn*): Just now as I was coming in I saw a young man in the garden. He was lying there with his eyes closed and his face so pale that I shouldn't think he'd last much longer. And they tell me this is our chairman's eldest son. Ah, it's a punishment, it's what he deserves!

FENG (*indignant*): How dare you — (*checking herself*) he treats people very decently, you know.

HAI: He can't be any good with a father who'll stoop to any dirty trick to make money!

FENG (*looking at him*): It's two years since I saw you last. You've changed a lot.

HAI: These past two years — (*he walks a few steps, then turns and looks her full in the face*) I think it's you that's changed.

(*Lu Gui reappears from the study.*)

35

贵：好容易客人刚走,我正要回话,又来了一位。(向大海)我看我们先下去待一会儿吧。

大：那我就先进去跟他谈谈。(要向书房门走。)

贵：(拦住他)干什么?

四：不,不。哥哥你先——

大：好,(沉吟一下)也好,不要叫他看着我们工人不懂规矩。

贵：你看你这点骨头!老头说不见就不见,到下房再等一等算什么!我跟你走,这么大院子,你别胡闯乱闯走错了。(走向中门,回头)四凤,你先别走,我就回来,你听见没有?

四：您去吧。

鲁贵,大海同下。

四凤厌倦地坐到沙发上。

听见外面花园里一个年轻的轻快的声音,唤着"四凤!"渐渐移到中间门口。

四：(有点惊慌)哦,二少爷。

周冲的声音：四凤!四凤!

LU: Well, the visitors went at last, but just as I was going to tell him you were here another one came in. (*Turning to Dahai.*) I think we'd better go out the back and wait.

HAI: In that case I'll go in and see him myself. (*He goes towards the door of the study.*)

LU (*blocking the way*): Where do you think you're going?

FENG: Stop, Dahai, don't go in. You'd better —

HAI: All right — (*after a moment's thought*) perhaps you're right: we don't want him thinking that miners have got on manners.

LU: Come down off your high horse! If the old man says he won't see you, then he won't. Now, why not go down and wait a bit longer in the servants' quarters? Come on, I'll take you along, otherwise in a big house like this you'll be losing your way and blundering into places where you shouldn't be. (*As he goes towards the centre door he calls over his shoulder to his daughter.*) You stay here, Sifeng. I won't be a minute. Got it?

FENG: Yes, all right.

(*Lu Gui and Lu Dahai go out.*)

(*Sifeng sits down wearily on a sofa.*)

(*A young man's cheerful voice is heard outside in the garden calling her name. It comes nearer and nearer until it is just outside the centre door.*)

FENG (*slightly alarmed*): Oh dear, it's Master Chong!

ZHOU CHONG'S VOICE: Sifeng! Sifeng!

四凤慌忙站起躲在沙发背后。

周冲——周朴园的小儿子,十七岁,穿着打球的白衣服,左腋下挟着一只球拍,一面用毛巾擦汗,快步走进。他有着一切孩子的空想,他的脸色通红,眼睛欣喜地闪动着。

冲:四凤!四凤!(四面张望)咦,不在这儿。(蹑足走向右边的饭厅,开开门,低声)四凤你出来,我告诉你一件事。(又轻轻地走到书房门口,更低声)四凤。

周朴园的声音:是冲儿么?

冲:(胆怯地)是我,爸爸。

周朴园的声音:你在干什么?

冲:我找四凤。

周朴园的声音:她不在这儿。

冲:(把头由门口缩回来,做了一个鬼脸)咦,奇怪。(失望地向右边的饭厅走去。)四凤看见周冲已走,嘘出一口气。鲁贵由中门进。

贵:(向四凤)刚才是谁在喊你?

四:二少爷。

(*Sifeng jumps hurriedly to her feet and hides behind the sofa.*)

(*Zhou Chong, Zhou Puyuan's seventeen-year-old younger son, comes briskly into the room. He is dressed for tennis and carries a racket under his left arm. He is mopping his perspiring face with a towel. Like all youngsters of his age, he is something of an idealist. Just now his face is flushed and his eyes are dancing merrily.*)

ZHOU CHONG: Sifeng! Sifeng! (*Looking all round the room.*) Oh, she's not here. (*Tiptoes across to the door of the dining-room, opens it, and speaks in a low voice.*) Come on out, Sifeng. I've got something to tell you. (*He now goes quietly across to the door of the study and speaks in a lower voice still.*) Sifeng.

ZHOU PUYUAN'S VOICE (*from inside the study*): Is that you, Chong?

CHONG (*timidly*): Yes, Father.

THE VOICE: What do you want?

CHONG: I'm looking for Sifeng.

THE VOICE: Well, she's not in here.

CHONG (*turning away from the door with a puzzled frown*): Well, that's odd. (*Disappointed, he walks across the room and disappears into the dining-room.*)

(*Now that he has gone, Sifeng comes out of her hiding-place and heaves a sigh of relief.*)

(*Lu Gui comes in through the centre door.*)

LU (*to Sifeng*): Who was that calling you just now?

FENG: Master Chong.

贵：他叫你干什么？

四：谁知道。

贵：(责备)你为什么不理他？

四：不是您叫我等着么？您有话就讲吧。

贵：你看，刚才我走到下房，这些王八蛋就堵着门口跟我要账，当着上上下下好些人，我看没有二十块钱，简直圆不下这个脸。

四：(拿出钱来)我的都在这儿。这是我回头预备给妈添衣服的，您先拿去吧。

贵：(假意)那你不是没有花的了么？

四：得了，您别这样客气啦。

贵：(笑着接下钱，数)就十二块？

四：(坦白地)现钱我只有这么一点。

贵：(故做为难的样子)那这些要账的，怎么打发呢？

四：(忍着气)您叫他们晚上到我们家里要吧。回头，见着妈，再想别的法子，这钱，您留着自己用吧。

贵：(高兴地)这给我啦，那我只当着你这是孝敬爸爸的。——好孩子，我早知道你有这份儿

LU: What did he want you for?

FENG: God knows.

LU (*reproachfully*): Why did you dodge him like that?

FENG: You told me to stay here, didn't you? Now, let's hear what you've got to say.

LU: Well, it's like this. When I went down to the servants' quarters just now I found all these bloody people I owe money to crowded round the door waiting for me. They stopped me in front of everybody and demanded their money back on the spot. Unless I can raise twenty dollars I won't be able to get rid of them.

FENG (*producing some money*): That's every penny I've got. I'd been keeping it to buy Mother a new dress, but you'd better have it.

LU (*hypocritically*): But won't that leave you broke?

FENG: Forget it. You're getting very considerate all of a sudden, aren't you?

LU (*taking the money with a smile and counting it*): Only twelve dollars?

FENG (*flatly*): It's all I've got.

LU (*trying to look as if the loan is more trouble than it is worth*): How am I going to get rid of these people, then?

FENG (*controlling herself with difficulty*): Tell them to come round to our place tonight. I'll see what I can do after Mother's arrived. You'd better keep this money for your own use.

LU (*delighted*): For me, eh? Then I'll accept it as a token of your affection for your father. I always

雷雨

孝心。

四：(没有办法)这回您让我上楼去了吧。(端起药碗。)

贵：你看，谁管过你啦。去吧，跟太太说一声，说鲁贵直惦记太太的病。

四：知道，忘不了。

贵：(得意)对了，四凤，我还告诉你一件事。

四：您留着以后再说吧。

贵：(暗示着)你看，这是你自己的事。(假笑。)

四：(沉下脸)我又有什么事？(放下药碗)好，我们今天都算清楚再走。

贵：你瞧瞧，又急了。真快成小姐了。耍脾气倒是聒聒叫啦。

四：您说吧。

贵：孩子，你别这样，(正经地)我劝你小心点。

四：(嘲弄地)我现在钱也没有了，还用得着小心干什么？

贵：我跟你说，太太这两天的神气有点不大对。

四：太太的神气不对有我什么关系？

贵：我怕太太看见你才有点不痛快。

四：为什么？

贵：为什么？我先提你个醒。老爷比太太岁数

knew you loved your old dad, my dear.

FENG (*helplessly*): Perhaps now you'll let me go upstairs after all that? (*She picks up the bowl of medicine.*)

LU: Why, who's stopping you? Go on, and tell the mistress that Lu Gui is anxious to know how she's getting on.

FENG: All right, I won't forget.

LU (*rather pleased with himself*): Oh yes, Sifeng, there's something else I want to tell you.

FENG: Couldn't you save it for later on?

LU (*mysteriously*): Ah, but this is something that concerns you. (*He smiles hypocritically.*)

FENG (*scowling*): Me again? Now what? (*Putting down the bowl.*) All right. Let's get everything cleared up once and for all before we go any; lf farther.

LU: There you go again. Flying off the handle at the slightest excuse! Quite the young lady, aren't you, with your airs and your tantrums!

FENG: Come on, out with it.

LU: Now don't be like that, my dear. (*Seriously.*) I just want to warn you to be on your guard.

FENG (*sarcastically*): What have I got to be on my guard for, now that you've cleaned me out?

LU: Listen. I don't think the mistress has been in a very good mood these last few days.

FENG: What's that got to do with me?

LU: It seems to upset her to have you around.

FENG: Why?

LU: Why? Let me remind you of one thing or two.

43

大得多,太太跟老爷不好。大少爷不是这位太太生的,他比太太的岁数差得也有限。

四:我都知道。

贵:你知道这屋子为什么晚上没有人来,老爷在矿上的时候,就是白天也是一个人也没有么?

四:不是半夜里闹鬼么?

贵:哼,鬼?一点也不错,我可看见过。

四:您看见来着?

贵:(自负地)嗯,这是你爸爸的造化。

四:怎么?

贵:那时你还没有来,老爷在矿上,那么阴森森的大院子,就太太,二少爷,大少爷住。那时这屋子就闹鬼,二少爷是小孩,胆小,叫我在他们口睡。是个秋天,半夜里二少爷忽然把我叫起来,说客厅又闹鬼,硬叫我去看看。我直发毛,可那会儿我刚来,少爷说了,我还能不去?

四:您去了?

贵:我就喝了两口烧酒壮壮胆子,穿过荷花池,

The master is years older than the mistress, and they don't get on very well with one another. Master Ping is only her stepson, and there's not much difference in their ages.

FENG: I know all that.

LU: But do you know why no one ever comes into this room after dark, and why it's not even used in the daytime all the time the master's away at the mine?

FENG: Well, it's because the room's haunted, isn't it?

LU: Haunted? Oh yes, it certainly is. And I've seen the ghosts, too.

FENG: You have?

LU (*complacently*): Yes, and lucky for me that I did.

FENG: How's that?

LU: It was before you came. The master was away at the mine, and the mistress and the two young gentlemen were left alone in this big, gloomy house. This room was already haunted then, and Master Chong, who was still only a child, was afraid and insisted I should sleep at his door to keep him company. I remember it was in the autumn. Well, one night, about midnight, he suddenly woke me up and said he'd heard ghosts in the drawing-room. He insited that I should go and have a look. I was shaking in my shoes at the thought of it, but I was new here then, and I didn't dare disobey the young master.

FENG: So you went, then?

LU: I had a little drink to steady my nerves, then I

偷偷地钻到这门外的走廊旁边。到门口,就听见这屋子里啾啾啾地像一个女鬼在哭。哭得惨!心里越怕,越想看。我就硬着头皮,从这窗缝里向里一望。

四:(紧张地望着他)您瞧见什么?

贵:就在这张桌上点着一枝要灭不灭的洋蜡烛。我恍恍惚惚地看见两个穿着黑衣裳的鬼,并排地坐着,像是一男一女,背朝着我。这个女鬼像是靠着男的身边哭,那个男鬼低着头直叹气。

四:真的。

贵:可不是!我就乘着酒劲儿,朝着窗户缝,轻轻地咳嗽一声。这两个鬼就飕一下子分开了,都朝我这边望。这一下子他们的脸清清楚楚地正对着我。这我可真见了鬼了!

四:什么样?

鲁贵停一下,四面望一望。

四:谁?

贵:我这才看见那个女鬼呀,(回头,低声)——

went round past the lotus-pond and crept up to the verandah outside this room. As soon as I got near the door, I heard a faint noise. It sounded like a woman sobbing her heart out. I was scared out of my wits, but the noise made me all the more determined to have a look. Finally, I plucked up courage and peeped in through this window here.

FENG (*gazing tensely at him*): What did you see?

LU: There was a candle on this table here. It had burned right down and it was just flickering as if it was going out. There was just enough light to make out two ghosts all in black sitting side by side with their backs towards me. They looked like a man and a woman. The woman seemed to be leaning on the man's shoulder and crying, and the man sat with his head bent, sighing to himself.

FENG: You're not making it all up?

LU: Of course not! Well, with the drink inside me, I managed to pluck up enough courage to put my face close to the window and give a little cough. The two ghosts sprang apart with a jerk and looked round towards me. Just for a moment I got a clear view of both their faces. — And then I really did think I was seeing things!

FENG: Why?

(*Lu Gui pauses and looks quickly all round.*)

FENG: Who were they?

LU: Well, the woman turned out to be — (*glancing over his shoulder, then dropping his voice to a*

是我们的太太。

四：太太？

贵：那个男鬼——就是大少爷。

四：他？

贵：就是他，他同他的后娘就在这屋子里闹鬼呢。

四：(故做不在意地)我不信，准是您看错了。

贵：没个错，你不用骗自己。所以孩子，你看开点，别糊涂，周家的人就是那么一回事。

四：不，不会。

贵：你忘了，大少爷比太太只小六七岁。

　　四凤摇头。

贵：好，信不信都在你，反正我先告诉你，太太的神气现在对你不大对，就是因为你，因为你同——

四：(连忙岔开)太太要知道是您，一定不会饶您的。

贵：是啊，我吓了一身汗，我没等他们来，我就跑了。

四：可是太太那个人她不会算了吧？

贵：她当然厉害，拿话套了我十几回，我一句话

whisper) the mistress herself!

FENG: The mistress?

LU: And the man — was Master Ping.

FENG: No!

LU: Yes, it was him all right. He and his stepmother were the ghosts who'd been haunting the place nights.

FENG (*with affected unconcern*): I don't believe it. You must have made a mistake.

LU: Not me. Don't you kid yourself. You see now, Sifeng, why I say you should come down to earth and stop being to silly. That's the Zhous for you!

FENG: No, it's impossible.

LU: You're forgeting that Master Ping is only six or seven years younger than the mistress.

(*Still refusing to believe it, Sifeng shakes her head.*)

LU: All right. Please yourself whether you believe it or not, but don't say I didn't warn you. The reason the mistress hasn't been in a very good mood about you lately is because you — er — because you and —

FENG (*hurriedly changing the subject*): If the mistress knew it was you, she'd never forgive you.

LU: You're telling me. Though I was in a cold sweat at the time, and I didn't wait to be caught. I got out, quick.

FENG: But I can't imagine the mistress letting it go at that.

LU: She was very worried about it, of course not. She kept on sounding me and trying to trap me in-

也没有漏出来。这两年过去,说不定他们倒以为那晚上真是鬼在咳嗽呢。

四:(自语)不,不,我不信。

贵:你不信?又做你的梦啦,不想想,你是谁?他是谁?你,就凭你没有个好爸爸,人家大少爷会……

四:(突然)您别说了! (站起来)妈今天回家,您看我太快活是么?您说这些瞎话——这些瞎话!

贵:你看你,告诉你真话,你倒生气了,唉,你呀! (傲然地扫四凤一眼,走到茶几旁,很熟练地偷了几支烟卷,放在自己的旧烟盒里。)

四:(望着他,冷冷地)没有话了吧,我走了。(拿起药碗就走。)

贵:别走,话还没完呢。(轻描淡写地)回头你妈就到这儿来找你。

四:(变色)什么?

贵:你妈一下火车,就到这儿公馆来。

四:妈不愿意我在公馆里帮人,您为什么叫她到这儿来找我?反正我每天晚上回家,您叫她

to saying something, but I didn't breathe a word. Still, that was very two years ago, and I expect by now they've decided it must have been a ghost they heard coughing that night.

FENG (*to herself*): No, no. I can't believe it.

LU: You can't? You and your day-dreams! Don't you realize who you are, and who he is? Do you imagine for one moment that a young gentleman in his position could ever be serious about you? Why, the mere fact that your father's no good is enough to —

FENG (*suddenly*): Stop it! I suppose you're talking all this silly nonsense to upset me just because I'm so happy about Mother coming home today! Lot of twaddle!

LU: There you go again! I tell you the truth, and you go off the deep end! Ah, I don't know. (*With a brief, supercilious glance at Sifeng be walks across to the low table and, with a practised hand, conveys some of the cigarettes on it to his own battered old cigarette-case.*)

FENG (*coldly, as she watches him*): If that's all, I'll be going. (*She picks up the bowl of medicine and turns to go.*)

LU: Wait a minute. I haven't finished yet. (*Casually.*) Your mother will be coming here to see you.

FENG (*turning pale*): What?

LU: She's coming straight here from the station.

FENG: What did you have to tell her to come here for? You know she never wanted me to go into service. Anyway, I always go home in the

雷雨

到这儿来干什么?

贵:不是我,孩子,是太太要我找她来的。

四:太太要她来?

贵:嗯,(神秘地)奇怪不是,没亲没故。你看太太偏要请她来谈一谈。

四:您别吞吞吐吐地成么?

贵:你知道太太为什么一个人在楼上,装病不下来?

四:老爷一回家,太太向来是这样。

贵:这次不对吧?

四:有什么不对?

贵:你一点不觉得?——大少爷没提过什么?

四:没有,我就知道这半年多,他跟太太不常说话。

贵:哦——那么太太对你呢?

四:这几天比往日特别地好。

贵:那就对了!——我告诉你,太太知道我不愿意你离开这儿。这次,她自己要对你妈说,叫她带着你卷铺盖滚蛋!

四:(低声)她要我走——可是——为什么?

贵:那你自己明白!

四:(低声)要妈来干什么?

evening, so what's the point of bringing her here?

LU: It's none of my doing, Sifeng. The mistress wanted me to fetch her here.

FENG: The mistress, did you say?

LU: That's right. (*Mysteriously*.) Queer, isn't it? She's no relation of your mother's, or friend either, and yet she goes out of her way to invite her here for a little chat.

FENG: Would you mind not being so mysterious about it and tell me what it's all about?

LU: Do you know why the mistress is hiding herself upstairs on her own and pretending to be ill?

FENG: Well, she always does that whenever the master comes home.

LU: Wouldn't you say it was different this time?

FENG: In what way?

LU: Don't you feel there's something wrong? — Hasn't Master Ping mentioned anythng?

FENG: No. All I know is, for the last six months or so he hasn't had much to say to the mistress.

LU: I see — and how's she been treating you?

FENG: Better than ever these last few days.

LU: Just as I thought! Now listen. She knows I don't want you to leave this job, so this time she's going to speak to your mother direct and get her to take you away, bag and baggage!

FENG (*in a low voice*): So she wants to get rid of me — but — but why?

LU: You know very well without me telling you.

FENG (*still in a low voice*): But what can she want Mother here for?

贵:她要告诉你妈一件事。

四:(突然明白)哦,爸爸,无论如何,我在这儿的事,不能让妈知道的。(惧悔交集,流下泪来)爸爸,您想,妈前年离开我的时候,她嘱咐过您,好好地看着我,不许您送我到公馆帮人。您不听,您要我来。妈不知道这些事,我死也不能叫妈知道这儿这些事情的。(扑在桌上)妈呀!

贵:孩子!(轻轻抚着四凤)你看现在才是爸爸好了吧,爸疼你,不要怕!她不敢怎么样,她不会辞你的。这儿呀,还有一个人叫她怕呢!

四:谁?

贵:哼,她怕你的爸爸!你忘了我告诉你那两个鬼哪。昨天晚上我替你告假,她说你妈来的时候,要我叫你妈来。我看她这两天的神气,我就猜着了一半,我顺便就把那天半夜的事提了两句,她是机灵人,不会不懂的。——哼,她要是跟我装蒜,现在老爷在家,咱们就是个麻烦。我知道她是个厉害

LU: She must have something to tell her.

FENG (*the truth suddenly dawning on her.*): Oh, Dad! Whatever happens, Mother mustn't find out what I've been up to here. (*Overcome by remorse and apprehension, she bursts into tears.*) Just think, Dad. When Mother went away two years ago, she told you to look after me and not bring me to this place to work. You didn't take any notice of what she said and you insisted on me coming here. Mother still doesn't know about it. I just couldn't bear her to find out just what I've been doing here. (*Flinging herself down on the table.*) Oh, Mother! Mother!

LU: There, there! (*Stroking her tenderly.*) Now, your dad's on your side, see? Your dad loves you, and you've got nothing to worry about. There's nothing she can do about it, and you won't get the sack. You see, there's one person in this house that she's afraid of.

FENG: Who's that?

LU: She's afraid of me. Remember the two ghosts I told you about? When I asked her to give you a day off last night, she said I could bring your mother here when she comes. Well, seeing what sort of a mood she'd been in these last few days, I put two and two together. Then, casual-like, I dropped a word or two about what happened that night. She's all there, you know, and she must have realized what I was getting at. — Humph! If she tries to come the old acid with me, she'll find herself in an awkward situation, especially with

四：(抬起头)您可不要胡来！

贵：这家除了老头，我谁也看不上眼。别着急，有你爸爸。再说，也许是我瞎猜，她原来就许没有这意思。她外面倒是跟我说，因为听说你妈会读个书写个字，才想见见谈谈。

四：(忽然谛听)您别说话，我听见好像有人在饭厅咳嗽似的。

贵：(听一下)别是太太吧？(走到通饭厅的门前，由锁眼窥视，忙回来)可不是她，奇怪，她下楼来了。别慌，什么也别提，我走了。

四：(擦干泪)嗯，妈来了，您先告诉我一声。

贵：对了，见着你妈，就当什么都不知道，听见了没有？(走到中门，又回头)别忘了，跟太太说鲁贵惦记着太太的病。(慌忙由中门下。)

the master at home now! I know she can be a nasty piece of work, but anybody who tries to push my daughter around will have me to deal with first!

FENG (*looking up*): Don't go doing anything rash, though!

LU: I don't think much of anybody in this house, except the old man. Don't worry, your dad'll look after you. Anyway, I may be wrong about her. Perhaps she isn't thinking of doing anything of the sort. In fact, she did say she only wanted to meet your mother because she'd heard your mother could read and write.

FENG (*suddenly straining her ears to listen*): Sh-h! I think I can hear someone coughing in the dining-room.

LU (*listening*): It's not the mistress, is it? (*He goes across to the door leading to the dining-room, peeps through the keyhole, and hurries back to her.*) It is, too. Funny, her coming downstairs like that. Now, don't panic and don't breathe a word to her about anything. I'd better make myself scarce now.

FENG (*drying her tears*): All right, but be sure to let me know the minute Mother arrives.

LU: Yes, and when she does come, pretend you haven't heard a thing. Got it? (*He goes across to the centre door, then speaks over his shoulder.*) And don't forget to tell the mistress that Lu Gui is anxious to know how she is. (*He hurries out through the centre door.*)

雷雨

四凤端着药碗向饭厅门走,至门前,周蘩漪进。她一望就知道是个果敢阴鸷的女人。她的脸色苍白,只有嘴唇微红,她的大而灰暗的眼睛同高高的鼻梁令人觉得很美,但是有些可怕。在眉目间,在那静静的长的睫毛下面,看出来她是忧郁的。有时为心中的郁积的火燃烧着,她的眼光会充满了一个年轻妇人失望后的痛苦与怨望。她的嘴角向后略弯,显出一个受抑制的女人在管制着自己。她那雪白细长的手,时常在她轻轻咳嗽的时候,按着自己瘦弱的胸。

直等自己喘出一口气来,她才摸摸自己胀得红红的面颊。她是一个中国旧式女人,有她的文弱,她的哀静,她的明慧,——她对诗文的爱好,但她也有更原始的一点野性:在她的心里,她的胆量里,她的狂热的思想里,在她莫名其妙的决断时忽然来的力量里。整个地来看她,她似乎是一个水晶,只能给男人精神的安慰,她的明亮的前

(*Sifeng picks up the bowl of medicine once again and goes towards the dining-room, but just as she reaches the door, it opens and Zhou Fanyi appears. She is obviously a woman of ruthless determination. The faint red of her lips is the only touch of colour in her otherwise pale face. Her large, dark eyes and straight nose give her face a certain beauty, though a beauty with a sinister cast to it. The eyes beneath her long, steady lashes betray her unhappiness. Sometimes, when the smouldering fires of misery in her heart blaze into life, these eyes will fill with all the anguish and resentment of a frustrated woman. The corners of her mouth are slightly drawn back, revealing her to be a repressed woman controlling herself with difficulty. Whenever she coughs in her quiet way, her slender, delicate white hands press against her flat, emaciated chest, and when the coughing is over, leaving her panting for breath, they will go up to feel her face, now flushed with coughing. With her delicate health, her secret sorrows, her intelligence and her love of poetry and literature, she is a woman of old China; yet there is a primitive wildness in her which shows in her courage, in her almost fanatical reasoning, and in her sudden, unaccountable strength in moments of crisis. The sum impression which one gains of her is of a crystalline transparency, as if she is the sort of woman who can offer a man no companionship but the platonic kind, and her*

额表现出深沉的理解;但是当她陷于情感的冥想中,忽然愉快地笑着;当她见着她所爱的,快乐的红晕散布在脸上,两颊的笑涡也显露出来的时节,你才觉得出她是能被人爱的,应当被人爱的,你才知道她到底是一个女人,跟一切年轻的女人一样。她爱起你来像一团火,那样热烈,恨起你来也会像一团火,把你烧毁的。然而她的外形是沉静的,忧烦的,她像秋天傍晚的树叶轻轻落在你的身旁,她觉得自己的夏天已经过去,生命的晚霞早暗下来了。

她通身是黑色。旗袍镶着银灰色的花边。她拿着一把团扇,挂在手指下,走进来,很自然地望着四凤。

四:太太!怎么您下楼来啦?我正要给您把药送上去呢!

繁:老爷在书房里么?

四:老爷在书房里会客呢。

繁:谁来了?

四:刚才是警察局长,现在不知道是谁。您要见他?

broad, unclouded forehead is expressive of a subtle intelligence; but when, lost in sentimental reverie, she breaks into a sudden smile of happiness, or when, at the sight of someone dear to her, a flush of pleasure suffuses her face and dimples appear on her cheeks, one feels for the first time that it would be possible to love her and that she does indeed deserve to be loved — one realizes, in fact, that she is a woman after all, a woman no different from all the others. When she loves, she loves with a fiery passion, and when she hates, she hates as fiercely, with a hatred which can destroy; yet on the surface she appears quiet and wistful, and when she stops beside one, it is like a leaf falling by one's side on a late autumn afternoon. She seems to feel that the summer of her life is now over, and that the shades of evening are falling around her.

She is dressed all in black, and her dress is trimmed with silver-grey pipings. A round fan hangs from her fingers. As she comes in she looks casually at Sifeng.)

FENG: Why, madam! I didn't know you'd come downstairs! I was just coming up with the medicine.

FANYI: Is the master in the study?

FENG: Yes, he's got a visitor.

FAN: Who is it?

FENG: Well, it was the police superintendent in there a minute ago, but I don't know who it is now. Did you want to see him?

繁:不。(又停一下,看看四面)两礼拜没下来,这屋子改了样子了。

四:是的,老爷说原来的样子不好看,又把您添的新家具搬走了几件。这是老爷自己摆的。

繁:(看看右面的衣柜)这只旧衣柜,又拿来了。(咳,坐下。)

四:太太,您脸上像是发烧,还是到楼上歇着吧。

繁:不,楼上太热。(咳。)

四:老爷说太太有病,嘱咐过请您好好地在楼上躺着。

繁:我不愿意躺在床上。——哦,我忘了,老爷哪一天从矿上回来的?

四:大前天晚上。老爷看您烧得厉害,叫我们别惊醒您,就一个人在楼下睡的。

繁:白天我像是没见过老爷来。

四:嗯,这两天老爷天天到省政府开会,到晚上才上楼看您。可是您又把门锁上了。

繁:(不经意地)哦,哦——怎么,楼下也这样闷热。

四:对了,闷的很。一早晨乌云就遮满了天,也

FAN: No. (*She pauses and looks all round.*) After two weeks upstairs, this room looks quite different.

FENG: I know. The master didn't like the way it was aranged before, so he had some of your new furniture moved out again. He's got the room arranged just the way he wants it.

FAN (*noticing the bureau on the right*): I see he's had that old bureau put back where it used to be. (*She coughs and sits down.*)

FENG: Your face looks feverish, madam. Wouldn't it be better if you went back upstairs and lay down?

FAN: No, it's too hot up there. (*She coughs again.*)

FENG: The master says that as you're not very well, madam, you'd best stay quietly upstairs in bed.

FAN: I don't want to stay in bed. — Oh, I forgot to ask you. When did the master get back from the mine?

FENG: Three days, ago, late at night. When he saw how feverish you were, he told us not to disturb you. He's been sleeping downstairs on his own.

FAN: But I don't seem to have seen him in the daytime, either.

FENG: Well, since he's back he's been out every day to meetings at the provincial government offices, and each time he's got home and gone up to see you in the evening your door's been locked.

FAN (*unconcernedly*): I see. — Why, it's just as stifling downstairs.

FENG: Yes, it's very close. But it's been very cloudy, dark and overcast since first thing this morning. I

许今儿个会下一场大雨。

繁：换一把大点的团扇,我简直有点喘不过气来。

四凤拿一把大蒲扇给繁漪,繁漪望着四凤,又故意地转过头去。

繁：怎么这两天没见着大少爷?

四：大概是很忙。

繁：听说他也要到矿上去,是么?

四：我不知道。

繁：你没有听见说么?

四：没有,倒是侍候大少爷的张奶奶这两天尽忙着给他捡衣裳。

繁：你父亲干什么呢?

四：不知道。——他说,他问太太的病。

繁：他倒是惦记着我。(停一下,忽然)他现在还没起来么?

四：谁?

繁：(没有想到四凤这样问,忙收敛一下)嗯——大少爷。

四：我不知道。

繁：(看了她一眼)嗯?

四：我没看见大少爷。

繁：他昨天晚上什么时候回来的?

四：(红脸)我每天晚上总是回家睡觉,我不知道。

繁：(不自主地)哦,你每天晚上回家睡!(觉得

expect we're in for a storm.

FNA: Give me a larger fan. I'm practically suffocating.

(*Sifeng hands her a large palm-leaf fan. Fanyi looks at her for a moment, then deliberately turns her face away.*)

FAN: How is it I haven't seen anything of Master Ping just lately?

FENG: He's probably very busy.

FAN: I hear he's off to the mine. Is that true?

FENG: I don't know.

FAN: Haven't you heard about it, then?

FENG: No. Though I do know his maid's been busy packing his things.

FAN: What's your father doing?

FENG: I don't know. — Oh, he said he was anxious to know how you're getting on.

FAN: Humph, he would be. (*After a pause, suddenly.*) Isn't he up yet?

FENG: Who?

FAN (*rather taken aback by the unexpected question, but hastily recovering herself*): Why — er — Master Ping.

FENG: I don't know.

FAN (*casting a swift glance at her*): You don't?

FENG: I haven't seen him.

FAN: What time did he get home last night?

FENG (*blushing*): I don't know. I sleep at home every night.

FAN (*forgetting herself*): Sleep at home every night, indeed! (*Realizing that she has made a faux*

失言)老爷回来,家里没有人会侍候他,你怎么天天要回家呢?

四:太太,不是您吩咐过,叫我回去睡么?

繁:那时是老爷不在家。

四:我怕老爷念经吃素,不喜欢我们侍候他。

繁:哦,(忽而抬起头来)这么说,他在这几天就走,究竟到什么地方去呢?

四:(胆怯地)您是说大少爷?

繁:(注视四凤)嗯!

四:我没听见。(嗫嚅地)他,他总是两三点钟回家,我早晨像是听见我父亲叨叨说下半夜给他开的门来着。

繁:他又喝醉了么?

四:我不清楚。(想找一个新题目)——太太,您吃药吧。

繁:谁说我要吃药?

四:老爷吩咐的。

繁:我并没请医生,哪里来的药?

四:老爷说您犯的是肝郁,今天早上想起从前您吃的老方子,就叫抓一副,给您煎上。

繁:煎好了没有?

四:煎好了,凉在这儿好半天啦。(递药给繁漪)

pas.) But why should you go home every night now that the master's at home with no one to wait on him?

FENG: But, madam, didn't you tell me to yourself?

FAN: Yes, but the master wasn't at home then.

FENG: I thought a religious man like the master wouldn't like having a girl staying on to wait on him.

FAN: I see. (*Suddenly looking up.*) Though if he is leaving in a day or two, where else can he be going?

FENG (*timidly*): Master Ping, you mean?

FAN (*staring hard at her*): Of course.

FENG: I haven't heard a thing. (*Hesitantly.*) He — he never gets in till two or three in the morning. This morning my father was muttering something about having to open the gate for him in the early hours of the morning.

FAN: Was he drunk again?

FENG: I'm not sure. (*Changing the subject.*) — Madam, what about having your medicine now?

FAN: Medicine? Whose idea's this?

FENG: The master had it made up for you.

FAN: But how can there be any medicine when I haven't even seen a doctor?

FENG: The master said it must be your liver again, and this morning he happened to remember about the prescription you had last time, so he sent out for the ingredients and had it made up for you.

FAN: Is it ready?

FENG: Yes. It's been here getting cool for some time

您喝吧。

繁：(喝一口)苦的很。谁煎的？

四：我。

繁：难喝，倒了它。

四：倒了？

繁：(想起周朴园严厉的脸)先放在那儿也好。不，(厌恶)还是倒了它。

四：(犹豫)嗯。

繁：这些年喝这种苦药，我大概是喝够了。

四：(拿着药碗)您忍一忍，喝了吧。药苦可能够治病。

繁：(忽然恨起来)谁要你劝我？倒掉！(自己觉得失了身份)这次老爷回来，我听老妈子说他瘦了。

四：嗯，瘦多了，也黑多了。听说矿上正在罢工，老爷很着急的。

繁：老爷很不高兴么？

四：老爷还是那样，除了会客，出门，在家里一句话也没说。

繁：没有跟少爷们说话么？

四：见了大少爷只点一点头，没说话，倒是问了

now. (*Handing her the bowl.*) Here you are, madam.

FAN (*taking a sip at it*): It's terribly bitter. Who made it up?

FENG: I did.

FAN: It tastes abominable. Pour it away.

FENG: Pour it away?

FAN (*deterred by the thought of her husband's stern face*): Oh, well, perhaps you'd better leave it on the table for the time being. — No. (*With loathing.*) You'd best pour it away.

FENG (*hesitantly*): All right, then.

FAN: For years I've been taking this revolting stuff. I've had more than enough of it already.

FENG (*holding out the bowl*): Now be brave, madam. Do try to take it. The worse it tastes, the more good it'll do you.

FAN (*flaring up*): Who asked you for advice? Pour it away, I say! (*Realizing that this outburst is rather undignified.*)

My maid tells me the master looks much thinner this time.

FENG: Yes, he is thinner, and darker in the face, too. I hear the miners are out on strike just now, and that the master's very worried about it.

FAN: Is he very cross?

FENG: He's the same as usual. Except for seeing visitors and going out, he hasn't said a word to anybody in the house.

FAN: Not even to Master Ping and Master Chong?

FENG: He just nodded when he saw Master Ping. He

二少爷学堂的事。——对了,二少爷今天早上还问您的病呢。

繁:你告诉他我很好就是了——回头叫账房拿四十块钱给二少爷,说是给他买书的。

四:二少爷想看看您。

繁:那就叫他到楼上来见我。——(站起来,踱了两步)哦,这屋子怎么这样闷气,里里外外,都像发了霉。

四:(想想)太太,今天我想跟您告假。

繁:是你母亲从济南回来了么?——你父亲说过来着。

花园里周冲的声音:四凤!四凤!

繁:你去看看,二少爷在喊你。

周冲的声音:四凤。

四:在这儿。

周冲由中门进。

冲:(进门只看见四凤)四凤,我找你一早晨。(看见繁漪)妈,怎么您下楼来了?

繁:冲儿,你怎么啦?一脸汗。

冲:我刚和一个同学打网球。(亲热地)我正有

didn't say a word to him. Only when he saw Master Chong he asked him about school. — Oh yes, that reminds me: Master Chong was asking after you only this morning.

FAN: You can tell him I'm quite well. — And tell them in the office to give him forty dollars. Say it's for him to buy books with.

FENG: Master Chong was hoping to have a word with you.

FAN: Tell him to come and see me upstairs, then. (*She stands up and walks a few steps.*) What a horribly stuffy room this is! The whole place smells so musty.

FENG (*after a moment's hesitation*): I wonder if I might have the afternoon off, madam?

FAN: Because your mother's coming back from Jinan, do you mean? Your father was saying something about it.

CHONG'S VOICE (*from the garden*): Sifeng! Sifeng!

FAN: That's Master Chong calling you. Go and see what he wants.

CHONG'S VOICE: Sifeng!

FENG: Here I am.

(*Zhou Chong comes in through the centre door.*)

CHONG (*seeing only Sifeng*): Ah, here you are, Sifeng. I've been looking for you all the morning. (*Noticing Fanyi.*) Mother! What are you doing downstairs?

FAN: Why, Chong, what have you been doing? Your face is streaming.

CHONG: Oh, I've just been playing tennis with a

许多话要跟您说。您好一点儿没有?（坐在繁漪身旁）这两天我到楼上看您,您怎么总把门关上?

繁:我想清净清净。你看我的气色怎么样?四凤,你给二少爷拿一瓶汽水。你看你的脸通红。

四凤由饭厅门口下。

冲:（高兴地）让我瞧瞧。我瞧您挺好,没有一点病。为什么他们总说您有病呢?您一个人躲在房里,父亲回家三天了,您都没有见着他。

繁:（忧郁地看着周冲）我心里不舒服。（忽然）冲儿,你是十七了吧?

冲:妈,您要再忘了我的岁数,我真得跟您生气啦!

繁:（笑笑）妈是不好,有时候连自己都忘了在哪儿。（沉思）——哦,十八年了,在这个家里,你看,妈老了吧?

冲:不,您想什么?

繁:不想什么。

四凤拿汽水上。

四:二少爷。

schoolfriend. (*Affectionately*.) I've been wanting to see you. I've got so many things to tell you about. Are you feeling any better now? (*He sits down beside her*.) I've been up to see you several times in the past few days, but your door's always locked.

FAN: I wanted to be left alone. How do you think I look? — Sifeng, you might fetch Master Chong a bottle of mineral water. Why, you're blushing!

(*Sifeng goes into the dining-room*.)

CHONG (*delighted*): Let me have a look at you. Well, so far as I can see, you're perfectly all right — nothing wrong with you at all. I don't see why they should always be saying you're ill. While you've been shut away in your room Father's been home three days and you haven't even seen him yet.

FAN (*looking at him sadly*): I don't feel myself, somehow. (*Suddenly*.) Chong, you're seventeen, aren't you?

CHONG: Now, Mother, if you forget my age again, I'll be really angry with you.

FAN (*smiling*): Yes, I know it's silly of me, but sometimes I even forget where I am. (*Lost in thought*.) Yes, it's now eighteen years since I came to live in this house. — But tell me: don't you think I'm getting old?

CHONG: No. Why, what's worrying you?

FAN: Nothing.

(*Sifeng comes in with the mineral water*.)

FENG: Here you are, Master Chong.

雷雨

冲：谢谢你。

四凤红脸，倒汽水。

冲：你给太太再拿一个杯子来，好么？

四凤下。

蘩：(目不转睛地看着四凤和周冲)冲儿，你们为什么这样客气？

冲：(喝水)妈，我就想告诉您，那是因为——

四凤进。

冲：——回头我跟您讲。怎么这屋子这样热？

蘩：大概是窗户没有开。

冲：我来开。

四：老爷说过不叫开，说外面比屋里热。

蘩：不，打开。他在外头一去就是两年不回家，这屋子里的死气他是不知道的。

四凤拉开窗前的帷幔。

冲：(见四凤很费力地移动窗前的花盆)四凤，你不要动。让我。(走过去。)

蘩：(转向四凤)你到厨房去看一看，看看给老爷做的什么素菜。

四凤由中门下。

蘩：冲儿！

周冲走回来。

CHONG: Thank you.

(*Blushing, Sifeng pours it out for him.*)

CHONG: Do you mind fetching another glass for the mistress?

(*Sifeng goes out.*)

FAN (*who has been watching them closely all this time*): Chong, why are you two being so polite to one another?

CHONG (*drinking*): Well, Mother, that's just what I wanted to tell you about. It's because —

(*Sifeng comes in again.*)

CHONG: — I'll tell you about it some other time. Why is it so stuffy in this room?

FAN: Probably because the windows are closed.

CHONG: I'll open them then.

FENG: The master said they weren't to be opened. He says it's hotter outdoors than in.

FAN: Nonsense. Let's have them open. He's usually away two years at a time, and doesn't realize how stale and airless this room can be.

(*Sifeng draws aside the curtains.*)

CHONG (*seeing that Sifeng is having some difficulty moving the flower-pots on the window-still*): Don't bother, Sifeng. I'll do it. (*He goes across to the window.*)

FAN (*turning to Sifeng*): Go down to the kitchen, will you, and see what they're getting for the master in the way of vegetarian food.

(*Sifeng goes out through the centre door.*)

FAN: Chong!

(*Zhou Chong comes back across the room to

繁：坐下。你说吧。

冲：（看着繁漪，带了希冀和快乐的神色）妈，我这两天很快活。

繁：在这家里你能快活，自然好。

冲：妈，我一向什么都不肯瞒着您，您不是一个平常的母亲，您最大胆，最有想像，又最同情我的思想的。

繁：嗯。

冲：妈，我要告诉您一件事——不，我要跟您商量商量。

繁：你先说给我听听。

冲：妈，（神秘地）您不说我么？

繁：不说，你讲吧。

冲：（高兴地）哦，妈——（迟疑着）不，我不说了。

繁：（笑了）为什么？

冲：我，我怕您生气。说了以后，你还是一样地喜欢我么？

繁：傻孩子，妈永远是喜欢你的。

冲：（笑）好妈妈。真的，您还喜欢我？不生气？

繁：当然，你说吧。

冲：说完了不许您笑话我！

繁：嗯，不笑话你。

her.)

FAN: Now, sit down and tell me all about it.

CHONG (*looking at her with eyes bright with hope and happiness*): Mother, I've been very happy these last few days.

FAN: If you can be happy in this house, so much the better.

CHONG: I've never had any secrets from you, Mother. You're not just an ordinary mother. You're the most courageous, the most imaginative, the most sympathetic of mothers — sympathetic to my ideas.

FAN: Go on, then.

CHONG: I want to tell you something — or rather, I want to talk something over with you.

FAN: Well, let's hear what it is.

CHONG: Mother — (*Guardedly*.) You won't be cross with me?

FAN: No. Go on.

CHONG (*elated*): Oh, Mother — (*He hesitates*.) No, I don't think I will tell you.

FAN (*breaking into a smile*): Why not?

CHONG: Well, I — I'm afraid you'll be angry. Will you still love me just the same after I've told you?

FAN: Of course I will, you silly boy. Always.

CHONG (*smiling*): Dear Mother! You mean that? You'll still love me? And not be angry?

FAN: Of course. Now tell me all about it.

CHONG: But you mustn't laugh at me when you hear what it is.

FAN: I won't.

冲：真的？

繁：真的！

冲：妈，我现在喜欢一个人。

繁：(证实了她的疑惧)哦！

冲：(望着繁漪的凝视的眼睛)妈，您看，您的神气又好像说我不应该似的。

繁：(摇头)没有啊，没有，你讲吧。(提起兴会)这个女孩子是谁？

冲：(拦不住的热情)她是世界上最，最——(看一看繁漪)反正她是我认为最满意的女孩子。她心地单纯，她懂得活着的快乐，她知道同情，她明白劳动有意义。最好的，她不是小姐堆里娇生惯养出来的人。

繁：(不经意地)你不是喜欢受过教育的人么？她念过书么？

冲：自然没念过书。这是她，也可说是她唯一的缺点，然而这并不怪她。

繁：哦。(眼睛暗下来，不得不问下去)冲儿，你说的不是——四凤？

冲：是，妈妈。——妈，我知道旁人会笑话我，您不会不同情我的。

繁：(惊愕，自语)怎么，我的孩子——真是怪事。

CHONG: Promise.

FAN: Yes, I promise.

CHONG: Well, Mother, I'm in love.

FAN (*her suspicions and fears confirmed*): Indeed!

CHONG (*meeting her stare*): Now, Mother! You're looking disapproving already.

FAN (*shaking her head*): Not at all. I want to hear more. (*More cheerfully.*) Who's the girl?

CHONG (*his enthusiasm undaunted*): Oh, she's the most — the most — (*casting a glance at his mother*) well, anyway, I think she's the most wonderful girl in the world. She has a heart of gold; she knows how to enjoy life; she's understanding and kind; and she realizes the importance of hard work. What's most important, she isn't one of these aristocratic young ladies who've been pampered and spoiled all their lives.

FAN (*casually*): I should have thought you'd prefer an educated girl. Has she been to school?

CHONG: Oh, no. Though that's her only — I mean it seems to be her only shortcoming. — Though you can't very well hold that against her.

FAN: I see. (*The sparkle has now faded from her eyes, but she cannot very well abandon her questioning now.*) Chong, I suppose you wouldn't be referring to — er — Sifeng?

CHONG: Yes, Mother, I am. — Oh, I know people will laugh at me, Mother, but I'm sure *you'll* understand.

FAN (*to herself, in a stunned voice*): But my own son — it's fantastic!

冲：(焦灼)您不愿意么？您以为我做错了么？

繁：不，不，那倒不。我怕她这样的孩子不会给你幸福的。

冲：不，她是个聪明有感情的人，并且她懂得我。

繁：你不怕父亲不满意你么？

冲：这是我自己的事情。

繁：别人知道了说闲话呢？

冲：那我更不放在心上。

繁：这倒像我自己的孩子。不过我怕你走错了。第一，她始终是个没受过教育的下等人。你要是喜欢她，她当然以为这是她的福气。

冲：妈，您以为她没有主张么？

繁：冲儿，你把什么人都看得太高了。

冲：妈，我认为您这句话对她用是不合适的。她是最纯洁，最有主张的好孩子，昨天我跟她求婚——

繁：(更惊愕)什么？求婚？(笑起来)你跟她求婚？

冲：(不喜欢母亲这样的态度)您不要笑！她拒绝我了。——可是我很高兴，这样我觉得她

CHONG (*becoming anxious*): Why, don't you approve? You don't think I've done wrong, do you?

FAN: No, no, it's not that. It's just that I doubt whether a girl like her could make you happy.

CHONG: But she will! She's intelligent and warmhearted — and she understands me.

FAN: You're reckoning without your father — he may not approve.

CHONG: This is my own affair.

FAN: And if people talk when they hear about it?

CHONG: That would worry me even less.

FAN: Like mother, like son. Though I'm afraid you're going the wrong way. In the first place, when all's said and done, she's still an uneducated girl from the lower classes. For a girl in her position it must seem a marvellous stroke of luck to have a young man like you fall in love with her.

CHONG: Now, Mother! Don't you think she has a mind of her own?

FAN: You're always setting people up on pedestals, Chong.

CHONG: I think you're doing her a great injustice, Mother. She's the purest, most independent, nicest girl alive. When I proposed to her yesterday —

FAN (*with growing astonishment*): What! Proposed to her? (*Laughing.*) You mean to say you proposed to her?

CHONG (*annoyed by his mother's attitude*): There's no need to laugh about it! She turned me down. — But I'm glad, in a way, because it strengthens

81

更高贵了。她说她不愿意嫁给我。

繁：哼。

冲：你以为她不答应我，是故意地虚伪么？不，她说，她心里另外有一个人。

繁：谁？她说？

冲：我没有问。总是她的邻居，常见的人吧。——不过真的爱情免不了波折，我爱她，她会渐渐地明白我，喜欢我的。

繁：(抑制不住)我的儿子要娶也不能娶她。

冲：(出乎意料)妈，您为什么这样？四凤是个好女孩子，她背地总是很佩服您，敬重您的。

繁：你现在预备怎么样？

冲：我预备把这个意思告诉父亲。

繁：你忘了你父亲是什么样一个人啦！

冲：我一定要告诉他的。我将来并不一定跟她结婚。如果她不愿意我，我仍然是尊重她，帮助她的。但是我希望她现在受教育，我希望父亲允许我把我的教育费分给她一半上学。

繁：你真是个孩子。

冲：(不高兴地)不，妈，我不是孩子了。

my conviction that she's a girl in a million. She said she didn't want to marry me.

FAN: Humph!

CHONG: Now, don't imagine she's just putting on an act by refusing, because it just isn't true. She said her heart belonged to another.

FAN: Who? Did she say?

CHONG: I didn't ask. Most probably some neighbour of hers, someone she sees every day. — Still, the course of true love never runs smooth. I love her, and gradually she'll come to understand me and love me in return.

FAN (*unable to control herself any longer*): No son of mine shall ever marry a girl like her!

CHONG (*taken aback*): Don't be like that about it, Mother! Sifeng's a decent girl. Whenever she mentions you behind your back it's always with the greatest deference and respect.

FAN: What are you going to do now?

CHONG: I intend to tell Father all about it.

FAN: You forget what sort of man your father is.

CHONG: I must tell him. Of course, it's not absolutely certain that I'll ever marry her, but even if she doesn't want me for a husband, I'll still have great respect for her and try to help her. In the meantime, I'd like to see her getting an education. I'm hoping that Father will let me give her half the money set aside for my education, so that she can go to school.

FAN: What a child you are!

CHONG (*crossly*): No, Mother, I'm not a child any

繁：你父亲一句话就把你所有的梦打破了。

冲：我不相信。——(有点沮丧)得了,我们不谈这个吧。妈,昨天我见着哥哥,你说他这次可要到矿上去做事了,他明天就走,他说他太忙,他叫我告诉您一声,他不上楼见您了。您不会怪他吧?

繁：为什么怪他?

冲：我总觉得您同哥哥的感情不如以前那样似的。妈,您想,他自幼就没有母亲,性情自然容易古怪。我想他的母亲一定也感情很重的,哥哥就是一个很有感情的人。

繁：你父亲回来了,你少说哥哥的母亲,免得你父亲又板起脸,叫一家子不高兴。

冲：妈,可是哥哥现在真有点怪,他喝酒喝得很多,脾气很暴,大前天他喝醉了,拉着我的手,跟我说,他恨他自己,说了许多我不大明白的话。

longer.

FAN: One word from your father, and all your castles in the air will collapse.

CHONG: I don't think so. (*A shade despondently.*) All right, don't let's talk about it any more. I say Ping yesterday, Mother. He said he really is going to the mine to work this time and that he's leaving tomorrow. He said would I tell you he's terribly busy and probably won't have time to go upstairs and say good-bye to you himself. You won't mind, I hope?

FAN: Why should I?

CHONG: Somehow I can't help feeling you don't get on with him as well as you used to. You know, Mother, when you consider that he lost his own mother when he was still a child, it's not really surprising that he should have such an odd disposition. His mother must have been a very emotional sort of woman, judging from what he's like.

FAN: Now that your father's at home, it would be better if you didn't mention Ping's mother; otherwise your father will be going around looking as black as thunder again and making everybody feel miserable.

CHONG: But there's no getting away from it that Ping has been acting rather oddly just lately. He's taken to drinking heavily and he'll snap your head off as soon as he looks at you. The other day, when he was drunk, he took me by the hand and told me he hated himself, and then reeled off a whole long rigmarole that I couldn't make head or tail

雷雨

繁：哦！

冲：最后他忽然说，他从前爱过一个他决不应该爱的女人！

繁：(自语)从前？

冲：说完就大哭，当时又逼着我离开他的屋子。

繁：以后还说什么话么？

冲：没有，他很寂寞的样子，我替他很难过，他到现在为什么还不结婚呢？

繁：(喃喃地)谁知道呢？谁知道呢？

冲：(听见门外脚步的声音，回头看)咦，哥哥进来了。

推开中门，周萍进。他约莫有二十八九，颜色苍白，躯干比他的弟弟略微长些。他的面目清秀，甚至于可以说美，但不是一看就使女人醉心的那种男子。他有宽而黑的眉毛，有厚的耳垂，粗大的手掌，乍一看，有时会令人觉得他有些憨气的。不过，若是你再长久地同他坐一坐，会感到他的气味不是你所想的那样纯朴可喜。在他灰暗的眼神里，你看见了不定，犹疑，怯弱同矛盾。他的唇角时常松弛地垂下来。一点疲乏会

of.

FAN: Oh!

CHONG: In the end he suddenly told me that he'd once loved a woman that he never should have loved!

FAN (*to herself*): Once?

CHONG: After that he burst into tears, and the next moment he bundled me out of his room.

FAN: Did he say anything more after that?

CHONG: No, nothing. He looked so forlorn that I felt really sorry for him. Why hasn't he ever got married?

FAN (*in a murmur*): Who knows? Who knows?

CHONG (*looking round at the sound of footsteps outside the door*): Why, if it isn't Ping himself!

(*The centre door is pushed open and Zhou Ping comes in. He is about twenty-eight, very pale, and slightly taller than his half-brother. His features are well formed — one might even say handsome, though he is not exactly the sort of young man who makes women swoon at a glance. His bushy black eyebrows, his thick-lobed ears, and his large, powerful hands may give one the impression, at first sight, of simple honesty; but if you remain in his company a little longer you will realize that his appearance of rough, likable simplicity is deceptive. In his dull, troubled eyes you will discover uncertainty, hesitation, timidity and conflict. The corners of his mouth droop slackly, and at the slightest fatigue his eyes will become set in a lifeless stare,*

使他眸发呆,叫你觉得他不能克制自己,也不能有规律地终身做一件事。他明白自己的病,他在改,不,不如说永远悔恨自己在过去铸成的错误。当着一个新的冲动来时,他的热情,他的欲望,整个又如潮水似地上来,淹没了他。他一星星的理智,只是一段枯枝卷在漩涡里。这样,很自然地一个大错跟着一上更大的错。但他认为自己是有道德观念的,有感情的,于是他痛苦,他恨自己,他羡慕一切没有顾忌,敢做坏事的人。他又羡慕一切能抱定一件事业向前做,依循着一般人所谓的道德,做模范市民,模范家长的人,于是他佩服他的父亲。他的父亲在他的见闻里,除了一点倔强,冷酷,——但是这个也是他喜欢的,因为这两种性格他觉得自己都没有——是一个无瑕的男子。他觉得他在那一方面欺骗他的父亲是不对了,他要把自己"拯救"起

so that you feel he is unable to exert any control over himself or settle down permanently to any regular occupation. He is conscious of his weakness and tries to remedy it — no, perhaps it would be more accurate to say that he suffers perpetual remorse for something wrong which he once did. Nevertheless, when some fresh impulse seizes him, all his passion and desire come flooding back in an overwhelming torrent, and what little is left of his reason becomes nothing more than a dead twig caught up in a whirlpool. Under these circumstances it is quite natural that one act of folly should be succeeded by an even greater one. And so, being in his own estimation a man with a moral outlook and a sensitive nature, he suffers agonies; he hates himslef; and he envies all those who, untroubled by scruples, dare abandon themselves to any wickedness. At the same time, he also envies those who can firmly embrace a career and forge steadily ahead with it, keep to the beaten track of what is generally accepted as morality, and finally emerge as model citizens and model family men. It is this that lies behind his admiration for his father, who, so far as he can judge from his own limited experience, is a man of flawless character — except for a certain amount of obstinacy and coldness, and he admires him even for this, for these are traits which he is conscious of lacking himself. He feels he has done wrong in deceiving his father, and wants to rid himself to

来,他需要新的"力",无论是什么,只要能帮助他,把他由矛盾的苦海中救出来。他愿意找,他找着四凤,他发现他最需要的那一点东西,是洋溢地流动着在四凤的身体里。他有"青春",有"美",有热情,固然他也觉得她粗,但是现在他觉到这才是他需要的,现在他厌恶一切忧郁过分的女人,同那些细致的情绪。

然而依然有一种不满的感情的波纹在他心里隐约地流荡着,潜伏着。当他认为四凤不能了解也不能安慰他的时候,他便不自主地纵酒,狂欢,沉缅在一切外面的刺激之中。于是他精神颓丧,永远成了不安定的神情。

现在他穿一件藏青的绸袍,西服裤,漆皮鞋,没有修脸,整个是不整齐。他打着呵欠。

冲:哥哥。

萍:你在这儿。

繁:(觉得没有理自己)萍!

萍:哦?(低了头,又抬起)您——您也在这儿。

繁:我刚下楼来。

萍:(转头问周冲)父亲没有出去吧?

this feeling, but for this he needs new strength-anything so long as it will help him extricate himself from the morass of tormenting indecision which is dragging him down. His search has brought him to Sifeng, and he has discovered in her the things, which he most desperately needs: for she has youth, beauty and passion in over-flowing abundance. It is true that he finds her rather unrefined, but he has now realized that this lack of refinement is just what he needs, and he has now come to loathe over-wistful women and the subtler emotions.

Yet his mind is still troubled by a hidden, fitful undercurrent of dissatisfaction. Whenever he becomes obsessed by the idea that Sifeng is incapable of understanding and comforting him, he plunges headlong into heavy drinking and all the usual round of riotous pleasure and debauchery. This leaves him more listless and depressed than ever, a prey to perpetual restlessness.

At the moment he is wearing a dark blue silk gown, European-style trousers, and patent leather shoes. He is unshaven and generally untidy. He is yawning.)

CHONG: Hullo, Ping.

ZHOU PING: So here you are.

FAN (*feeling slighted*): Ping!

PING: Oh. (*Lowers his eyes, then looks up again.*) I — er — I didn't know you were here too.

FAN: I've just come downstairs.

PING (*turning to Zhou Chong*): I suppose Father's

雷雨

冲：没有，你预备见他么？

萍：我想在临走以前跟父亲谈一次。(一直走向书房。)

冲：你不要去。

萍：他老人家干什么呢？

冲：他大概跟一个人谈公事。我刚才见着他，他说他一会儿会到这儿来，叫我们在这儿等他。

萍：那我先回到我屋子里写封信。(要走。)

冲：不，哥哥，母亲说好久不见你。你不愿意一齐坐一坐，谈谈么？

繁：你看，你让哥哥歇一歇，他愿意一个人坐着的。

萍：(有些烦)那也不见得，我总怕父亲回来，您很忙，所以——

冲：你不知道母亲病了么？

繁：你哥哥怎么会把我的病放在心上？

冲：妈！

萍：您好一点了么？

繁：谢谢你，我刚刚下楼。

萍：对了，我预备明天离开家里到矿上去。

繁：哦，(停)好得很。——什么时候回来呢？

still here?

CHONG: Yes, he is. Did you want to see him?

PING: I was thinking of having a chat with him before I go.
(*Walks straight towards the door of the study.*)

CHONG: You can't go in now.

PING: Why, what's Father doing, then?

CHONG: Probably having a business discussion with a visitor. When I saw him a moment ago, he said he'd be out soon and told us to wait for him here.

PING: I'd better get back to my room and write a letter first, then. (*Turns to go.*)

CHONG: Oh no, you don't. Mother says she hasn't seen you for a long time. Why not sit down with us and have a chat?

FAN: Don't stop him, Chong. Let him go and have a rest if he wants to. I expect he wants to be left alone.

PING (*somewhat nettled*): Not at all. It's just that I thought you'd be very busy now that Father's at home, and I —

CHONG: But don't you realize Mother's been ill?

FAN: Why should *he* worry his head about my being ill?

CHONG: Mother!

PING: Are you better now?

FAN: Yes, thank you. I've just this moment come downstairs.

PING: Good. I'm leaving for the mine tomorrow.

FAN: Oh. (*After a pause.*) That'll be nice for you.
— When do you expect to be back?

萍：不一定，也许两年，也许三年。哦，这屋子怎么闷气得很。

冲：窗户已经打开了。——我想，大概是大雨要来了。

繁：(停一停)你在矿上做什么呢？

冲：妈，你忘了，哥哥是专门学矿科的。

繁：这是理由么，萍？

萍：(拿起报纸)说不出来，像是家里住得太久了，烦得很。

繁：(笑)我怕你是胆小吧？

萍：怎么讲？

繁：这屋子曾经闹过鬼，你忘了。

萍：没有忘。但是这儿我住厌了。

繁：(笑)假若我是你，这周围的人我都会厌恶，我也离开这个死地方的。

冲：妈，我不要您这样说话。

萍：(忧郁地)哼，我自己对自己都恨不够，我还配说厌恶别人？——(叹一口气)弟弟，我想回屋去了。(起立。)

　　书房门开。

冲：别走啦，大概是爸爸来了。

周朴园的声音：我的意思是这么办，没有问题

PING: Job to say, really. I may be gone two years, perhaps three. Whew, it's suffocating in here!

CHONG: Well, we've opened all the windows. — Seems to me we're in for a heavy storm.

FAN (*after a pause*): What will you be doing at the mine?

CHONG: Don't forget, Mother, that Ping specialized in mining when he was at the university.

FAN: Is that the reason why you're going, Ping?

PING (*picking up a newspaper*): I don't quite know how to put it. I feel I've been at home too long and I'm getting fed up.

FAN (*with a smile*): I rather think it's because you're afraid.

PING: How do you mean?

FAN: You've forgotten that this room was haunted once.

PING: No, I haven't forgotten. I've lived here long enough, that's all.

FAN (*smiling*): If I were in your place I'd be absolutely sick and tired of everybody here, and I'd get out of this ghastly place, too.

CHONG: You mustn't say such things, Mother.

PING (*gloomily*): Ah, I can't hate myself enough: Who am I to be sick and tired of other people? (*Heaving a sigh.*)

— Well, Chong, I'm off back to my room. (*He stands up.*)

(*The door of the study opens.*)

CHONG: Don't go. I think Father's coming out now.

ZHOU PUYUAN'S VOICE: Well, I think if we do it like

了,很好,再见吧,不送。

门大开,周朴园进。他约莫有五六十上下,鬓发已经斑白,带着椭圆形的金边眼镜,一对沉鸷的眼在底下闪铄着。像一切起家立业的人物,他的威严在儿孙面前格外显得峻厉。他穿的衣服,还是二十年前的新装,一件团花的官纱大褂,底下是白纺绸的衬衫,长衫的领扣松散着,露着颈上的肉。他的衣服很舒展地贴在身上,整洁,没有一些尘垢。他有些胖,背微微地伛偻,腮肉松弛地垂下来。眼眶下陷,眸子却闪闪地放着光彩。他的脸带着多年的世故和劳碌,一种冷峭的目光和偶然在嘴角上逼出的冷笑,看出他平日的专横,自是和倔强。年轻时一切的冒失狂妄,已经为脸上的皱纹深深遮盖着,再也寻不着一点痕迹,只有他的半白的头发还保持昔日的丰采,很润泽地分梳到后面。在阳光底下,他的脸呈着银白色,一般人说这就是贵人的特征,所以他才有这样大的矿产。

that it'll be plain sailing. Right, well, good-bye.... Find your own way out?

(*The door opens wide and Zhou Puyuan appears. He could be anywhere between fifty and sixty. His hair is already greying at the temples. He wears oval, gold-rimmed spectacles, and his deep-set eyes flash with a hawk-like intensity. Like all founders of family fortunes, his forbidding presence overawes his chidren. He is dressed in the latest fashion of twenty years ago — a patterned satin gown with a white silk shirt underneath and the collar unbuttoned to reveal a fleshy neck. His clothes, neat and spotlessly clean, look roomy and comfortable. He is rather fat, and has a slight stoop and a' loose, flabby jowl. His eyes are sunken, yet they glitter hard and keen. The lines on his face tell a tale of long years of toiling and scheming, and his cold, insolent stare and the sardonic smile which occasionally twists the corners of his mouth proclaim his tyrannical temper, self-righteousness and obsinacy. All signs of the wild abandon of his youth are now buried deep beneath his wrinkles, except that his hair, though greying, still retains its youthful lustre. It is neatly parted and combed back from the forehead sleek and glossy. In the sunlight his face will take on that silvery sheen which is popularly supposed to be the distinguishing mark of a man of wealth and position. This is the secret of his success as a mine-owner, no doubt.*)

萍,冲:爸。

冲:客走了?

朴:(点头,转向蘩漪)你怎么今天下楼来了,完全好了么?

蘩:病原来不重——回来身体好么?

朴:还好。——你应当再到楼上去休息。冲儿,你看你母亲的气色比以前怎么样?

冲:母亲原来就没有什么病。

朴:(不喜欢儿子们这样回答老人的话)谁告诉你的?我不在的时候,你常来问你母亲的病么?(坐在沙发上。)

蘩:(怕他又来教训)朴园,你的样子像有点瘦了似的。——矿上罢工的事怎么样?

朴:昨天早上已经复工,不成问题。

冲:爸爸,怎么鲁大海还在这儿等着要见您呢?

朴:谁是鲁大海?

冲:鲁贵的儿子。前年荐进去,这次当代表的。

朴:这个人!我想这个人有背景,厂方已经把他

PING: Hullo, Father.
CHONG: Hullo, Father.
CHONG: Your visitor gone?
ZHOU (*nodding, then turning to Fanyi*): I'm surprised to see you up. Better?
FAN: Oh, I wasn't so very ill in any case. How are you this time?
ZHOU: Well enough. — I think you ought to go back upstairs and rest, though. Well, Chong, how do you think your mother looks compared with her usual self?
CHONG: There's never been anything wrong with her at all.
ZHOU (*who does not like having his sons answer him back like this*): Where did you get that idea from? I hope you made it your business to inquire after your mother's health all the time I was away. (*He sits down on a sofa.*)
FAN (*sensing that one of his usual lectures is imminent*): Puyuan, you seem to have got thinner since last time. — What's happened about the strike at the mine?
ZHOU: Oh, they've been back at work since yesterday morning. It's all blown over now.
CHONG: Then why is Lu Dahai still here waiting to see you, Father?
ZHOU: Who's Lu Dahai?
CHONG: Lu Gui's son. You know: Lu Gui got you to give him a job the year before last. He's just turned up as the miners' representative.
ZHOU: Oh, him! Put up to it by somebody outside,

开除了。

冲：开除！爸爸，这个人脑筋很清楚，我方才跟他谈了一回。代表罢工的工人并不见得就该开除。

朴：哼，现在一般青年人，跟工人谈谈，说两三句不关痛痒，同情的话，像是一件很时髦的事情！

冲：我以为这些人替自己的一群人努力，我们应当同情的。并且我们这样享福，同他们争饭吃，是不对的。这不是时髦不时髦的事。

朴：（眼翻上来）你知道社会是什么？你读过几本关于社会经济的书？我记得我在德国念书的时候，对于这方面，我自命比你这种半瓶醋的社会思想要彻底的多！

冲：（被压制下去，然而）爸，我听说矿上对于这次受伤的工人不给一点抚恤金。

朴：（头一扬）我认为你这次说话说得太多了。（向蘩漪）这两年他学得很像你了。（看钟）十分钟后我还有一个客来，嗯，你们关于自

unless I'm much mistaken. Anyway, he's already been sacked.

CHONG: Sacked! But Father, the man knows what he's talking about. I've just this moment had a chat with him. You can hardly sack a man just because he's a strikers' representative.

ZHOU: H'm! It seems to be quite the fashion nowadays for young men to hobnob with the workers and go around mouthing meaningless words of sympathy with them!

CHONG: I think we ought to sympathize with them. After all, they're only doing their best to help their own people. Besides, it's not right that people who are as well off as we are should grudge them enough to keep body and soul together. And it's not a matter of fashion, either.

ZHOU (*turning up his eyes*): What do you know about society? How many books on sociology and economics have you read? I rememher now I used to have the same sort of ideas when I was a student in Germany — except that my ideas were much more thorough than your half-baked notions!

CHONG (*thoroughly browbeaten, yet firing a parting shot*): Father, I hear the miners who were injured this time didn't get a penny in the way of compensation.

ZHOU (*looking swiftly up*): I think you've said more than enough for the time being. (*Turning to Fanyi.*) He's been getting just like you these past two years. (*Looking at the clock.*) I've got an-

己有什么话说么?

萍:爸,刚才我就想见您。

朴:哦,什么事?

萍:我想明天就到矿上去。

朴:这边公司的事,你交代完了么?

萍:差不多完了。我想请父亲给我点实在的事情做,我不想看看就完事。

朴:(停一下,看周萍)苦的事你成么?要做就做到底。我不愿意我的儿子叫旁人说闲话的。

萍:这两年在这儿做事太舒服,心里很想在内地乡下走走。

朴:让我想想。——(停)你可以明天起身,做哪一类事情,到了矿上我再打电报给你。

四凤由饭厅门入,端了碗普洱茶。

冲:(犹豫地)爸爸。

朴:(知道他又有新花样)嗯,你?

冲:我现在想跟爸爸商量一件很重要的事。

朴:什么?

other appointment in ten minutes' time. Now, have any of you got anything to see me about?

PING: Yes, I wanted to see you, Father.

ZHOU: Oh, yes? What about?

PING: I want to leave for the mine tomorrow.

ZHOU: Have you finished handing over at Head Office?

PING: Just about. I hope you'll give me some real work to do this time. I don't want to just stand by and watch.

ZHOU (*pausing a moment, then looking him full in the face*): You think you're up to a really tough job? There'd be no backing out once you'd taken it on, you know. I won't have a son of mine make a fool of himself.

PING: I've been having much too easy a time here these last two years, and I'm really keen no getting away from the city and having a spell in the interior.

ZHOU: Now let me think. (*A pause.*) Yes, you may as well leave tomorrow if you want to. I'll send you a wire when you get there and let you know exactly what you job will be.

(*Sifeng comes in from the dining-room with a bowl of Yunnan tea.*)

CHONG (*hesitantly*): Er, Father.

ZHOU (*sensing fresh trouble from this quarter*): What is it now?

CHONG: There's something rather important I'd like to discuss with you.

ZHOU: Well?

冲：(低下头)我想把我的学费的一部分分出来。

朴：哦？

冲：(鼓起勇气)把我的学费拿出一部分送给——

四凤端茶，放在周朴园面前。

朴：四凤，——(向周冲)你先等一等。——(向四凤)叫你给太太煎的药呢？

四：煎好了。

朴：为什么不拿来？

四凤看繁漪，不说话。

繁：(觉出空气不对了)她刚才给我倒来了，我没有喝。

朴：为什么？(停，向四凤)药呢？

繁：(忙说)倒了，我叫四凤倒了。

朴：(慢)倒了？哦？——(向四凤)药还有么？

四：药罐里还有一点。

朴：倒了来。

繁：(反抗地)我不愿意喝这种苦东西。

朴：(向四凤)倒了来。

四凤走到左面倒药。

冲：爸，妈不愿意，您何必这样强迫呢？

朴：你同你母亲都不知道自己的病在哪儿。(向

CHONG (*banging his head*): I'd like to share my allowance with someone.
ZHOU: Eh?
CHONG (*screwing up his courage*): My school allowance. I'd like to share it with —
(*Sifeng places the tea in front of Zhou Puyuan.*)
ZHOU: Sifeng — (*to Zhou Chong*) just a minute — (*to Sifeng again*) what about the medicine I told you to get ready for the mistress?
FENG: I've done it.
ZHOU: Then why isn't it here?
(*Sifeng says nothing, but looks at Fanyi.*)
FAN (*sensing a certain tension in the air*): She got it for me just a short while ago, but I didn't take it.
ZHOU: Why not? (*Pauses, then turns to Sifeng.*) Where is it now?
FAN (*quickly*): Down the sink. I told her to pour it away.
ZHOU (*slowly*): Pour it away? I — see! (*To Sifeng.*) Is there any of it left?
FENG: There's still a little drop left in the jar.
ZHOU: Go and get it.
FAN (*protesting*): I won't touch it — it's too bitter.
ZHOU (*to Sifeng*): Go on.
(Sifeng walks across to the left and pours the medicine into a small bowl.)
CHONG: But, Father! If Mother doesn't want it, there's no need to force her to take it.
ZHOU: Neither you nor your mother knows what's wrong with either of you. (*To his wife, in a low*

繁漪,低声)你喝了,就会完全好的。(见四凤犹豫,指药)送到太太那里去。

繁:(忍顺地)好,先放在这儿。

四凤放下药碗。

朴:(不高兴地)你最好现在喝了它吧。

繁:(忽然)四凤,你把它拿走。

朴:(忽然严厉地)喝了它,不要任性,当着这么大的孩子。

繁:(声颤)我不想喝。

朴:冲儿,你把药端到母亲面前去。

冲:(反抗地)爸!

朴:(怒视)去!

周冲只好把药端到繁漪面前。

朴:说,请母亲喝。

冲:(拿着药碗,手发颤)爸,您不要这样。

朴:你说什么?

萍:(低头,至周冲前,低声)听爸爸的话吧,爸爸的脾气你是知道的。

冲:(含着泪,向着母亲)您喝吧,为我喝一点吧,要不然,父亲的气是不会消的。

繁:(恳求地)留着我晚上喝不成么?

voice.) Come now, it'll make you quite well again if you'll only take it. (*Seeing that Sifeng seems still undecided, he points to the medicine bowl.*) Hand it to the mistress.

FAN (*forcing herself to agree to it*): All right. Put it down here for the moment.

(*Sifeng puts down the bowl.*)

ZHOU (*with annoyance*): I think you'd better take it at once.

FAN (*bursting out*): Sifeng, take it away!

ZHOU (*with a sudden harshness*): Take it, I say! Don't be so headstrong. And in front of the children, too!

FAN (*her voice trembling*): But I don't want it.

ZHOU: Chong, hand your mother the medicine.

CHONG (*protesting*): Now, Father!

ZHOU (*glaring*): Go on!

(*Zhou Chong reluctantly takes the medicine across to Fanyi.*)

ZHOU: Now ask her to take it.

CHONG (*holding the medicine bowl with trembling hands*): Father, you're taking it too far!

ZHOU: What's that?

PING (*going across with bent head to Zhou Chong and speaking in an undertone*): You'd better do as Father says. You know what he's like.

CHONG (*to his mother, with tears in his eyes*): Please take it, Mother, if only for my sake. Father won't let up until you do.

FAN (*pleading*): Can't I leave it now and take it in the evening?

朴:(冷峻地)蘩漪,当了母亲的人,处处应当替孩子着想,就是自己不保重身体,也应当替孩子做个服从的榜样。

蘩:(望望周朴园,又望望周萍,拿起药又放下)不!我喝不下!

朴:萍儿,劝你母亲喝下去。

萍:爸!我——

朴:去,跪下,劝你的母亲。

萍:(走至蘩漪前;向周朴园,求恕地)爸爸!

朴:(高声)跪下!

周萍望着蘩漪;蘩漪泪痕满面。周冲气得发抖。

朴:叫你跪下!

周萍正要向下跪。

蘩:(望着周萍,急促地)我喝,我现在喝!(喝了两口,眼泪又涌出来,望一望周朴园的峻厉的眼和苦恼着的周萍,咽下愤恨,一气喝下)哦……(哭着,由右边饭厅跑下。)半晌。

朴:(看表)还有三分钟。(向周冲)你刚才说的事呢?

ZHOU (*with icy severity*): Fanyi, as a mother, you've got to be constantly thinking of the children. Even if you don't particularly care about your own health, you should at least set the children an example by being obedient.

FAN (*looking from Zhou Puyuan to Zhou Ping, then picking up the bowl and putting it down again*): No! I can't!

ZHOU: Ping, persuade your mother to take it.

PING: But Father, I —

ZHOU: Go on! Down on your knees and persuade her!

PING (*going across to Fanyi, then looking appealingly towards Zhou Puyuan*): Father!

ZHOU (*shouting*): Down on your kness!

(*Zhou Ping looks dumbly at Fanyi, who is in tears, while Zhou Chong trembles with rage.*)

ZHOU: Down on your knees, I said!

(*Zhou Ping is about to kneel down, when —*)

FAN (*hurriedly, her eyes on Zhou Ping*): All right! I'll take it now. (*She takes a couple of sips, but immediately the tears stream down her cheeks again. Then, with a glance at her harsh-eyed husband and the distressed Zhou Ping, she swallows her resentment and finishes the medicine at a single gulp.*) Oh — oh — oh — (*She runs out weeping through the dining-room door.*)

(*A long silence.*)

ZHOU (*looking at his watch*): There's still three minutes to spare. (*To Zhou Chong.*) You were saying?

冲：(抬头,慢慢地)什么?

朴：你说把你的学费分出一部分?——嗯,是怎么样?

冲：(低声)我现在没有什么事情啦。

朴：真没有什么新鲜的问题啦么?

冲：(哭声)没有什么,没有什么,——妈的话是对的。(跑向饭厅。)

朴：冲儿,上哪儿去?

冲：到楼上去看看妈。

朴：就这么跑了么?

冲：(抑制着自己,走回去)是,爸,我要走了,您有事吩咐么?

朴：去吧。

周冲向饭厅走了两步。

朴：回来。

冲：爸爸。

朴：你告诉你的母亲,说我已经请德国的克大夫来给她看病。

冲：妈不是已经吃了您的药了么?

朴：我看你的母亲,精神有点失常,病像是不轻。(回头向周萍)我看,你也是一样。

萍：爸,我想下去歇一会。

CHONG (*looking up, slowly*): Eh?

ZHOU: You were saying something about wanting to share your allowance with someone. — Well, what's it all about?

CHONG (*in a low voice*): I've changed my mind about it now.

ZHOU: You're quite sure there's nothing worrying you?

CHONG (*with a sob in his voice*): No, nothing, nothing. — Mother was right. (*He hurries towards the dining-room.*)

ZHOU: Chong! Where are you going?

CHONG: Upstairs to see Mother.

ZHOU: Just like that? Where are your manners?

CHONG (*controlling himself and turning back*): Sorry, Father. May I be excused?

ZHOU: All right. You may go now.

(*Zhou Chong turns and makes for the dining-room again.*)

ZHOU: Come back.

CHONG: Yes, Father?

ZHOU: Tell your mother I've asked Dr. Kramer to come and have a look at her.

CHONG: But she's already taken the medicine you got for her.

ZHOU: I think your mother's becoming mentally unbalanced. It looks serious to me. (*Over his shoulder to Zhou Ping.*) And the same goes for you, too.

PING: Well, Father, I think I'll go back to my room for a rest.

朴：不，你不要走。我有话跟你说。（向周冲）你告诉她，说克大夫是个有名的脑病专家，我在德国认识的。来了，叫她一定看一看，听见了没有？

冲：听见了。（走了两步）爸，没有事啦？

朴：上去吧。

周冲由饭厅下。

朴：（回头向四凤）四凤，我记得我告诉过你，这个房子你们没有事就得走的。

四：是，老爷。（也由饭厅下。）

鲁贵由书房上。

贵：（见着老爷，便不自主地好像说不出话来）老，老爷。客，客来了！

朴：哦，先请到大客厅里去。

贵：是，老爷。（下。）

朴：怎么这窗户谁开开了？

萍：弟弟跟我开的。

朴：关上。（擦眼镜）这屋子不要底下人随便进来，回头我预备一个人在这里休息的。

萍：是。

朴：（擦着眼镜，看周围的家具）这间屋子的家具

ZHOU: No, don't go yet. I want to have a talk with you. (*To Zhou Chong.*) Tell her Dr. Kramer is a famous German psychiatrist — a specialist. I knew him when I was in Germany. When he calls, she must see him without fail. Got it?

CHONG: Yes, all right. (*Turning back after a few steps.*) Anything else, Father?

ZHOU: No. Off you go.

(*Zhou Chong goes out into the dining-room.*)

ZHOU (*turning and finding Sifeng still there*): Sifeng, I seem to rememher telling you once that the servants are not to hang around in this room when they're not wanted.

FENG: Very well, sir. (*She also goes out through the dining-room door.*)

(*Lu Gui enters from the study.*)

LU (*becoming incoherent upon suddenly finding himself confronted by his master*): Oh, er, a — a gentleman to see you, sir.

ZHOU: Oh, show him into the big drawing-room.

LU: Very good, sir. (*He goes out.*)

ZHOU: Hullo! Who's been opening the windows?

PING: Chong and I opened them.

ZHOU: Shut 'em. (*Taking off his spectacles and wiping them.*) I don't want the servants running in and out of this room all the time. I shall be resting in here presently and I don't want to be disturbed.

PING: I'll see to it.

ZHOU (*still wiping his spectacles, and looking all round at the furniture*): Most of the things in this

多半是你生母顶喜欢的东西。我从南边移到北边,搬了多少次家,总是不肯丢下的。(戴上眼镜,咳嗽一声)这屋子摆的样子,我愿意总是三十年前的老样子,这叫我的眼看着舒服一点。(踱到桌前,看桌上的相片)你的生母永远喜欢夏天把窗户关上的。

萍:(强笑)不过,爸爸,纪念母亲也不必——

朴:(突然抬起头来)我听人说你现在做了一件很对不起自己的事情。

萍:(惊)什——什么?

朴:(走到周萍的面前)你知道你现在做的事是对不起你的父亲么?并且——(停)——对不起你的母亲么?

萍:(失措)爸爸。

朴:(仁慈地)你是我的长子,我不愿意当着人谈这件事。(稍停,严厉地)我听说我在外边的时候,你这两年来在家里很不规矩。

萍:(更惊恐)爸,没有的事,没有。

朴:一个人敢做,就要敢当。

萍:(失色)爸!

room were your own mother's favourites. That's why, when we moved up here from the south, and all the times we've moved house since then, I've never been able to bring myself to part with any of it. (*He puts on his spectacles and coughs.*) I want the furniture in this room kept just the way it was arranged thirty years ago. It makes me feel better to see it like that. (*He strolls across to the bureau and looks at the photograph on it.*) Your own mother always liked the windows closed in summer.

PING (*with a forced smile*): Though even if you do want to keep up Mother's memory, I still don't see why you've got to —

ZHOU (*suddenly looking up*): I hear you've been behaving rather discreditably.

PING (*alarmed*): Wh — What!

ZHOU (*walking up to him*): Do you realize that what you're doing is a disgrace to your father? And also (*pauses*) — to your mother?

PING (*beginning to panic*): Father!

ZHOU (*kindly*): You're my eldest son, and I don't think this need go any farther than the two of us. (*He pauses a moment, then his voice becomes stern.*) I hear your private life's been highly irregular while I've been away these last two years.

PING (*the colour draining from his cheeks*): Father!

ZHOU: If a man takes a risk, he must be prepared to accept the consequences.

PING (*with growing alarm*): Oh, no, Father, it just isn't true!

朴：公司的人说你总是在跳舞场里鬼混，尤其是这两三个月，喝酒，赌钱，整夜地不回家。

萍：哦，(放下心)您说的是——

朴：这些事是真的么？(半晌)说实话！

萍：真的，爸爸。(红了脸。)

朴：将近三十的人应当懂得"自爱"！——你还记得你的名字为什么叫萍么？

萍：记得。

朴：你自己说一遍。

萍：那是因为母亲的名讳是侍萍，母亲临死，自己替我起的名字。

朴：那我请你为你的生母，把现在的行为完全改过来。

萍：是，爸爸，那是我一时的荒唐。

鲁贵由书房上。

贵：老爷。客人——等，等了好半天啦。

朴：知道。

鲁贵退。

朴：我的家庭是我认为最圆满，最有秩序的家庭，我的儿子我也认为都还是健全的子弟，我教育出来的孩子，我绝对不愿叫任何人说他们一点闲话的。

萍：是，爸爸。

朴：来人啦。(自语)哦，我有点累啦。

ZHOU: They told me at Head Office that you spend all your time hanging around the dance-halls, and that the last two or three months you've got worse: out all night drinking and gambling.

PING: Oh, that. (*With obvious relief.*) You mean —

ZHOU: Is all this true? (*After a long pause.*) Come on, I want the truth!

PING: It's quite true, Father. (*He blushes.*)

ZHOU: A man approaching thirty should have learned a certain amount of self-respect! — Do you rememher why you were named Ping?

PING: Yes.

ZHOU: Tell me why, then.

PING: It's because Mother's name was Shiping. She gave me the name "Ping" herself, on her death-bed.

ZHOU: Then perhaps you'll mend your ways out of respect for your own mother.

PING: I will, Father. It was only a momentary lapse.

(*Lu Gui enters from the study.*)

LU: Excuse me, sir, but the visitor's — er — he's been here some time now.

ZHOU: All right.

(*Lu Gui withdraws.*)

ZHOU: I pride myself on having one of the most satisfactory and well-behaved families possible, and I think my sons are both good, healthy lads. I've brought the two of you up, and I won't have you giving anybody an excuse to gossip about you.

PING: No, Father.

ZHOU: Hullo, there, a servant! (*To himself.*) Why, I

雷雨

周萍扶周朴园至沙发坐下。

鲁贵上。

贵：老爷。

朴：你请客到这边来坐。

贵：是，老爷。

萍：爸，您歇一会吧。

朴：不，你不要管。（向鲁贵）去，请进来。

贵：是，老爷。（下。）

周朴园拿出一支雪茄，周萍为他点上；周朴园徐徐抽烟，端坐。

——幕落

feel suddenly tired.

(*Zhou Ping takes his father's arm and steers him to a sofa, where he sits down.*)

(*Lu Gui comes in.*)

LU: Yes, sir?

ZHOU: Show the visitor in here.

LU: Very good, sir.

PING: Won't you have a rest first, Father?

ZHOU: No. Don't worry about me. (*To Lu Gui.*) Show him in, then.

LU: Yes, sir. (*He goes out.*)

(*Zhou Puyuan produces a cigar, and Zhou Ping gives him a light. He sits sedately, puffing slowly at the cigar.*)

(*Curtain*)

雷雨

第二幕

午饭后,天气很阴沉,更郁热,低沉湿潮的空气,使人烦躁。周萍一个人由饭厅走上来,望望花园,冷清清的,没有一个人。偷偷走到书房门口,书房里是空的,也没有人。忽然想起父亲在别的地方会客,他放下心,又走到窗户前开窗门,看着外面绿荫荫的树丛。他吹出一种奇怪的哨声,低低地叫了两三声"四凤"。

四凤由外面轻轻地跑进来。

萍:(回头,低声,热烈地)凤儿!(拉着四凤的手。)

四:不,(推开他)不。(谛听,四面望)看看,有人!

萍:没有,凤,你坐下。(推她到沙发前。)

四:(不安地)老爷呢?

萍:在大客厅会客呢。

Act Two

After lunch. Beneath a dark, overcast sky, the afternoon is even more sultry and oppressive than the morning has been. The close, damp air is of the kind that makes one lose one's temper on the slightest provocation. Zhou Ping appears from the dining-room. He is alone. He peers out at the garden: it is silent and deserted. He tiptoes across to the door of the study: the study: the study is empty. He suddenly remembers that his father is seeing visitors in another part of the house. Reassured by this thought, he goes over to the window again, opens it, and looks out at the green, tree-canopied garden. He gives a peculiar whistle and calls "Sifeng!" several times in a low voice.

Sifeng slips stealthily into the room.

PING (*turning and speaking softly and with warmth*): Sifeng! (*He takes her bands in his.*)
FENG: No. (*Pushing him away.*) Don't. (*Listening tensely and glancing all round.*) There may be someone about.
PING: Not a soul, Feng. Come and sit down. (*He steers her to a sofa.*)
FENG (*uneasily*): Where's the master, then?
PING: Oh, he's seeing visitors in the large drawing-room.

四:(坐下,叹一口长气,望着)总是这样偷偷摸摸的。

萍:嗯。

四:你连叫我都不敢叫。

萍:所以我要离开这儿哪。

四:(想一下)哦,太太怪可怜的。为什么老爷回来,头一次见太太就发这么大的脾气?

萍:父亲就是这个样,他的话,向来不能改的。他的意见就是法律。

四:(怯懦地)我——我怕得很。

萍:怕什么?

四:我怕万一老爷知道了,我怕。有一天,你说过,要把我们的事情告诉老爷的。

萍:(摇头,深沉地)可怕的事不在这儿。

四:还有什么?

萍:(忽然地)你没有听见什么话?

四:什么?(停)没有。

萍:关于我,你没有听见什么?

四:没有。

萍:从来没听见过什么?

四:(不愿提)没有——你说什么?

萍:那——没什么!没什么!

四:(真挚地)我信你,我相信你以后永远不会骗我。这我就够了。——刚才,我听你说,你明天就要到矿上去。

FENG (*sitting down, then looking up into his face with a long sigh*): It's always like this, always so underhand.

PING: Mm.

FENG: You don't even dare call out my name.

PING: That's why I'm leaving.

FENG (*after a moment's thought*): I'm really sorry for the mistress after the way the master lost his temper with her. It's the first time he's seen her since he's been back, too.

PING: That's Father all over. His word is law, and he'll never take anything back once he's said it.

FENG (*nervously*): I — I'm terribly afraid.

PING: What of?

FENG: In case the master should find out about us. I'm terrified. You said once you'd tell him about us.

PING (*shaking his head, darkly*): There are worse things than that to worry about.

FENG: Such as?

PING (*suddenly*): You haven't heard anything?

FENG: Eh? (*After a pause.*) Why, no.

PING: Nothing about me?

FENG: No.

PING: Have you never heard anything at all?

FENG (*finding the topic distasteful to her*): No, never. — What do you mean, anyway?

PING: Well, er — oh, nothing. Nothing at all.

FENG (*earnestly*): I trust you. I trust you to be true to me, always. That's all I want. — A little while ago you were saying you'd be leaving for the mine tomorrow.

萍：我昨天晚上已经跟你说过了。

四：(爽直地)你为什么不带我去？

萍：因为(笑)因为我不想带你去。

四：这边的事我早晚是要走的。——太太，说不定今天就要辞掉我。

萍：(没想到)她要辞掉你，——为什么？

四：你不要问。

萍：不，我要知道。

四：自然因为我做错了事。我想，太太大概没有这个意思。也许是我瞎猜。(停)萍，你带我去好不好？

萍：不。

四：(温柔地)萍，我好好地侍候你，你要这么一个人。我给你缝衣服，烧饭做菜，我都做得好，只要你叫我跟你在一块儿。

周萍不做声。

四：我知道你一个人在外头是不成的。

萍：凤，你看不出来，现在我怎么能带你出去？——你这不是孩子话么？

PING: I told you all about it last night.

FENG (*coming straight to the point*): Why won't you take me with you?

PING: Because — (*he smiles*) because I don't choose to.

FENG: But you know I'll have to leave this job sooner or later. Any day now the mistress is likely to give me the sack — perhaps even today.

PING (*to whom such a possibility has never occurred*): Give you the sack! — But why should she want to do that?

FENG: Never you mind why.

PING: But I want to know.

FENG: Well, for not doing my job properly, of course. Though I may be wrong — making wild guesses. — I don't expect she will, though. (*After a pause.*) You will take me with you, won't you, Ping?

PING: No.

FENG (*tenderly*): I'll do everything I can to make you comfortable, Ping. You need someone like me to look after you. I'll cook for you and sew on your buttons and darn your socks for you — I'm very good at all that sort of thing — if only you'll let me go with you!

(*Zhou Ping says nothing.*)

FENG: I know for certain that once you get away from home you'll be lost without someone to look after you.

PING: But don't you see, Feng? I just can't take you with me. — Now don't you think you're being

四：萍，你带我走！我不连累你，要是外面因为我，说你的坏话，我立刻就走。你——你不要怕。

萍：(急躁地)凤，你以为我这么自私自利么？你不该这么看我。——哼，我怕什么？(管不住自己)这些年，我的心都死了，我恨极了我自己。现在我刚刚有点生气，我能放开胆子喜欢一个女人，我反而怕人家骂？哼，让大家说吧，周家大少爷看上他家里面的女下人，怕什么，我喜欢她。

四：(安慰地)萍，不要难过。你做了什么，我也不怨你的。(想。)

萍：(平静下来)你现在想什么？

四：他又把前一个月的话跟我提了。

萍：他说，他爱你？

四：不，他问我肯嫁他不肯。

萍：你呢？

四：我说我许了人家了。

萍：他没有问旁的？

四：没有，他倒说，要供我上学。

rather childish about it?

FENG: Do take me with you, Ping! I promise I won't be any trouble to you. If people started gossiping about you because of me, I'd go away at once. You needn't be afraid of scandal.

PING (*irritably*): Now, Feng! You don't imagine I'm that selfish, do you? You mustn't think I'm that sort. — Humph. Afraid of scandal indeed! (*Unable to restrain himself.*) For years now my heart has been dead, and for years I've hated myself with all the hatred I could muster. Do you imagine that now, now that I've begun to revive and summoned up the courage to fall in love with a woman — do you imagine I'm going to start worrying about what people say? Huh! Let'em say! Let them say what they like about "young Mr. Zhou falling for one of the servants" — what do I care? I love her.

FENG (*soothingly*): There, Ping. Don't let it upset you. Whatever you've done, I won't hold it against you. (*She becomes lost in thought.*)

PING (*calmer now*): Penny for your thoughts?

FENG: He's repeated what he said a month ago.

PING: You mean that he loves you?

FENG: No, he's proposed.

PING: And what did you say to that?

FENG: I said I was already engaged to somebody else.

PING: Didn't he want to know more?

FENG: No. Though he did say he'd like to pay for me to go to school.

萍:上学?(笑)这孩子!——可是,谁知道,你听了他的话,也许很喜欢的。我已经快三十了,你才十八,我也不比他的将来有希望,并且我做过许多——见不得人的事。

四:萍,你不要同我瞎扯,我现在心里很难过。你得想法子,他是个小孩,老是这样装着腔,对付他,我实在不喜欢。你又不许我跟他说明白。

萍:我没有叫你不跟他说。

四:可是你每次见我跟他在一块儿,你的神气,偏偏——

萍:我的神气那自然是不快活的。我看见我最喜欢的女人时常跟别人在一块儿,哪怕他是我的亲弟弟,我也不情愿!

四:你看你又扯到别处。你不要扯,你现在到底对我怎么样?你要跟我说明白。

萍:我对你怎么样?(他笑了,他讲不出来,他觉得女人们都有些呆气,这一句话有一个女人也这样问过他)要我说出来?(笑)那么,你要我怎么说呢?

四:(苦恼地)萍,你别这样待我好不好?你明明知道我现在什么都是你的,你还——你还这样欺负人。

PING: Go to school? (*He laughs.*) The young idiot! — Still, who knows? You may find you're better off with him after all. I'm almost thirty, and you're only eighteen. And my prospects are no better than his, either. Besides, I've done a lot of — of unspeakable things.

FENG: Oh, do be serious, Ping. I'm really worried about it all. You must help me find a way out. He's still only a boy, you see, and I just hate having to keep him on a piece of string like this all the time, and you not letting me tell him the truth.

PING: I never said you couldn't tell him.

FENG: But every time you see me with him, you *will* look so — so —

PING: Well, naturally I look unhappy. When I see the girl I love best of all always going about with someone else, even if he is my own brother, well, of course I don't like it.

FENG: There you go again, getting away from the subject. Let's get down to brass tacks. Tell me honestly how you really feel about me.

PING: How I feel about you? (*He smiles as he remembers another woman who once asked him the same question, and decides that all women have a touch of stupidity about them.*) You want me to tell you honestly? (*He laughs.*) Well, what do you want me to say?

FENG (*unhappily*): I wish you wouldn't treat me like this, Ping. You know very well that I'm yours now, all yours, and yet you — you keep on taking the rise out of me.

萍:(不喜欢她这样讲,同时还以为她究竟有些不明白他)哦!(叹一口气)天哪!

四:萍,我父亲只会跟人要钱,我哥哥瞧不起我,说我没有志气,我母亲如果知道了这件事,她一定不要我。没有你就没有我。他们也许有一天会不理我,你不能够,你不能够的。(抽咽。)

萍:四凤,不,不,你让我好好地想一想。

四:我的妈最疼我,我的妈不愿意我在公馆里做事,我怕她万一看出你同我的事,……你又不是真心,……那我——那我就伤了我妈的心了。(哭)还有,……

萍:(立起)凤,你别这样疑心我。我告诉你,今天晚上我预备到你那里去。

四:不,我妈今天回来。

萍:那么,我们在外面会一会好么?

四:不成,我妈晚上一定会找我谈话的。

萍:我可明天早车就要走了。

四:你真不预备带我走么?

萍:孩子!那怎么成?

PING (*annoyed at this, and feeling at the same time that she still misunderstands him to a certain extent*): Eh? (*Heaving a sigh.*) Oh, God!

FENG: You know how it is, Ping: my father's only interested in cadging money off me; my brother looks down on me because he says I haven't got any character; and my mother, if she found out about us, she certainly wouldn't have anything more to do with me. You're all I have, Ping. They may throw me over one day, but you can't, you can't. (*She breaks down sobbing.*)

PING: Now, just a minute, Feng. Just give me time to think things out.

FENG: My mother really does love me. She was always against me going into service, and I'm afraid she might find out about us and — and that you may not be serious about me at all. If that happened it — it would break her heart. (*Sobbing.*) And besides —

PING (*rising*): Don't be so suspicious of me, Feng. Tell you what: I'll come round to your place tonight.

FENG: You can't: Mother's coming home today.

PING: What about meeting somewhere outside, then?

FENG: No go. Mother's bound to want to have a chat with me this evening.

PING: But I'm leaving on the first train tomorrow morning.

FENG: So you've made up your mind not to take me with you, then?

PING: But my dear girl! How can I take you?

四：那么，你——你叫我想想。

萍：我先要一个人离开家，过后，再想法子跟父亲说明白，把你接出来。

四：(看着他)也好吧，今天晚上你只好到我家里来。我想，爸爸跟妈一定在外房睡，哥哥总是不在家睡觉，我的房子在半夜一定是空的。

萍：那么，我来还是先吹哨，你听得清楚吧？

四：嗯，我要是叫你来，我的窗上一定有个灯。要是没有灯，那你千万不要来。

萍：不要来？

四：那就是我改了主意，家里一定有许多人。

萍：好，就这样。十一点钟。

四：嗯，十一点。

鲁贵由中门上。

贵：哦！(向四凤)我正要找你。(向周萍)大少爷，您刚吃完饭。

四：找我有什么事？

贵：你妈来了。

四：(喜形于色)妈来了，在哪儿？

贵：在门房，跟你哥哥刚见面，说着话呢。

四凤跑向中门。

FENG: In that case, you — let me think about it.

PING: Now, my idea is that I leave home first, and then, once I'm out of it, I can find some way of talking Father round and getting him to let you come out and join me.

FENG (*looking him in the eye*): Oh, all right, then, I suppose you'd better come round to my place tonight. I expect Dad and Mum will be sleeping in the front room, and Dahai never sleeps at home, so by midnight I should have the back room all to myself.

PING: Well, then, shall I whistle first, as usual? You'll be able to hear me all right, won't you?

FENG: No, don't. If the coast is clear, I'll have lamp in the window. If there's no lamp there when you come, you mustn't come near the place.

PING: No?

FENG: No, because that'll mean that I've got company and I've changed my mind.

PING: All right, as you say. Eleven o'clock, then.

FENG: Yes, eleven.

(*Lu Gui appears through the centre door.*)

LU: Oh! (*To Sifeng.*) I was just looking for you. (*To Zhou Ping.*) Good afternoon, Master Ping.

FENG: What did you want me for?

LU: Your mother's arrived.

FENG (*her face lighting up with delight*): She's here? Where is she?

LU: In the porter's lodge. Your brother's just gone down to see her, and they're having a chat.

(*Sifeng hurries towards the centre door.*)

133

萍:四凤,见着你妈,给我问问好。

四:谢谢您,回头见。(下。)

贵:大少爷,您是明天起身么?

萍:嗯。

贵:让我送送您。

萍:不用,谢谢你。

贵:不时总是您心好,照顾着我们。您这一走,我同我这丫头都得惦记着您了。

萍:(笑)你又没钱了吧?

贵:大少爷,您这可是开玩笑了。——我说的是实话,四凤知道,我总是背后说大少爷好的。

萍:好吧。——你没有事么?

贵:没事,没事,我只跟您商量点闲拌儿。您知道,四凤的妈来了,楼上的太太要见她,……

繁漪由饭厅门上,鲁贵一眼看见,话说成一半,又吞进去。

贵:哦,太太下来了!太太,您病完全好啦?

繁漪点一点头。

贵:鲁贵直惦记着。

繁:好,你下去吧。

鲁贵鞠躬,由中门下。

繁:(向周萍)他上哪儿去了。

萍:(莫名其妙)谁?

繁:你父亲。

萍:他有事情,见客,一会儿就回来。弟弟呢?

PING (*calling after her*): Give my regards to your mother, Sifeng.
FENG: Thank you. See you later. (*She goes out.*)
LU: Is it tomorrow you're leaving, sir?
PING: Um.
LU: May I see you off at the station?
PING: Don't bother. Thanks all the same.
LU: You've always been so kind to us. My daughter and I will miss you.
PING (*smiling*): You mean you're broke again, eh?
LU: You're pulling my leg, sir. — I really mean what I said. Sifeng can tell you how highly I always speak of you, sir.
PING: Mm, yes. — You're not — after anything, are you?
LU: Oh no, nothing like that. I just thought you might be able to spare a moment for a little chat. As you know, Sifeng's mother's here — the mistress wants to see her — (*He breaks off: out of the corner of his eye he has glimpsed Fanyi coming in from the dining-room.*) Why, madam! You're downstairs! Are you quite well again, madam? (*Fanyi nods briefly.*)

LU: I kept inquiring how you were.
FAN: All right, you may go now.
(*Lu Gui bows and goes out through the centre door.*)
FAN (*to Zhou Ping*): Where's he gone?
PING (*blankly*): Who?
FAN: Your father.
PING: Oh, he's busy — got a visitor. Shouldn't be

繁：他只会哭，他走了。

萍：(怕和她一同在这间屋里)哦。(停)我要走了，我要收拾东西去。(走向饭厅。)

繁：等一会儿。

周萍停步。

繁：我请你略微坐一坐。

萍：什么事？

繁：(沉郁地)有话说。

周萍走回，站着不语。

繁：我希望你明白方才的情形。这不是一天的事情。

萍：(躲避地)父亲一向是那样，他说一句就是一句的。

繁：可是人家说一句，我就要听一句，那是违背我的本性的。

萍：我明白你。(强笑)你不要听他的话就是了。

繁：萍，我盼望你还是从前那样诚恳的人。顶好不要学着现在那种玩世不恭的态度。你知道我没有你在我面前，我已经很苦了。

萍：所以我就要走了。不要再多见面，互相提醒我们最后悔的事情。

long. Where's Chong?

FAN: He's gone out, the cry-baby.

PING (*ill at ease now that he is left alone with her in the room*): Oh, I see. (*Pauses.*) I must be going now: I've got some packing to do. (*He goes towards the dining-room.*)

FAN: Just a moment.

(*Zhou Ping stops.*)

FAN: I wish you'd stay with me a moment.

PING: What for?

FAN (*unhappily*): I want to talk to you.

(*Zhou Ping walks back to her and stands there in silence.*)

FAN: I hope you fully realize what that scene this morning was all about. It's not just an isolated incident, you know.

PING (*evasively*): Oh, well, Father's always been like that. What he says goes.

FAN: It's not in my nature to do just as I'm told by anybody.

PING: Yes, I know what you're like. (*Forcing a smile.*) Just don't take any notice of him, then.

FAN: Oh, Ping, I wish you'd be as warm and human as you used to be. I don't like to see you adopting this attitude of blase cynicim that's so fashionable these days. You must realize that it's bad enough for me as it is, not being able to have you near me.

PING: That's why I'm going away. So that we won't have to keep seeing one another and being reminded of what we most regret.

繁：我不后悔,我向来做事没有后悔过。

萍：(不得已地)我想,我很明白地对你表示过。这些日子我没有见你,我想你很明白。

繁：很明白。

萍：那么,我是个最糊涂,最不明白的人。我后悔,我认为我生平做错一件大事。我对不起自己,对不起弟弟,更对不起父亲。

繁：(低沉地)但是你最对不起的人,你反而轻轻地忘了。

萍：还有谁?

繁：你最对不起的是我,是你曾经引诱过的后母!

萍：(有些怕她)你疯了。

繁：你欠了我一笔债,你对我负着责任,你不能看见了新的世界,就一个人跑。

萍：我认为你用的这些字眼,简直可怕。这种字句不是在父亲这样——这样体面的家庭里说的。

繁：(气极)父亲,父亲,你撇开你的父亲吧!体面?你也说体面?(冷笑)我在这样的体面家庭已经十八年啦。周家的罪恶,我听过,我见过,我做过。我始终不是你们周家的人。我做的事,我自己负责任。不像你们的

FAN: I don't regret it. I've never regretted anything.

PING (*somewhat reluctantly*): I think I've made my position quite clear now. I've been keeping out of your way all these days — I think you understand why.

FAN: Only too well.

PING: I've been stupid, an utter fool. Now I'm sorry, because I realize I've made such a mess of my life. I'm a disgrace to myself, to my brother, and what's worse, to my father.

FAN (*in an ominously low voice*): But you're forgetting the person you disgraced most of all. A little too readily, I think.

PING: Why, who do you mean?

FAN: Me, your stepmother, the woman you seduced!

PING (*uneasily*): You must be mad.

FAN: You're in my debt. You've incurred certain responsibilities. You can't just run off on your own the moment the chance of a new life offers itself.

PING: That's an outrageous thing to say! You can't talk like that in a — a respectable family like Father's.

FAN (*furious*): "Father"! "Father"! To hell with your father! "Respectable"! From you of all people! (*With a sneer.*) Eighteen years now I've been in this "respectable family" of yours. I've heard all about the sins of the Zhous — and seen them — and committed them myself. Not that I've ever considered myself one of you: what I've done I've done on my own responsibility. No, I'm not like your grandfather, or your great-uncle,

祖父,叔祖,同你们的好父亲,偷偷做出许多可怕的事情,外表还是一副道德面孔,慈善家,社会上的好人物。

萍:大家庭里自然不能个个都是好人。不过我们这一房……

繁:都一样,你父亲是第一个伪君子,他从前就引诱过一个下等人的姑娘。

萍:你不要扯这些个。

繁:你就是你父亲的私生子!

萍:(惊异而无主地)你瞎说,你有什么证据?

繁:请你问你的体面父亲,这是他十五年前喝醉了的时候告诉我的。(指桌上相片)你就是这年轻的姑娘生的小孩。她因为你父亲又不要她,就自己投河死了。

萍:你,你,你简直……——好,好,(强笑)我都承认。你预备怎么样?你要跟我说什么?

繁:你父亲对不起我,他用同样手段把我骗到你们家来,我逃不开,生了冲儿。十几年来就像刚才一样的凶横,把我渐渐地磨成了石头

or your dear father himself — doing the most atrocious things in private, and wearing a mask of morality in public. Philanthropists, respectable citizens, pillars of society!

PING: Well, of course, you have the occasional black sheep in any big family, but our branch —

FAN: You're all the same, and your father's the biggest hypocrite of the lot. Years ago now he seduced a girl from the lower classes.

PING: There's no need to go dragging up that sort of thing.

FAN: And you — you're the illegitimate child he gave her!

PING (*overwhelmed and helpless with astonishment*): You're lying! What proof have you got?

FAN: Go and ask your "respectable" father yourself. He told me all about it one night fifteen years ago, when he was drunk. (*Pointing to the photograph on the bureau.*) That girl was your mother. Your father turned her out, so she drowned herself.

PING: You're — you're — you're just — oh, all right, all right — (*he smiles wryly*) I'll take your word for it. Well, what are you going to do? What is it you want with me?

FAN: Your father let me down. He tricked me into coming here — the same old wiles. There was no escape for me, and so I had Chong. All these years he's been the hateful tyrant that you saw this morning. He gradually ground me down until I became as cold and dead as a stone. Ten, sud-

样的死人。你突然从家乡出来,是你,是你把我引到一条母亲不像母亲,情妇不像情妇的路上去。是你引诱的我!

萍:引诱!我请你不要用这两个字好不好?你知道当时的情形怎么样?

繁:你忘记了在这屋子里,半夜,你说的话么?你说你恨你的父亲,你说过,你愿他死,就是犯了灭伦的罪也干。

萍:你忘了,那是我年轻,我一时冲动,说出来这样糊涂的话。

繁:你忘了,我虽然比你只大几岁,那时,我总还是你的母亲。你知道你不该对我说这种话么?

萍:年轻人一时糊涂,做错了的事,你就不肯原谅么?(苦恼地皱着眉。)

繁:这不是原谅不原谅的问题,我已经安安静静地等死,一个人偏把我救活了又不理我,撇得我枯死,慢慢地渴死。让你说,我该怎么办?

萍:那,那我也不知道,你来说吧!

denly, you appeared from our place in the country, where you'd been living. It was you who made me what I am, half stepmother, half mistress. It was you who seduced me!

PING: "Seduced" indeed! I'd rather you didn't use that word, if you don't mind. Do you remember what actually took place?

FAN: Have you forgotten what you told me here in this very room, in the middle of the night? You said you hated your father. You said you wished he were dead. You said that even the prospect of putting yourself beyond the pale wouldn't deter you from loving me.

PING: Ah, but don't forget I was much younger then. I came out with all this nonsense on the impulse of the moment.

FAN: Aren't you forgetting something? There may have been only a few years between us, but that doesn't alter the fact that I was still your stepmother. Don't you see you had no right to say such things to me?

PING: You mean you can't forgive a young man for doing wrong in a moment of folly? (*He frowns uncomfortably.*)

FAN: It's not a question of forgiving anything. I'd resigned myself to my fate, when along came someone who must need revive me — and then tire of me and cast me aside, and leave me to wither away and slowly die of thirst. Now you can tell me what I should do.

PING: Er, well — I've no idea. What do you think?

繁:(一字一字地)我希望你不要走。

萍:怎么,你要我陪着你,在这样的家庭,每天想着过去的罪恶,这样活活地闷死么?

繁:你既然知道这家庭可以闷死人,你怎么肯一个人走,把我丢在这里?

萍:你没有权利说这种话,你是冲弟弟的母亲。

繁:我不是!我不是!自从我把我的性命,名誉,交给你,我什么都不顾了。我不是他的母亲,不是,不是,我也不是周朴园的妻子。

萍:(冷冷地)如果你以为你不是父亲的妻子,我自己还承认我是我父亲的儿子。

繁:(不曾想到他会说这一句话,呆了一下)哦,你是你的父亲的儿子。——这些日子,你特别不来看我,是怕你的父亲?

萍:也可以说是怕他,才这样的吧。

繁:你这一次到矿上去,也是学着你父亲的英雄榜样,把一个真正明白你,爱你的人丢开不管?

萍:这么解释也未尝不可。

繁:(冷冷地)这么说,你到底是你父亲的儿子。(笑)父亲的儿子!(忽然冷静地)哼,都是些

FAN (*hammering out her words one by one*): I don't want you to go away.

PING: Eh? You mean you want me to stay here with you, in this god-forsaken place? So that every day we're reminded of our past sins, until they gradually suffocate us?

FAN: But if you realize what a soul-destroying place this is, how can you have the heart to go away on your own and leave me here?

PING: You've no right to say that. You're still Chong's mother.

FAN: No! I'm not! Ever since I placed my life and my reputation in your hands I've shut myself off from everything else. No, I'm not his mother, no more than I'm Zhou Puyuan's wife!

PING (*icily*): Even if you don't regard yourself as my father's wife, I still recognize myself as his son.

FAN (*rendered speechless for a moment by this unexpected remark*): I see, so you're your father's son. — I suppose the reason you've made a point of not coming to see me lately is that you're afraid of your father?

PING: I suppose you could put it like that.

FAN: And the reason why you're going away to the mine is that you're following your father's heroic example and throwing over the one person who really understands and loves you?

PING: I see no reason why you shouldn't interpret it like that, if you want to.

FAN (*coldly*): Spoken like a true son of your father. (*She laughs.*) His father's son! (*Suddenly*

没有用,胆小怕事,不值得人为他牺牲的东西!我恨我早没有知道你!

萍:那么你现在知道了!我对不起你,我已经同你详细解释过,我厌恶这种关系。我告诉你,我厌恶。你说我错,我承认。然而叫我犯了那样的错,你也不能完全没有责任。你是我认为最聪明,最能了解人的女子,所以我想,你最后会原谅我。我的态度,你现在骂我玩世不恭也好,不负责任也好,我告诉你,我盼望这一次的谈话是我们最末一次谈话了。(走向饭厅门。)

繁:(沉重的语气)等一等。

周萍立住。

繁:我希望你明白我刚才说的话,我不是请求你。我盼望你用你的心,想一想,过去我们在这屋子说的(停,难过)许多,许多的话。一个女子,你记着,不能受两代的欺侮,你可以想一想。

萍:我已经想得很透彻。我自己这些天的痛苦,我想你不是不知道。好,请你让我走吧。(由饭厅下。)

繁漪望着周萍出去,流下泪来,忍不住伏在沙发上哭泣。

calm.) Pah! You're both the same. Useless, cowardly creatures, not worth anyone's self-sacrifice! I'm only sorry I didn't find you out sooner!

PING: Well, you know now, don't you! As for wronging you, I've explained to you at great length that I find this relationship between us repugnant. Yes, repugnant. You say I did wrong, and I freely admit it: but you cannot disclaim all responsibility for what I did. I've always looked upon you as a very intelligent and understanding woman, and so I'm sure that one day you'll understand and forgive me. I expect you'll accuse me of being cynical or irresponsible, but I want to tell you this: I hope this meeting will be our last.

(*He goes towards the dining-room door.*)

FAN (*in a heavy voice*): Wait.

(*Zhou Ping stops.*)

FAN: I hope you understand what I meant just now. I'm not asking you for anything. I just want you to think back, and go over in your mind all the (*she pauses, distressed*) — all the things we ever said to one another in this room. Rememher, no woman can be expected to submit to humiliation at the hands of two generations. Just think it over.

PING: I've already thought it over — from top to bottom. I don't think you can be entirely unaware of the torment I've gone through these past few days. And now perhaps you'll excuse me. (*He disappears into the dining-room.*)

(*As Fanyi watches him go, tears start to her eyes. She buries her face in the sofa and sobs.*)

鲁贵偷偷地由中门走进来,看见太太在哭。

贵:(低声)太太!

繁:(站起)你来干什么?

贵:鲁妈来了好半天啦。

繁:谁?谁来好半天啦。

贵:我家里的,太太不是说过要我叫她来么?

繁:你为什么不早点来告诉我?

贵:我倒是想着,可是我(低声)刚才瞧见太太跟大少爷说话,所以就没敢惊动您。

繁:啊,你,你刚才——

贵:我?我在大客厅伺候老爷见客呢!(故意地不明白)太太有什么事么?

繁:没什么,那么你叫鲁妈进来吧。

贵:(谄笑)我们家里是个下等人,说话粗里粗气,您可别见怪。

繁:都是一样的人。我不过想见一见,跟她谈谈闲话。

贵:是,那是太太的恩典。对了,老爷刚才跟我说,怕要下大雨,请太太把老爷的那一件旧雨衣拿出来。

繁:四凤给老爷捡的衣裳,四凤不会拿么?

贵:我也是这么说啊,您不是不舒服么?可是老

(*Lu Gui comes in stealthily through the centre door and sees that she is weeping.*)

LU (*softly*): Madam!

FAN (*starting up*): What are you doing here?

LU: Lu Ma's here. She's been here some time.

FAN: Who? Who's been here some time?

LU: My wife. You asked me to bring her here, I believe, madam.

FAN: Why didn't you tell me earlier?

LU: I meant to, only I — (*lowering his voice*) I saw you were having a conversation with Master Ping, I didn't like to disturb you.

FAN: Oh, so you — you were — ?

LU: Me? Ho, I've been waiting on the master and his visitor in the main drawing-room. (*Pretending not to understand her suggestion.*) Why, did you want me for something, madam?

FAN: No. Well, you'd better show Mrs. Lu in.

LU (*smiling obsequiously*): You mustn't mind my wife, madam: she's no class, really, and she hasn't much idea of how to behave.

FAN: She's a human being the same as anyone else. I only want to make her acquaintance and have a little chat with her.

LU: It's very kind of you, madam. — Oh, and while I think of it, madam, the master told me to ask you to find that old raincoat of his, as he thinks we're in for a storm.

FAN: Sifeng looks after his clothes. Can't she get it for him?

LU: Well, that's what I said to the master, seeing that

149

爷吩咐,要太太自己拿。

繁:那么,我一会儿拿。

贵:老爷吩咐,说现在就要,说不定老爷就要出去。

繁:哦,好,我就去吧。——你现在叫鲁妈进来,叫她在这房里等一等。

贵:是,太太。(下。)

蘩漪的脸更显得苍白,她在极力压制自己的烦郁。

繁:(吸一口气,自语)热极了,闷极了,这日子真过不下去了。(茫然望着窗外。)

鲁贵上。

贵:刚才小当差来,说老爷催着要。

繁:(抬头)好,你先去吧。我叫陈妈送去。(由饭厅下。)

鲁贵由中门下。移时鲁妈——即鲁侍萍——与四凤上。鲁妈的年纪约有四十六七,鬓发有点斑白,面貌白净,看上去也只有三十八九岁的样子。她的眼有些呆滞,时而呆呆地望着前面,但是在那秀长的睫毛,和

you're no feeling very well, but he insists that you should get it, madam.

FAN: Oh, well, I'll get it presently.

LU: The master says he wants it now. He may be going out any minute.

FAN: Oh, I see. Well, I'd better go and get straight away. — Ask your wife to come in and wait in here.

LU: Very good, madam. (*He goes out.*)

(*Fanyi's face is paler than ever now; she is making a great effort to suppress her feelings of resentment.*)

FAN (*drawing a deep breath and speaking to herself*): God, this heat! It's absolutely stifling! — I can't go on much longer like this! (*She gazes listlessly out of the window.*)

(*Lu Gui re-enters.*)

LU: The master's just sent somebody along about the raincoat: he insists on having it at once.

FAN (*lifting her head*): All right. You needn't wait. I'll have it sent along by one of the maids. (*She goes out through the dining-room.*)

(*Lu Gui goes out through the centre door.*)

(*After a while, Lu Ma — Lu Shiping — comes in with Sifeng. She is about forty-seven, and her hair is beginning to grey at the temples. Her complexion is fair and clear, and makes her look eight or nine years younger. Her eyes are dull and lifeless, and from time to time will become fixed in an unseeing stare; yet there is something about the long, delicate lashes and the*

她圆大的眸子间,还寻得出她少年时的神韵。她的衣服朴素,洁净,穿在身上,像一个由大家门户落魄的妇人。

她头上包着一条白毛巾,怕是坐火车时围着遮土的。她说话总爱微微地笑,声音很低,很沉稳,语音像一个南方人在北方落户久了,夹杂着一些模糊,轻快的南方口音,但是她的字句说得很清楚。她的牙齿非常整齐,笑的时候在嘴角旁露出一对深深的笑涡。

鲁妈拉着女儿的手,四凤亲热地偎在她身边走进来。后面跟着鲁贵,提着一个旧包袱。

四:太太呢?

贵:就下来。

四:妈,您坐下。

　　鲁妈坐下。

四:累了吧?

鲁:不累。

四:(高兴地)妈,您坐一坐。我给您倒一杯冰镇的开水。

鲁:不,不要走,我不热。

贵:凤儿,你给你妈拿一瓶汽水来,(向鲁妈)这

large, round pupils that tells us of the charm and sparkle that must have been hers in her younger days. Her clothes are plain but neat, and she wears them like a woman of good family who has fallen on evil days. Around her head is a white towel, apparently there to keep the dust off her hair during her train journey. Whenever she speaks, the faintest of smiles comes to her lips. Her voice is low and steady, and her accent is that of a southerner who has lived a long time in the north: only the occasional peculiarity and the generally lighter intonation betray her place of birth. She speaks clearly, never swallowing her syllables. Her teeth are good and evenly set, and when she smiles deep dimples appear at the corners of her mouth. She comes in hand-in-hand with her daughter Sifeng, who is nestling affectionately up against her. Lu Gui comes in behind them carrying a bundle wrapped in an old piece of cloth.)

FENG: Where's the mistress?

LU: She'll be down in a minute.

FENG: Sit down, Mother.

(*Lu Ma sits down.*)

FENG: You're tired, I expect.

LU MA: Not a bit.

FENG (*in high spirits*): Well, just wait there a minute while I get you a glass of iced water.

MA: No, don't bother. I don't feel hot.

LU: Get your mother a bottle of mineral water, Sifeng. (*To his wife.*) In a big house like this

153

儿公馆什么没有？一到夏天，柠檬水，果子露，西瓜汤，橘子，香蕉，鲜荔枝，你要什么，就有什么。

鲁：不，不，你别听你爸爸的话。这是人家的东西。你在我身旁跟我多坐一会，回头跟我同——同这位周太太谈谈，比喝什么都强。

贵：太太就会下来，你看你，那块白包头，总舍不得拿下来。

鲁：(和蔼地笑着)真的，说了那么半天，……(笑望着四凤)连我在火车上搭的白手巾都忘了取啦。(取下白毛巾)你看我的脸脏么？火车上尽是土，你看我的头发，不要叫人家笑。

四：不，不，一点都不脏。两年没见您，您还是那个样。

贵：(轻蔑地)你看你们这点穷相，走到大家公馆，不来看看人家的阔排场，尽在一边闲扯。四凤，你先把你这两年做的衣裳给你妈看看。

四：妈不希罕这个。

贵：你不也有点首饰么？你拿出来给你妈开开

they have everything! Now that it's summer, there's lemonade, fruit juice, watermelon, oranges, bananas, fresh litchis — have what you like.

MA: No, don't, Sifeng. Don't listen to your father. We've no right to help ourselves to other people's things. You just stay here with me a little longer and then, when Mrs. Zhou comes, we can see her together. I'll enjoy that more than all your cold drinks.

LU: The mistress should be down any minute now. What about your headscarf? You don't seem in much of a hurry to take it off.

MA (*with a good-natured smile*): Well, well. That's what comes of talking so much. (*Beaming at Sifeng*). Fancy me forgetting that. I only put it on for the train. (*She removes it.*) No smuts on my face, are there? It was so dusty on the train. Does my hair look all right? I don't want to look a sight.

FENG: No, you're perfectly all right. You know, you haven't changed a bit these two years you've been away.

LU (*contemptuously*): Well, don't just sit there chattering away in a corner like a couple of poor relations when you should be making the most of being in a big house and admiring your splendid surroundings. Sifeng, show your mother all the clothes you've bought these last two years.

FENG: Mother's not interested in such things.

LU: And haven't you got a bit of jewellery of your own, too? Bring it out and show her, and then see

眼。看看还是我对,还是把女儿关在家里对?

鲁:(向鲁贵)我走的时候嘱咐过你,这两年写信的时候也总不断地提醒你,我不愿意我的女儿叫人家使唤。你偏——(忽然觉得这不是谈家事的地方,回头向四凤)你哥哥呢?

四:不是在门房里等着我们么?

贵:不是等着你们,人家等着见老爷呢。(向鲁妈)去年我叫人捎个信,告诉你,大海也在矿上找上事了,那都是我在这儿嘀咕上的。

四:(厌恶她父亲又表白自己的本领)爸爸,别再扯了,您看看哥哥去吧。

贵:真他妈的,这孩子我倒忘了。(走向中门,回头)你们好好在这屋子坐一会,别乱动,太太一会儿就下来。(下。)

鲁妈和四凤见鲁贵走后,都舒展多了。母女二人相对凄然地笑了一笑。

鲁:(伸出手来,向四凤)孩子,让我好好看看你。

who she thinks was right: her, who wanted to keep you shut up at home, or me?

MA (*to Lu Gui*): I told you before I went that I wouldn't have my daughter go into service, and every time I've written to you over the past two years I've reminded you about it. Yet you still go and — (*Suddenly breaking off as she remembers that this is no place to discuss family matters, and turning to her daughter instead.*) Where's Dahai?

FENG: I thought he was waiting for us at the porter's lodge.

LU: It's not you two he's waiting for, it's the master he wants to see. (*To his wife.*) I sent word to you last year about Dahai. He managed to get a job in the mine. — Only because I put in a word for him here, though.

FENG (*finding her father's repeated boasting distasteful*): You needn't keep harping on that, Dad. Hadn't you better go and look after Dahai?

LU: Oh, well. I'd forgotten all about him. (*Going towards the centre door, then stopping and turning for a last few words.*) You'd better stay here in this room for the time being and not go roaming around all over the place, because the mistress will be down any minue. (*He goes out.*)

(*Once he is out of the room, Lu Ma and her daughter relax. They look at each other with a wry smile.*)

MA (*holding out her hands to Sifeng*): Let me have a good look at you, child.

157

四凤走到鲁妈面前。

四：妈，您不怪我吧？

鲁：不，做了就做了。——不过为什么这两年你一个字也不告诉我？

四：我怕您生气，不敢告诉您。——其实，妈，就是像我这样帮帮人，我想也没有什么关系。

鲁：你以为妈怕穷么？怕人家笑我们穷么？不，孩子，妈最看得开，不过，我怕你太年轻，容易一阵子犯糊涂，(叹一口气)好，我们先不提这个。(站起来)这位太太真怪，她要见我干什么？

四：是啊。(恐惧来了，但是愿意向好的一面想)不，妈，这边太太没有多少朋友，她听说妈也会写字，念书，也许觉着很相近，所以想请妈来谈谈。

鲁：哦？(慢慢看这屋子的摆设，指着有镜台的柜)这屋子倒是很雅致的。就是家具太旧了点。

四：可不是，都是三十年前的老东西了，听说是

(*Sifeng goes across to her mother.*)

FENG: You're not cross with me, are you, Mother?

MA: No. What's done is done. — But why have you kept quiet about it all this time?

FENG: I didn't dare tell you, because I was afraid you'd be angry with me. — Though I don't see that it matters all that much really that I should be in service like this.

MA: You don't imagine it's because I don't like being poor, do you? Or that I'm afraid of having people laugh at us because we're poor? No, child, it's not that at all, I've learned to accept all that. The thing that really worries me is that you're still very young, and you might easily go and do something foolish. (*Heaving a sigh.*) Well, there's no need to talk about is now. (*She gets up.*) I wonder what your mistress wants to see me about. Strange, isn't it?

FENG: I suppose it is. (*Becoming apprehensive, but still trying to be optimistic.*) Though, you know, Mother, the mistress here hasn't got many friends. She's heard that you can read and write, so perhaps she feels you've got something in common and wants to have a little chat with you about that.

MA: Don't you think so? (*She looks slowly round the room at the furniture, then points to the old bureau with the mirror on it.*) This room's very elegantly furnished — though the furniture looks rather too old.

FENG: It is, too. It's all thirty years old. They say his

从前的第一个太太,就是大少爷的母亲,顶爱的东西。您看,从前的家具多笨哪。

鲁:(用手巾擦擦汗)奇怪——为什么窗户还关上呢?

四:您也觉得奇怪不是?这是我们老爷的怪脾气,一到夏天就要关窗户。

鲁:(回想)凤儿,这屋子我像是在哪儿见过似的。

四:(笑)真的?您大概是想我想的,梦里到过这儿。

鲁:对了,做梦似的。——奇怪,这地方好眼熟。(低下头。)

四:(慌)妈,您不舒服?您别是受了暑,我给您拿一杯冷水吧。

鲁:不,不是,你别去。

四:妈,您怎么啦?

鲁:(注意看着房中的一切,沉思着)奇怪——(伸手拉四凤)四凤!

四:(摸鲁妈的手)您手冰凉,妈。

鲁:不要紧的,妈不怎么样。真是,真好像我的魂来过这儿似的。

first wife was very fond of all these things — the young master's mother, that is. They did have some clumsy furniture in those days, didn't they?

MA (*dabbing her face with a handkerchief*): That's funny — why should all the windows be kept closed in this weather?

FENG: Yes, it is queer, isn't it? One of the master's queer notions. He will have the windows closed in the summer.

MA (*trying to remember something*): You know, Feng, I seem to have seen this room somewhere before.

FENG (*laughing*): Have you? You must have been thinking about me too much, and come here in a dream.

MA: Yes, it does seem like a dream. — I can't get over it, it all looks so familiar. (*She hangs her head.*)

FENG (*alarmed*): Ma, Mother, are you feeling all right? It must be the heat. Shall I go and get you a glass of water?

MA: No, I'm all right. Don't go.

FENG: What's the matter with you, Mother?

MA (*scrutinizing everything in the room and lost in thought*): Strange — (*reaching out and grasping Sifeng by the hand*) Sifeng!

FENG (*feeling her mother's hands*): Why, your hands are like ice, Mother.

MA: Don't worry. I'm all right. It really does seem as if I've been here before, though — if not in body, then in spirit.

四:妈,您别瞎说啦,您怎么来过?他们二十年前才搬到北方来,那时候,您不是还在南方么?

鲁:不,不,我来过。这些家具,我想不起来——我在哪儿见过。

四:妈您看什么?

鲁:那个柜,那个柜。(声音愈低,努力地回想着。)

四:那——那是从前死了的太太的东西。

鲁:(自语)不能够,不能够。

四:(怜惜她的母亲)别多说话了,妈,歇一会儿吧。

鲁:不要紧的。——刚才我在门房听见这家还有两位少爷?

四:嗯,妈,都很好,周家的人都很和气的。

鲁:周?这家姓周?

四:妈,您看您,您刚才不是问着周家的门进来的么?怎么会忘了?妈,您准是路上受热了。我给您拿点水来喝。(走过柜前)妈,您看这就是周家第一个太太的相片。(拿相片过来,站在鲁妈背后,给她看。)

FENG: Oh, don't be so silly, Mother. How can you have been here before? It's twenty years since they moved up north here, and you were still living down south then, weren't you?

MA: I can't help that. I still say I've been here before. These pieces of furniture — I've seen them before somewhere — though where, I just can't think.

FENG: What are you looking at, Mother?

MA: The bureau, that bureau there. (*Her voice dwindles to a whisper as she racks her brains to remember.*)

FENG: Oh, that used to belong to the first mistress, the one who died.

MA (*to herself*): No, it can't be, it can't be.

FENG: (*feeling sorry for her mother*): Don't talk any more, Mother. Just relax for a while.

MA: It's all right. — I gathered when I was down at the porter's lodge just now that there are two sons.

FENG: Yes, there are. Very nice, both of them. In fact, all the Zhous are very nice people.

MA: The Zhous? Is that their name?

FENG: Now Mother. Didn't you have to ask the way to the Zhous' when you came. You can't have forgotten already. You must have got a touch of the sun on your way here. I'll get you a drink of water. (*As she goes past the bureau.*) Look, Mother, here's a photo of the master's first wife. (*She brings the photograph across and holds it over her mother's shoulder from behind for her*

鲁:(拿着相片,看)哦!(惊愕得说不出话来。)

四:(站在鲁妈背后)您看她多好看,这就是大少爷的母亲,他们说还有点像我呢。可惜她死了。

鲁妈拿相片的手有些发颤。

四:妈!

鲁:给我点水喝。

四:妈,您到这边来!(扶鲁妈到一个大的沙发前。)

鲁妈手里还紧紧地拿着相片。

四:妈,您在这儿躺一躺。我给您拿水去。(由饭厅门忙跑下。)

鲁:哦,天哪。我是死了的人!这是真的么?这张相片?这些家具?——哦,天底下地方大得很,怎么熬过这几十年,偏偏又把我这个可怜的孩子,放回到他——他的家里?哦,天哪!

四凤拿水上。

四:妈,您喝。

鲁妈喝水。

四:好一点了么?

鲁:嗯,好,好啦。孩子,你现在就跟我回家。

to look at.)

MA (*taking the photograph and looking at it.*): Oh! (*She is too astonished to say another word.*)

FENG (*still standing behind her*): You can see how good-looking she was. She was the eldest son's mother. They say I look like her. It's a pity about her dying.

(*Lu Ma's hand trembles as it holds the photograph.*)

FENG: Mother!

MA: Get me a drink of water.

FENG: You'd better come over here. (*She takes her mother's arm and leads her across to the large sofa.*)

(*Lu Ma still has the photograph clutched tightly in her hand.*)

FENG: Just lie down here for a minute. I'll go and get you some water. (*She hurries out into the dining-room.*)

MA: Oh, my God! ... So I'm dead. — But this photo, and this furniture.... Can it be true? Oh, isn't the world big enough to — ? To think that after all these years of misery my own poor child should have to go and find herself in his — his house of all places. Oh, God!

(*Sifeng comes in with the water.*)

FENG: Here you are, Mother.

(*Lu Ma drinks.*)

FENG: Feel a bit better now?

MA: Mm, yes, I'm all right now. You're coming straight home with me, Sifeng.

雷雨

四：（惊讶）妈，您怎么啦？

由饭厅传出繁漪的声音："四凤！"

四：（听）太太。

繁漪的声音：四凤！

四：唉。

繁漪的声音：四凤，你来，老爷的雨衣你给放在哪儿啦？

四：（大声）我就来。（向鲁妈）妈等一等，我就回来。

鲁：你去吧。

四凤下。鲁妈周围望望，走到柜前放下相片。忽然听见屋外花园里走路的声音，她转过身来，等候着。

鲁贵由中门上。

贵：四凤呢？

鲁：这儿的太太叫了去啦。

贵：你回头告诉太太，说找着雨衣不用送去了；老爷自己到这儿来，还有话跟太太说。

鲁：老爷要到这屋里来？

贵：嗯，你告诉清楚了，别回头老爷来了，太太不在，老头儿又发脾气了。

鲁：你跟太太说吧。

贵：这上上下下多少听差都得我支派，我忙不

FENG (*surprised*): Why, what's the matter now?
(*Fanyi's voice calls "Sifeng!" from the dining-room.*)
FENG (*stopping to listen*): It's the mistress.
FANYI'S VOICE: Sifeng!
FENG: Yes, madam?
FANYI'S VOICE: Come here, Sifeng, where have you put the master's raincoat?
FENG (*loudly*): I'm just coming. (*To her mother.*) I won't be a minute, Mother.
MA: Go on, then.
(*Sifeng goes out. Lu Ma looks all round the room, then goes across to the bureau and puts the photograph back. Suddenly hearing footsteps from the garden, she turns round, waiting.*)
(*Lu Gui comes in through the centre door.*)
LU: Where's Sifeng?
MA: Her mistress shouted for her.
LU: Well, when you see the mistress presently, tell her she needn't send the raincoat along when she's found it, because the master will be coming along here himself as he wants to see her about something.

MA: You say the master's coming along to this room here?
LU: Yes, and make sure you tell her properly, because if you don't and she's not here when he comes, the old man will go right up in the air.
MA: You'd better tell her yourself.
LU: I'm up to my eyes in work with all these servants to look after. I haven't got time to stand about

雷雨

开,我可不能等。

鲁:我要回家去,我不见太太了。

贵:为什么?这次太太叫你来,我告诉你,就许有点什么很要紧的事跟你谈谈。

鲁:我预备带着凤儿回去,叫她辞了这儿的事。

贵:什么?你看你这点——

　　蘩漪由饭厅上。

贵:太太。

蘩:(向门内)四凤,你先把那两件也拿出来,问问老爷要哪一件。(向鲁妈)这就是四凤的妈吧?叫你久等了。

贵:应当的。太太准她来跟您请安就是老大的面子。

　　四凤拿着雨衣由饭厅门进。

蘩:请坐,你来了好半天啦。

鲁:(只在打量着,没有坐下)不多一会,太太。

四:太太,把这三件雨衣都送给老爷那边去么?

贵:老爷说就放在这儿,老爷自己来拿,还请太太等一会,老爷见您有话说呢。

here.

MA: Well, I'm going home. I won't be seeing your mistress after all.

LU: But why not? She's sent for you, and you never know: She might have something important to see you about.

MA: I'm taking Sifeng home with me. She won't be working here any longer.

LU: What! Who d'you think you —

(*Fanyi enters from the dining-room.*)

LU: Madam!

FAN (*speaking back into the dining-room*): Bring the other two as well, Sifeng, and let the master choose. (*Turning to Lu Ma.*) Ah, you'll be Sifeng's mother, I think? I'm sorry I've kept you waiting all this time.

LU: You shouldn't apologize to her, madam. You've done her a great honour by allowing her to come and pay her respects to you.

(*Sifeng enters from the dining-room with the raincoats.*)

FAN: Won't you sit down? You must have been waiting a long time.

MA (*looking Fanyi up and down, but not sitting down*): Only a few moments, madam.

FENG: Shall I take all three raincoats along to the master, madam?

LU: The master wants them left here as he's coming along for them himself. Oh, and madam: he said would you please wait for him here, as he'd like to have a word with you.

繁:知道了。(向四凤)你先到厨房,把晚饭的菜看看,告诉厨房一下。

四:是,太太。(望着鲁贵,又疑惧地望着繁漪,由中门下。)

繁:鲁贵,告诉老爷,说我同四凤的母亲谈话,回头再请他到这儿来。

贵:是,太太。(但不走。)

繁:(见鲁贵不走)你有什么事么?

贵:太太,今天早上老爷吩咐请德国克大夫来。

繁:二少爷告诉过我了。

贵:老爷刚才吩咐,说来了就请太太去看。

繁:我知道了。你去吧。

鲁贵由中门下。

繁:(向鲁妈)坐下谈,不要客气。(自己坐到沙发上。)

鲁:(坐在旁边一张椅子上)我刚下火车,就听说您要我来见见您。

繁:我常听四凤提到你,说你念过书,从前是个很好的人家。

鲁:(不愿提起从前的事)四凤这孩子很傻,不懂事,这两年叫您多操心。

FAN: Very well. (*To Sifeng*). Go to the kitchen and see how they're getting on with dinner. Make sure they know what's wanted.

FENG: Very good, madam. (*Shooting a glance first at Lu Gui and then, apprehensively, at Fanyi, she goes out through the centre door.*)

FAN: Lu Gui, tell the master I'm engaged here with Sifeng's mother and that I'll let him know when I'm ready to see him.

LU: Very good, madam. (*He does not move.*)

FAN (*seeing that he is still there*): Was there something else you wanted to see me about?

LU: Yes, madam: this morning the master had me make an appointment for you with the German doctor.

FAN: I know. Master Chong's already told me about it.

LU: The master was just saying that he'd like you to see the doctor as soon as he arrives, madam.

FAN: All right. You can go now.

(*Lu Gui goes out through the centre door.*)

FAN (*to Lu Ma*): Let's sit down, then. Make yourself at home. (*She sits down on a sofa.*)

MA (*sitting down on a nearby chair*): The moment I got off the train, I was told you wanted to see me.

FAN: Yes, I'd heard so much about you from Sifeng: she tells me you've had an education and that you come from a very good family.

MA (*not wishing to bring up the past*): Sifeng's a silly child. Not much sense. She must have been

繁：不，她非常聪明，我也很喜欢她。这孩子不应当叫她侍候人，应当替她找一个正当的出路才好。

鲁：是的，我一直也是不愿意这孩子帮人。

繁：这一点我很明白。我知道你是个知书达礼的人，一看就看出是个直爽人，我就不妨把请你来的原因现在跟你说一说。

鲁：(疑虑地)是不是我这小孩平时的举动有点叫人说闲话？

繁：(笑着，故做肯定地说)不，不是。

鲁贵由中门上。

贵：太太。

繁：什么事？

贵：克大夫已经接来了，现时在小客厅等着呢。

繁：我有客。

贵：客？——老爷说请太太就去。

繁：我知道，你先去吧。

鲁贵下。

繁：(向鲁妈)我先把我家里的情形说一说。我家里的女人很少的。

鲁：是的。

繁：老爷，两个少爷，除了我和一两个老妈子以

a great trial to you.

FAN: On the contrary, she's very intelligent and I'm very fond of her. I don't think a girl like her should be in service at all. She should be given a better start in life.

MA: I realize that. I've been against her going into service all along.

FAN: I know just what you mean. Now, I know you're an educated, sensible person, and one can tell at a glance that you're not one for beating about the bush, so I may as well tell you straight out why I asked you to come.

MA (*having misgivings*): Why, has this girl of mine been behaving in a way that causes gossip?

FAN (*smiling and assuming an air of complete assurance*): Oh no, nothing like that.

(*Lu Gui comes in through the centre door.*)

LU: Madam.

FAN: What is it?

LU: Dr. Kramer's here. He's waiting in the small drawing-room.

FAN: I have a visitor.

LU: A visitor? — But the master would like you to see the doctor now, madam.

FAN: All right. You needn't wait.

(*Lu Gui goes out.*)

FAN (*to Lu Ma*): Well, I'd better tell you something about the family first. You see, there are hardly any women in the house.

MA: I suppose not.

FAN: In fact, there's only myself and one or two

鲁：哦。

蘩：四凤的年纪很轻，她才十九岁，是不是？

鲁：十八。

蘩：(委婉地)那就对了，我记得好像她比我的孩子是大一岁的样子。这样年轻的孩子，在外边做事，又生得很秀气的。

鲁：(急切地)四凤有什么不检点的地方么？请您千万不要瞒我。

蘩：不，不，(又笑了)她很好的。我只是说说这个情形。我自己有一个儿子，他才十七岁——恐怕刚才你在花园见过——是个不大懂事的孩子。

鲁贵自书房门上。

贵：老爷催着太太去看病。

蘩：没有人陪着克大夫么？

贵：张局长刚走，老爷自己在陪着呢。

蘩：你跟老爷说，说我没有病，我自己并没要请医生来。

贵：是，太太。(但不走。)

蘩：(看鲁贵)你在干什么？

贵：我等太太还有什么事要吩咐。

maids. Then there's my husband, and my two sons. That leaves the rest of the servants — all men.

MA: I see.

FAN: Sifeng's very young; only nineteen, isn't she?

MA: Eighteen.

FAN (*with artful guile*): Oh yes, that's right. I remember now, she does look about a year older than my son. Yes, so young, so attractive — and working away from home.

MA (*anxiously*): Look, if Sifeng's done anything that she shouldn't have, you must tell me. Please don't keep anything from me.

FAN: No, it's nothing like that. (*She smiles again.*) She's a very nice girl. I'm only telling you how things are here. I've got a son, just seventeen — you may have seen him in the garden when you came in — not particularly bright.

(*Lu Gui comes in from the study.*)

LU: The master's becoming insistent about you seeing the doctor, madam.

FAN: Is there no one to keep the doctor company?

LU: Yes, the master's with him himself. The superintendent's just left.

FAN: You can tell the master that I'm not ill, nor have I asked for a doctor.

LU: Very good, madam. (*He remains where he is.*)

FAN (*looking round at him*): What are you waiting for?

LU: I thought there might be something further, madam.

繁：(忽然想起来)有,你跟老爷回完话之后,你出去叫一个电灯匠来。刚才我听说花园藤萝架上的旧电线落下来了,走电,叫他赶快收拾一下,不要电了人。

鲁贵由中门下。

繁：(见鲁妈立起)鲁奶奶,你还是坐呀。哦,这屋子又闷热起来啦。(走到窗户前,把窗户打开,回来)这些天我就看着我这孩子奇怪,谁知这两天,他忽然跟我说他很喜欢四凤。

鲁：(吃一惊)啊?

繁：他要帮助她学费,叫她上学。他还说——(笑笑)这孩子!——要娶四凤。

鲁：您不必往下说,我都明白了。

繁：四凤比我的孩子大,四凤又是很聪明的女孩子,这种情形——

鲁：(不喜欢繁漪的暧昧的口气)我的女儿,我总相信是个懂事,明白大体的孩子。我向来不愿意她到大公馆帮人,可是我信得过,我的女儿就帮这儿两年,她总不会做出一点糊涂事的。

FAN (*struck by a sudden thought*): Yes, there is something. After you've told the master what I said, go and find an electrician. I've just heard that an old electric cable on the wistaria-trellis has snapped. It's trailing loose and it's live. Tell him to get it mended as soon as possible. We don't want any accidents.

(*Lu Gui goes out through the centre door.*)

FAN (*seeing that Lu Ma is on her feet*): There's no need to get up, Mrs. Lu. Phew, this room's getting more stifling than ever. (*She goes across to a window, opens it, then returns to her seat.*) Just lately I've noticed that my son isn't quite his usual self. Well, to my great surprise, he suddenly tells me that he's very fond of Sifeng.

MA (*startled*): What!

FAN: He wants to share his school allowance with her to pay for her education. He even says — (*with a smile*) silly boy! — that he wants to marry her.

MA: You needn't go on. I quite understand.

FAN: Sifeng is older than my son, and she's a very intelligent girl. In a situation like this —

MA (*resenting Fanyi's mysterious tone of voice*): I think I can trust my daughter. I'm satisfied that she's a sensible girl and knows the difference between right and wrong. I've always been against her going into service in a big house, but I've got confidence in her and I don't think she could have done anything foolish in the two years that she's been with you.

177

繁：鲁奶奶，我也知道四凤是个明白的孩子，不过有了这种不幸的情形，我的意思，是非常容易叫人发生误会的。

鲁：(叹气)今天我到这儿来是万没想到的事，回头我就预备把她带走，现在就请您准了她的长假。

繁：哦，——如果你以为这样办好，我也觉得很妥当的。不过有一层，我怕，我的孩子有点傻气，他还是会找到你家里见四凤的。

鲁：您放心，我后悔得很。我不该把这个孩子一个人交给她父亲管的。大后天我就要离开此地，不会再见着周家的人。太太，我想现在带着我的女儿走。

繁：那么，也好，回头我叫账房把工钱算出来。她自己的东西，我可以派人送去，我有一箱子旧衣服，也可以带着去，留着她以后在家里穿。

鲁：(自语)我的可怜的孩子！

繁：(走到鲁妈面前)不要伤心，鲁奶奶。如果钱上有什么问题，尽管到我这儿来，一定有办法。好好地带她回去，有你这样一个母亲教育她，自然比在这儿好的。

FAN: Yes, Mrs. Lu, I agree that Sifeng's a sensible girl; but now that this unfortunate situation has arisen, well, I'm afraid it rather lends itself to misunderstanding.

MA (*with a sigh*): I never expected to find myself here today. I'm thinking of taking her with me when I go back, so if you'd be kind enough to let her leave you at once....

FAN: Well — if you think it would be for the best, I've got nothing against it. Though there is one thing: my son's rather wild, and I'm afraid he may try to see Sifeng at your home.

MA: You needn't worry about that. I can see now how stupid I was: I should never have left her for her father to look after. I'm leaving here in three days' time, so I don't think she'll ever see anything more of the Zhous. Madam, I'd like to take her away from here at once.

FAN: Well, if you insist. I'll get the office to make up her wages, and her personal belongings can be taken round to your house by a servant. — And I'll send a suitcase of some of my old clothes which she may have some use for at home.

MA (*to herself*): My poor child!

FAN (*going up to her*): Don't take it so much to heart, Mrs. Lu. If you have any difficulty with money because of this, please don't hesitate to come and see me. You can rely on me to help you. Now, take her home where you can look after her. With a good mother like you to guide her, she'll be much better off than working here.

周朴园由书房门上。

朴:蘩漪!

蘩漪转身。鲁妈闪在一旁。

朴:你怎么还不去?

蘩:(故意地)上哪儿?

朴:克大夫还在等着,你不知道么?

蘩:克大夫? 谁是克大夫?

朴:从前给你看病的克大夫。

蘩:我现在没有病。

朴:(忍耐)克大夫是我在德国的好朋友,对于脑科很有研究。你的神经有点失常,他一定治得好。

蘩:(爆发)谁说我的神经失常? 你们为什么这样咒我? 我没有病,告诉你,我没有病!

朴:(冷酷地)你当着人这样胡喊乱闹,你自己有病,偏偏要讳病忌医,不肯叫医生治,这不就是神经上的病态么?

蘩:哼,我假若是有病,也不是医生治得好的。(向饭厅门走。)

朴:(大声喊)站住! 你上哪儿去?

蘩:(不在意地)到楼上去。

朴:(命令地)你应当听话。

蘩:你! (不经意地打量他)你忘了你自己是怎

(*Zhou Puyuan enters from the study.*)

ZHOU: Fanyi!

(*Fanyi turns, while Lu Ma slips away into a corner.*)

ZHOU: Why haven't you gone yet?

FAN (*all innocence*): Gone where?

ZHOU: Aren't you aware you're keeping Dr. Kramer waiting?

FAN: Dr. Kramer? Who's he?

ZHOU: Why, the Dr. Kramer that you saw before.

FAN: But there's nothing wrong with me now.

ZHOU (*patiently*): Dr. Kramer's been a good friend of mine since we first met in Germany. Specializes in nervous troubles. Your nerves are a little upset, but I'm sure he'll soon put you right.

FAN (*exploding*): What do you mean, my nerves are upset? Why must you all keep saying such wicked things about me? There's nothing the matter with me, I tell you, nothing at all!

ZHOU (*coldly*): Well, you've got all the symptoms of being neurotic — raving and screaming in front of other people, and refusing to have a doctor when you're ill, or even admit that you're ill.

FAN: Humph! If there *were* anything the matter with me, it wouldn't be anything a doctor could cure.

(*She goes towards the dining-room door.*)

ZHOU (*at the top of bis voice*): Stop! Where do you think you're going?

FAN (*nonchalantly*): I'm going upstairs.

ZHOU (*imperiously*): Do as you're told!

FAN: Take orders from you? (*She looks him dis-*

样一个人啦!(迳自由饭厅门下。)

朴:来人!

仆人上。

仆人:老爷!

朴:太太现在在楼上。你叫大少爷陪着克大夫到楼上去给太太看病。

仆人:是,老爷。

朴:叫大少爷告诉克大夫,说我有点累,不陪他了。

仆人:是,老爷。(下。)

朴:(点着一支吕宋烟。看见桌上的雨衣,向鲁妈)这是太太找出来的雨衣么?

鲁:(看着他)大概是的。

朴:不对,不对,这都是新的。我要我的旧雨衣,你回头跟太太说。

鲁:嗯。

朴:(看她不走)你不知道这间房子底下人不准随便进来么?

鲁:不知道,老爷。

朴:你是新来的下人?

鲁:不是的,我找我的女儿来的。

朴:你的女儿?

鲁:四凤是我的女儿。

朴:那你走错屋子了。

鲁:哦。——老爷没有事了?

朴:(指窗)窗户谁叫打开的?

dainfully up and down.) And who, pray, do you think you are? (*Without more ado she goes out through the dining-room.*)

ZHOU: Here, somebody!

(*A servant appears.*)

SERVANT: Yes, sir?

ZHOU: The mistress is upstairs. Tell Master Ping to take Dr. Kramer up to her room.

SERVANT: Very good, sir.

ZHOU: And tell Master Ping to ask the doctor to excuse me. I'm tired and I'll have to leave him on his own.

SERVANT: Very good, sir. (*He goes out.*)

ZHOU (*lights a cigar, then, noticing the raincoats on the table, addresses Lu Ma*): Are these the raincoats the mistress hunted out?

MA (*looking at him*): I think so.

ZHOU: Well, they're the wrong ones. They're all new ones. It's my old one that I want, tell her.

MA: Um.

ZHOU (*seeing that she does not stir*): Don't you know that servants aren't allowed to be in this room unless they're sent for?

MA: No, I didn't know that, sir.

ZHOU: Are you a new servant here?

MA: No, I came to see my daughter.

ZHOU: Your daughter?

MA: My daughter Sifeng.

ZHOU: Then you've got into the wrong room.

MA: Oh. — Will that be all, sir?

ZHOU (*indicating the open window*): Who's opened

鲁:哦。(很自然地走到窗前,关上窗户,慢慢地走向中门。)

朴:(看她关好窗门,忽然觉得她很奇怪)你站一站。

鲁妈停。

朴:你——你贵姓?

鲁:我姓鲁。

朴:姓鲁。你的口音不像北方人。

鲁:对了,我不是,我是江苏的。

朴:你好像有点无锡口音。

鲁:我自小就在无锡长大的。

朴:(沉思)无锡?嗯,无锡,(忽而)你在无锡是什么时候?

鲁:光绪二十年,离现在有三十多年了。

朴:哦,三十年前你在无锡?

鲁:是的,三十多年前呢,那时候我记得我们还没有用洋火呢。

朴:(沉思)三十多年前,是的,很远啦,我想想,我大概是二十多岁的时候。那时候我还在无锡呢。

鲁:老爷是那个地方的人?

朴:嗯,(沉吟)无锡是个好地方。

鲁:哦,好地方。

朴:你三十年前在无锡么?

鲁:是,老爷。

朴:三十年前,在无锡有一件很出名的事情——

that window?

MA: Oh, yes. (*She strolls across to the window as if quite at home here, closes it, then goes slowly towards the centre door.*)

ZHOU (*suddenly struck by something odd about the way she closes the window*): Wait a minute. (*Lu Ma stops.*)

ZHOU: Who — what's your name?

MA: Lu.

ZHOU: I see, Lu. You don't sound like a northerner from your accent.

MA: You're quite right: I'm not. I'm from Jiangsu.

ZHOU: It sounds rather like a Wuxi accent.

MA: Well, I was born and bred in Wuxi.

ZHOU (*deep in thought*): Wuxi, eh? Wuxi.... (*Suddenly.*) When were you there, in Wuxi?

MA: About thirty years ago.

ZHOU: So you were in Wuxi thirty years ago, eh?

MA: Yes. Thirty years ago. I remember we still didn't use matches in those days.

ZHOU (*deep in thought again*): Thirty years ago.... Yes, it's a long time. Let's see, I must have been in my twenties then. Yes, I was still in Wuxi then.

MA: So you're from Wuxi too, aren't you, sir?

ZHOU: Yes. (*Meditatively.*) Nice place, Wuxi.

MA: Yes, very nice.

ZHOU: And you say you were there thirty years ago?

MA: That's right, sir.

ZHOU: Something happened in Wuxi thirty years ago, quite a to-do —

雷雨

鲁：哦。

朴：你知道么？

鲁：也许记得，不知道老爷说的是哪一件？

朴：哦，很远了，提起来大家都忘了。

鲁：说不定，也许记得的。

朴：我问过许多那个时候到过无锡的人，我也派人到无锡打听过。可是那个时候在无锡的人，到现在不是老了就是死了。活着的多半是不知道的，或者忘了。不过也许你会知道。三十年前在无锡有一家姓梅的。

鲁：姓梅的？

朴：梅家的一个年轻小姐，很贤慧，也很规矩。有一天夜里，忽然地投水死了。后来，后来，——你知道么？

鲁：不敢说。

朴：哦。

鲁：我倒认识一个年轻的姑娘姓梅的。不过那是在二十七年前。

朴：哦？你说说看。

鲁：可是她不是小姐，她也不贤慧，并且听说是不大规矩的。

朴：也许，也许你弄错了，不过你不妨说说看。

MA: Oh.

ZHOU: You know the incident I mean?

MA: Well, I might still remember if I knew what you were referring to, sir.

ZHOU: Oh, it happened so long ago that I expect everyone's forgotten all about it.

MA: You never know. There may be someone who still remembers it.

ZHOU: I've asked dozens of people who were in Wuxi at that time, and I've sent people down to make inquiries on the spot; but the people who were there at the time are either getting on in years or else they're dead, and the few who are still alive either knew nothing about it or else they've forgotten all about it. Though you might know. Well, there was a family in Wuxi thirty years ago called the Meis.

MA: The Meis?

ZHOU: There was a young lady in the family, a clever girl, and very decently behaved, too. One night, she suddenly went and drowned herself. Then, afterwards — you heard about it?

MA: I don't think so.

ZHOU: Oh.

MA: Though I did know a girl by the name of Mei, but that was twenty-seven years ago.

ZHOU: Oh? Tell me about her.

MA: But she wasn't a lady, and not particularly clever — and not very well behaved either, by all accounts.

ZHOU: Perhaps — perhaps you're talking about the

鲁：这个梅姑娘倒是有一天晚上跳的河，可是不是一个，她手里抱着一个刚生下三天的男孩。听人说她生前是不规矩的。

朴：(苦痛)哦！

鲁：她是个下等人，不很守本分的。听说她跟那时周公馆的少爷有点不清白，生了两个儿子。生了第二个，才过三天，忽然周少爷不要她了。大孩子就放在周公馆，刚生的孩子她抱在怀里，在年三十夜里投河死的。

朴：(汗涔涔地)哦。

鲁：她不是小姐，她是无锡周公馆梅妈的女儿，她叫侍萍。

朴：(抬起头来)你姓什么？

鲁：我姓鲁，老爷。

朴：(喘出一口气，沉思地)侍萍，侍萍，对了。这个女孩子的尸首，说是有一个穷人见着埋了。你可以打听到她的坟在哪儿么？

鲁：老爷问这些闲事干什么？

朴：这个人跟我们有点亲戚。

wrong girl. — Though I'd like you to go on, all the same.

MA: Well, this girl Mei threw herself in the river one night, though she wasn't alone: she was holding in her arms a three-day-old baby boy. She's been leading a rather irregular life, so they said.

ZHOU (*wincing*): Oh?

MA: She was a low-class girl who'd been getting above herself. It seems she'd been having an affair with a gentlemans's son by the name of Zhou, and that she'd had two sons by him. Well, a matter of three days after the second one was born, this young Mr. Zhou suddenly turned her out. The elder child was left with the family, but the new-born baby was in her arms when she threw herself in the river. That was on a New Year's Eve.

ZHOU (*with beads of perspiration on his forehead*): Oh!

MA: But she was no lady, only the daughter of a maid at the Zhous' in Wuxi. Her name was Shiping.

ZHOU (*looking up*): What's your name?

MA: My name's Lu, sir.

ZHOU (*heaving a sigh and becoming lost in thought*): Yes, Shiping, Shiping, that was the name. They say some poor man found her body and had it buried. Could you make inquiries and find out where her grave is?

MA: But I don't see why you take such an interest in all this business, sir.

ZHOU: She was a sort of relative of ours.

鲁：亲戚？

朴：嗯，——我们想把她的坟墓修一修。

鲁：哦，——那用不着了。

朴：怎么？

鲁：这个人现在还活着。

朴：(惊愕)什么？

鲁：她没有死。

朴：她还在？不会吧？我看见她河边上的衣服，里面有她的绝命书。

鲁：她又被人救活了。

朴：哦，救活啦？

鲁：以后无锡的人是没见着她，以为她那夜晚死了。

朴：那么，她呢？

鲁：一个人在外乡活着。

朴：那个小孩呢？

鲁：也活着。

朴：(忽然立起)你是谁？

鲁：我是这儿四凤的妈，老爷。

朴：哦。

鲁：她现在老了，嫁给一个下等人，又生了个女孩，境况很不好。

朴：你知道她现在在哪儿？

鲁：我前几天还见着她？

朴：什么？她就在这儿？此地？

鲁：嗯，就在此地。

MA: A relative?
ZHOU: Yes, er — we'd like to look after her grave.
MA: Oh, but there's no need to do that.
ZHOU: How do you mean?
MA: She's still alive.
ZHOU (*shaken*): What!
MA: She never died.
ZHOU: Still alive, you say? But I don't see how she can be. I saw her clothes on the bank of the river, and inside them was a note she'd left.
MA: She was rescued, though.
ZHOU: She was?
MA: But as she was never seen in Wuxi again after that, everybody there thought she was dead.
ZHOU: Where is she now, then?
MA: She's living alone, miles away from Wuxi.
ZHOU: What about the baby?
MA: He's alive, too.
ZHOU (*suddenly standing up*): Who are you, anyway?
MA: I am Sifeng's mother, sir.
ZHOU: H'm.

MA: She's getting on now. She's married to a poor man and they've got a daughter. She doesn't have an easy time of it.
ZHOU: Have you any idea where she is at the moment?
MA: I saw her only the other day.
ZHOU: What! You mean she's here of all places? In the city?
MA: Yes, not far from here.

雷雨

朴：哦！

鲁：老爷，您想见一见她么？

朴：（连忙）不，不，不用。

鲁：她的命很苦。离开了周家，周家少爷就娶了一位有钱有门第的小姐。她一个单身人，无亲无故，带着一个孩子在外乡，什么事都做：讨饭，缝衣服，当老妈子，在学校里伺候人。

朴：她为什么不再找到周家？

鲁：大概她是不愿意吧。为着她自己的孩子，她嫁过两次。

朴：嗯，以后她又嫁过两次。

鲁：嗯，都是很下等的人。她遇人都很不如意，老爷想帮一帮她么？

朴：好，你先下去吧。

鲁：老爷，没有事了？（望着周朴园，泪要涌出。）

朴：啊，你顺便去告诉四凤，叫她把我樟木箱子里那件旧雨衣拿出来，顺便把那箱子里的几件旧衬衣也捡出来。

鲁：旧衬衣？

朴：你告诉她在我那顶老的箱子里，纺绸的补衣，没有领子的。

鲁：老爷那种绸衬衣不是一共有五件？您要哪一件？

朴：要哪一件？

ZHOU: Well, I'm damned!

MA: Would you like to see her, sir?

ZHOU (*hurriedly*): No, no, not particularly.

MA: Times are hard for her now. After she left the Zhous, the young Mr. Zhou married a rich, well-connected young lady. But this girl Mei was on her own, far from home, without a single relative or friend to help her. And she had this child to support. She did everything — from begging to sewing, from working as a maid to being a servant in a school.

ZHOU: But why didn't she go back to the Zhous?

MA: I don't expect the idea appealed to her. For the child's sake she got married twice.

ZHOU: She did, eh?

MA: Yes, and both times to very low-class people. She's been unlucky in her husbands. Perhaps you'd like to help her in some way, sir?

ZHOU: Well, I think you'd better go now.

MA: Will that be all, sir? (*She gazes at him, her eyes filling with tears.*)

ZHOU: Er — oh, you can tell Sifeng to get my old raincoat out of the camphor-wood chest — and she can fish out those old shirts while she's about it.

MA: Old shirts, did you say?

ZHOU: Yes, tell her they're in the very old chest — silk ones, with on collars.

MA: But aren't there five of those silk shirts, sir? Which one did you want?

ZHOU: What do you mean, "which one"?

鲁：不是有一件，在右袖襟上有个烧破的窟窿，后来用丝线绣成一朵梅花补上的？还有一件——

朴：(惊愕)梅花？

鲁：旁边还绣着一个萍字。

朴：(徐徐立起)哦，你，你，你是——

鲁：我是从前伺候过老爷的下人。

朴：哦，侍萍！(低声)是你？

鲁：你自然想不到，侍萍的相貌有一天也会老得连你都不认识了。

周朴园不觉地望望柜上的相片，又望鲁妈。半晌。

朴：(忽然严厉地)你来干什么？

鲁：不是我要来的。

朴：谁指使你来的？

鲁：(悲愤)命，不公平的命指使我来的！

朴：(冷冷地)二十多年的工夫你还是找到这儿来了。

鲁：(愤怨)我没有找你，我没有找你，我以为你早死了。我今天没想到到这儿来，这是天要我在这儿又碰见你。

朴：你可以冷静点。现在你我都是有子女的人。如果你觉得心里有委屈，这么大年纪，我们

MA: Well, hasn't one of them got a hole burnt in the right sleeve, and wasn't it mended by having a plum-blossom embroidered over the hole? And then there's the one —

ZHOU (*startled*): A plum-blossom, you say?

MA: Yes, and the name "Ping" was embroidered beside it, too.

ZHOU (*rising slowly to his feet*): Then you — then you — you're —

MA: I used to be one of your servants.

ZHOU: Shiping! (*In a low voice.*) So it is you, then?

MA: Of course you never expected to see Shiping looking so old that even you wouldn't recognize her.

(*Zhou Puyuan glances automatically at the photograph on the bureau, them looks back at Lu Ma.*) (*There is a long pause.*)

ZHOU (*suddenly stern*): What did you come here for?

MA: I didn't ask to come.

ZHOU: Who sent you here, then?

MA (*bitterly*): Fate! Unjust fate brought me here!

ZHOU (*coldly*): So you've found me, after more than twenty years.

MA (*indignantly*): But I haven't, I haven't been looking for you. I thought you were dead long ago. I never expected to find myself here today. It's fate that meant us to meet again.

ZHOU: Well, you might be a bit calmer about it. We've both got families of our own now. If you think you've got a grievance, let's at least begin by dis-

先可以不必哭哭啼啼的。

鲁：哼，我的眼泪早哭干了，我没有委屈，我有的是恨，是悔，是二十多年来一天一天我自己受的苦。你大概已经忘了你做的事了！二十七年前，过年三十的晚上我生下你的第二个儿子才三天，你为了要赶紧娶那位有钱有门第的小姐，你们逼着我冒着大雪出去，要我离开你们周家的门。

朴：从前的旧恩怨，过了几十年，又何必再提呢？

鲁：那是因为周大少爷一帆风顺，现在也是社会上的好人物。可是自从我被你们家赶出来以后，我没有死成，我把我的母亲可给气死了，我亲生的两个孩子你们家里逼着我留在你们家里。

朴：你的第二个孩子你不是已经抱走了么？

鲁：那是你们老太太看着孩子快死了，才叫我带走的。（自语）哦，天哪，我觉得我像在做梦。

朴：我看过去的事不必再提起来吧。

鲁：我要提，我要提，我闷了二十多年了！你结

pensing with all these tears. We're a bit too old for that sort of thing.

MA: Tears? I've cried my eyes dry long ago. No, I've got no grievance: all I've got left is hatred, and regret, and the memory of the misery I've gone through, day in day out, for the past twenty years and more. Though I expect you've forgotten what you did: twenty-seven years ago, on New Year's Eve, just three days after I'd given birth to your second child, you turned me out of your house in a snow-storm, because you were in a hurry to get rid of me so that you could marry a young lady with money and position.

ZHOU: What's the point of raking up old scores after all these years?

MA: The point? Because our young Mr. Zhou has been a success in life and is now a respectable member of society! I didn't succeed in killing myself after I was turned out by your family, but the shock killed my mother. And your family forced me to leave my two babies behind at your house.

ZHOU: But you took the younger one with you, didn't you?

MA: Yes, your mother eventually let me take him — but only because she thought he wouldn't survive long. (*To herself.*) My God! It all seems like a bad dream!

ZHOU: I don't see the need to go on raking up the past like this.

MA: But I do! I do! I've kept it pent up inside me

了婚，就搬了家，我以为这一辈子也见不着你了；谁知道我自己的孩子偏偏要跑到周家来，又做我从前在你们家里做过的事。

朴：怪不得四凤这样像你。

鲁：我伺候你，我的孩子再伺候你生的少爷们。这是我的报应，我的报应。

朴：你静一静。把脑子放清醒点。你不要以为我的心是死了，你以为一个人做了一件于心不忍的事就会忘了么？你看这些家具都是你从前顶喜欢的东西，多少年我总是留着，为着纪念你。

鲁：(低头)哦。

朴：你的生日——四月十八——每年我总记得。一切都照着你是正式嫁过周家的人看，甚至于你因为生萍儿，受了病，总要关窗户，这些习惯我都保留着，为的是不忘你，弥补我的罪过。

鲁：(叹一口气)现在我们都是上了年纪的人，这些话请你也不必说了。

朴：那更好了。那么我们可以明明白白地谈一谈。

鲁：不过我觉得没有什么可谈的。

朴：话很多。我看你的性情好像没有大改，——

more than twenty years, and now it's got to come out! After you married and moved out of the district I thought I'd never see you again for the rest of my life. The last thing I expected was that my own daughter would come to work in your house of all places and follow in her mother's footsteps.

ZHOU: No wonder Sifeng's the image of you.

MA: I waited on you, and now my child is waiting on your sons. It's a punishment. That's what it is: a punishment.

ZHOU: Now, steady on. Let's be sensible about it. I'm not as cold-blooded as you think. You don't imagine anyone can stifle his conscience as easily as that? You've only got to look at this room: all your favourite furniture of the old days is here. I've kept it all these years to remember you by.

MA: (*with bent head*): Um.

ZHOU: I always remember your birthday, April the eighteenth. So far as everyone here is concerned you were my lawful wedded wife. Remember how you insisted on keeping the windows closed because of your delicate health after you had Ping? Well, I still keep them closed in memory of you to help make up for the wrong I did you.

MA: (*with a sigh*): Please don't go on. We're both too old for that sort of thing.

ZHOU: I couldn't agree more. Now we can have a straight talk.

MA: I don't think there's anything to talk about.

ZHOU: On the contrary. You don't seem to have al-

鲁贵像是个很不老实的人。

鲁：你不要怕。他永远不会知道的。

朴：那双方面都好。再有，我要问你的，你自己带走的儿子在哪儿？

鲁：他在你的矿上做工。

朴：我问，他现在在哪儿？

鲁：就在门房等着见你呢？

朴：什么？鲁大海？他！我的儿子？

鲁：就是他！他现在跟你完完全全是两样的人。

朴：（冷笑）这么说，我自己的骨肉在矿上鼓动罢工，反对我！

鲁：你不要以为他还会认你做父亲。

朴：（忽然）好！痛痛快快的！你现在要多少钱吧！

鲁：什么？

朴：留着你养老。

鲁：（苦笑）哼，你还以为我是故意来敲诈你，才来的么？

朴：也好，我们暂且不提这一层。那么，我先说我的意思。你听着，鲁贵我现在要辞退的，四凤也要回家。不过——

鲁：你不要怕，你以为我会用这种关系来敲诈你么？你放心，我不会的。大后天我就带着四凤回到我原来的地方。这是一场梦，这地方

tered much in temperament — Lu Gui strikes me as being rather a shifty character.

MA: You've got nothing to worry about on that score. He'll never know anything about it.

ZHOU: Which is a good thing for both of us. There is one other thing I'd like to know: what's become of the boy you took with you?

MA: He's working at your mine.

ZHOU: I mean, where is he at this moment?

MA: In the porter's lodge, waiting to see you.

ZHOU: What! Lu Dahai? You mean — he's my son?

MA: He certainly is! Only he and you are poles apart.

ZHOU (*wryly*): And so my own flesh and blood turns against me and foments a strike in my mine!

MA: Don't think he'll own you as his father, though.

ZHOU (*suddenly*): All right! Let's have it! How much do you want?

MA: What do you mean?

ZHOU: To keep you in your old age.

MA (*with a twisted smile*): Ha! So you still think I came here purposely to blackmail you, do you?

ZHOU: All right, let's say no more about that for the moment. I'll tell you first of all what I propose to do. Well now, Lu Gui will have to go, and Sifeng can't very well stay here, either. However —

MA: You needn't be afraid. You think I'd blackmail you with our relationship? Don't worry, I won't. In three days' time I'll be going back to where I came from, and I'll be taking Sifeng with me. This is all a bad dream. I just couldn't bear to

我绝对不会再住下去。

朴：好得很，那么一切路费，用费，都归我担负。

鲁：什么？

朴：这于我的心也安一点。

鲁：你？（笑）二十七年我一个人都过了，现在我反而要你的钱？

朴：好，好，好，那么，你现在要什么？

鲁：(停一停)我，我要点东西。

朴：什么？说吧。

鲁：(泪满眼)我——我——我只要见见我的萍儿。

朴：你想见他？

鲁：嗯，他在哪儿？

朴：他现在在楼上陪着他的母亲看病。我叫他，他就可以下来见你。不过是——(顿)他很大了，——(顿)并且他以为他母亲早就死了的。

鲁：哦，你以为我会哭哭啼啼地叫他认母亲么？我不会那样傻的。我难道不知道这样的母亲只给自己的儿子丢人么？我明白他的地位，他的教育，不容他承认这样的母亲。这些年我也学乖了，我只想看看他，他究竟是

stay in the place any longer.

ZHOU: Good idea. I'll pay all your fares and expenses.

MA: You'll do what?

ZHOU: It'll make me feel a bit better.

MA: Oh no, you don't! (*She laughs derisively.*) Do you imagine I'd fall back on your charity now, after managing single-handed for twenty-seven years?

ZHOU: All right, all right. What is it you want, anyway?

MA (*after a pause*): Well, there is — there is one thing I'd like.

ZHOU: And what's that? — Mum?

MA (*blinded by tears*): I — I just want to have a last look at my son Ping.

ZHOU: You want to see him?

MA: Yes. Where is he?

ZHOU: He's upstairs with his stepmother and her doctor. I can send for him now if you like. Though — (*he hesitates*) he's grown up now, and he — (*hesitating*) he thinks his mother's been dead for years now.

MA: Now you don't imagine I'm going to fall on his neck in a flood of tears and tell him I'm his long-lost mother, do you? I'm not as silly as that. I quite realize that I'm not the sort of mother that any son could feel proud of. I appreciate that his position in life and his education wouldn't allow him to own such a woman as me as his mother. I have learned a thing or two all these years, you

我生的孩子。你不要怕,我就是告诉他,白白地增加他的烦恼,他自己也不愿意认我的。

朴:那么,我们就这样解决了。我叫他下来,你看一看他,以后鲁家的人永远不许再到周家来。

鲁:好,我希望这一生不至于再见你。

朴:(由衣内取出支票,签好)很好,这是一张五千块钱的支票,你可以先拿去用。算是弥补我一点罪过。

鲁妈接过支票,把它撕了。

朴:侍萍。

鲁:我这些年的苦不是你拿钱算得清的。

朴:可是你——

外面争吵声。大海的声音:"放开我,我要进去。"三四个男仆声:"不成,不成,老爷睡觉呢。"门外有男仆等与大海挣扎声。

朴:(走至中门)来人!

仆人由中门进。

朴:谁在吵?

仆人:就是那个工人鲁大海!他不讲理,非见老

know. No, all I want is just to see him. After all, he is my own child. You've got nothing to worry about, though: even if I did spoil everything for him by telling him, he'd still never own me.

ZHOU: So that's settled, then. I'll have him down here and let you have a look at him, and after that, no Lu will ever set foot inside this house again.

MA: All right, then. And I hope I'll never set eyes on you again as long as I live.

ZHOU (*taking a cheque-book from an inside pocket and making out a cheque*): Fair enough. Here's a cheque of five thousand dollars, which I hope you'll accept. I hope it'll help to make up for the wrong I've done you.

(*Lu Ma takes the cheque and tears it up.*)

ZHOU: Shiping!

MA: No amount of your money can cancel out all these years of heart-break.

ZHOU: But you —

(*He is cut short by angry voices outside. Lu Dahai's voice is heard shouting "Get out of my way. I'm going in." Then come the voices of several footmen: "Stop. You can't go in. The master's resting." The noise of a struggle follows.*)

ZHOU (*going to the centre door*): Come here, somebody!

(*A servant appears in the doorway.*)

ZHOU: Who's that making all that noise?

SERVANT: It's that miner, Lu Dahai. He won't be reasonable about it, but insists on seeing your now,

雷雨

爷不可。

朴：哦。（沉吟）那你就叫他进来吧。等一等，叫人到楼上请大少爷下来，我有话问他。

仆人：是，老爷。（由中门下。）

朴：（向鲁妈）侍萍，你不要太固执。这一点钱你不收下，将来你会后悔的。

鲁妈望着周朴园，一句话也不说。

仆人领大海进，大海站在左边，三四个仆人立一旁。

大：（见鲁妈）妈，您还在这儿？

朴：（打量大海）你叫什么名字？

大：你不要同我摆架子，你难道不知道我是谁么？

朴：我只知道你是罢工闹得最凶的工人。

大：对了，一点也不错，所以才来拜望拜望你。

朴：你有什么事吧？

大：董事长当然知道我是为什么来的。

朴：（摇头）我不知道。

大：我们老远从矿上来，今天我又在你府上大门房里从早上六点钟一直等到现在，我就是要问问董事长，对于我们工人的条件，究竟是

sir.

ZHOU: I see. (*He hesitates a moment.*) You'd better let him come in, then. Wait a minute: send someone upstairs for Master Ping. I want to see him.

SERVANT: Very good, sir. (*He goes out through the centre door.*)

ZHOU (*to Lu Ma*): Don't be so pig-headed, Shiping. If you don't take the money, you'll regret it one day.

(*Lu Ma looks at him without so much as a word.*)

(*Three or four servants bring in Lu Dahai. He stands on the left with the servants clustering round him.*)

HAI (*noticing his mother*): Mother, I didn't know you were still here.

ZHOU (*sizing him up*): What's your name?

HAI: Don't you put on airs with me. Are you trying to tell me you don't know who I am?

ZHOU: All I know is that you were the biggest troublemaker during the strike.

HAI: Precisely. That's why I've come to pay you a visit.

ZHOU: What is it you want?

HAI: As chairman of the board of directors you know very well what I want.

ZHOU (*shaking his head*): I'm afraid I don't.

HAI: We've come all this way from the mine, and since six o'clock this morning I've been cooling my heels in your porter's lodge, just so that I can ask you, Mr. Chairman, what exactly you're going

允许不允许？

朴：哦，——那么，那三个代表呢？

大：我跟你说吧，他们现在正在联络旁的工会呢。

朴：哦，——他们没有告诉你旁的事情么？

大：告诉不告诉于你没有关系。——我问你，你的意思，忽而软，忽而硬，究竟是怎么回子事？

周萍由饭厅上，见有人，想退回。

朴：（看周萍）不要走，萍儿！（望了一下鲁妈。）

萍：是，爸爸。

朴：（指身侧）你站在这儿。（向大海）你这么只凭意气是不能交涉事情的。

大：哼，你们的手段，我都明白。你们这样拖延时候，不过是想去花钱收买少数不要脸的败类，暂时把我们骗在这儿。

朴：你的见地也不是没有道理。

大：可是你完全错了。我们这次罢工是有团结的，有组织的。我们代表这次来，并不是来求你们。你听清楚，不求你们。你们允许就

to do about our demands. Do you accept them or not?

ZHOU: H'm. — What's become of the other three representatives, then?

HAI: I'll tell you: they're busy enlisting the support of other trade unions.

ZHOU: I see. But didn't they tell you anything else?

HAI: It's none of your business what they told me. — And now I want to know what exactly you think you're playing at, blowing hot and cold all the time. (*Zhou Ping comes in from the diningroom. Seeing that his father has company, he turns to go.*)

ZHOU (*catching sight of Zhou Ping*): Don't go, Ping. (*He glances at Lu Ma.*

PING: Very well, Father.

ZHOU (*gesturing to one side*): Come and stand here by me. (*To Dahai.*) You'll find you need something more than mere emotion if you're going to be a negotiator.

HAI: Humph! Don't think I don't know your tricks! I know them all. All this hanging about and putting off is to give you time to buy over a few miserable blacklegs. You're just keeping us here out of the way until you've done it.

ZHOU: I must admit that that supposition is not entirely inaccurate.

HAI: But you're wasting your time. The miners are solid behind the strike this time, and they're properly organized. This time we representatives are not coming to you on our bended knees. Get

允许;不允许,我们一直罢工到底,我们知道你们不到两个月整个地就要关门的。

朴:你以为你们那些代表们,那些领袖们都可靠么?

大:至少比你们只认识洋钱的结合要可靠得多。

朴:那么我给你一件东西看。

周朴园在桌上找电报,仆人递给他;此时周冲偷偷由左书房进,在旁谛听。

朴:(给大海电报)这是昨天从矿上来的电报。

大:(拿过去读)什么?他们又上工了。(放下电报)不会。

朴:矿上的工人已经在昨天早上复工,你当代表的反而不知道么?

大:(怒)怎么矿上警察开枪打死三十个工人就白打了么?(笑起来)哼,这是假的。你们自己假作的电报来离间我们的。你们这种卑鄙无赖的行为!

萍:(忍不住)你是谁?敢在这儿胡说?

朴:没有你的话!(向大海)你就这样相信你那

that straight: we're not on our bended knees. If you accept our demands, well and good; if not, then the strike goes on until you do. We know just how long you can last out: two months, and you'll have to close down.

GHOU: So you think all these representatives and leaders of yours are reliable, eh?

HAI: At least they're much more reliable than anybody in your money-grabbing concerns.

ZHOU: Then let me show you something.

(*He looks for a telegram on the table. A servant hands it to him. Just at this moment Zhou Zhong slips unobtrusively in from the study and stands there listening.*)

ZHOU (*handing the telegram to Lu Dahai*): This telegram came from the mine yesterday.

HAI (*reading it*): What! They've gone back! (*Putting the telegram down.*) They can't have done.

ZHOU: The miners went back yesterday morning. You mean to say you didn't know, and you one of their representatives?

HAI (*angrily*): So the mine police can get away with opening fire on the miners and killing thirty of them, eh? (*He bursts out laughing.*) Huh, it's a fake. You faked this telegram yourselves to split us. What a dirty, low trick!

PING (*unable to contain himself any longer*): Who do you think you are? How dare you speak like that!

ZHOU: You keep out of this! (*To Lu Dahai.*) So you have complete confidence in the other represent-

同来的几个代表么?

大:你不用多说,我明白你这些话的用意。

朴:好,那我把那复工的合同给你瞧瞧。

大:(笑)你不要骗小孩子,复工的合同没有我们代表的签字是不生效力的。

朴:合同!

仆人进书房把合同拿给周朴园。

朴:你看,这是他们三个人签字的合同。

大:(看合同)什么?(慢慢地)他们三个人签了字。(伸手去拿,想仔细看一看)他们怎么会不告诉我,自己就签了字呢?他们就这样把我不理啦?

朴:(顺手抽过来,交给仆人)对了,傻小子,没有经验只会胡喊是不成的。

大:那三个代表呢?

朴:昨天晚车就回去了。

大:(如梦初醒)他们三个就骗了我了,这三个没有骨头的东西,他们就把矿上的工人们卖了。哼,你们这些不要脸的董事长,你们的钱这次又灵了。

萍:(怒)你混账!

atives who came with you, eh?

HAI: All right, don't waste your breath: I know what you're getting at.

ZHOU: Very well, then what if I show you the written agreement to call off the strike?

HAI (*laughing*): You needn't try and bluff me: I wasn't born yesterday. An agreement doesn't mean a thing without the representatives' signatures on it.

ZHOU: Get the agreement.

(*A servant goes into the study and returns with a document, which he hands to Zhou Puyuan.*)

ZHOU: There you are: the agreement, complete with the signatures of the other three.

HAI (*looking at it*): What! (*Slowly.*) They've signed it. All three of them. (*Reaching out for the document to examine it more closely.*) How could they just sign like that, without consulting me? They can't just ignore me like this!

ZHOU (*whipping the document away and handing it to a servant*): So there you are, you young fool. Shouting and blustering won't get you anywhere: experience is what you want.

HAI: Where are the other three?

ZHOU: They caught a train back last night.

HAI (*as the scales finally fall from his eyes*): So the three of them have double-crossed me, the spineless rats! And sold their mates, too! So your money's done the trick again, you nasty pieces of work! You're all the same, you bosses!

PING (*angered*): Why, you insolent scoundrel!

朴：不许多说话。(回头向大海)鲁大海,你现在没有资格跟我说话——矿上已经把你开除了。

大：开除了!?

冲：爸爸,这是不公平的。

朴：(向周冲)你少多嘴,出去!

周冲愤然由中门下。

大：好,好。(切齿)你的手段我早明白,只要你能弄钱,你什么都做得出来。你叫警察杀了矿上许多工人,你还——

朴：你胡说!

鲁：(至大海前)走吧,别说了。

大：哼,你的来历我都知道,你从前在哈尔滨包修江桥,故意叫江堤出险,——

朴：(厉声)下去!

仆人们：(拉大海)走!走!

大：你故意淹死了两千二百个小工,每一个小工的性命你扣三百块钱!姓周的,你发的是绝子绝孙的昧心财!你现在还——

萍：(冲向大海,打了他两个嘴巴)你这种混账东

ZHOU: Hold your tongue. (*Turning back to Lu Dahai.*) You're no longer in a position to speak to me, Lu Dahai — the firm's already sacked you.

HAI: Sacked me!

CHONG: That's not playing the game, Father.

ZHOU (*turning to Zhou Chong*): You shut up and get out! (*Zhou Chong departs in high dudgeon through the centre door.*)

HAI: All right, then. (*Grinding his teeth.*) Your dirty tricks are nothing new to me. You'd stoop to anything so long as there was money in it. You get the police to mow down your men, and then you —

ZHOU: How dare you!

MA (*going to Lu Dahai*): Come on, let's go. That's enough.

HAI: Yes, and I know all about your record too! When you contracted to repair that bridge over the river at Harbin, you deliberately breached the dyke —

ZHOU (*harshly*): Get out of here!

SERVANTS (*tugging at Lu Dahai*): Come on! Outside! Out!

HAI: You drowned two thousand two hundred coolies in cold blood, and for each life lost you raked in three hundred dollars! I tell you, creature, you've made your money by killing people, and you and your sons stand accursed for ever! And now on top of that you —

PING (*hurling himself on Lu Dahai and striking him twice in the face*): Take that, you lying

雷雨

西!

大海还手,被仆人们拉住。

萍:打他!

大:(向周萍)你!

仆人们一齐打大海。大海流了血。

朴:(厉声)不要打人!

仆人们住手,仍拉住大海。

大:(挣扎)放开我,你们这一群强盗!

萍:(向仆人们)把他拉下去!

鲁:(大哭)这真是一群强盗!(走至周萍面前)你是萍,——凭——凭什么打我的儿子?

萍:你是谁?

鲁:我是你的……你打的这个人的妈……。

大:妈,别理这东西,小心吃了他们的亏。

鲁:(呆呆地望着周萍的脸,又哭起来)大海,走吧,我们走吧!

大海为仆人们拥下,鲁妈随下。台上只有周朴园与周萍。

萍:(过意不去地)父亲。

朴:你太莽撞了。

萍:可是这个人不应该乱侮辱父亲的名誉啊。

半晌。

swine!

(*Lu Dahai returns a blow, but is seized and held by the servants.*)

PING: Give him what for!

HAI (*to Zhou Ping*): You — !

(*The servants set upon him. Blood appears on his face.*)

ZHOU (*harshly*): Stop! Leave him alone!

(*The servants stop but still keep hold of Lu Dahai.*).

HAI (*struggling*): Let go of me, you hooligans!

PING (*to the servants*): Hustle him outside!

MA (*breaking down*): You *are* hooligans, too! (*Going across to Zhou Ping.*) You're my — mighty free with your fists! What right have you to hit my son?

PING: Who are you?

MA: I'm your — your victim's mother.

HAI: Take no notice of the rat, Mother. You don't want them setting on to you, as well.

MA (*staring dazedly at Zhou Ping's face, then bursting into tears again*): Oh, Dahai, let's go! Let's get out of here! (*Lu Dahai is shepherded out by the servants, followed by Lu Ma. Only Zhou Puyuan and Zhou Ping remain on the stage.*)

PING (*apologetically*): Father.

ZHOU: You might have been less impetuoous.

PING: But the fellow had no right to throw mud at you like that.

(*A pause.*)

雷雨

朴：克大夫给你母亲看过了么？

萍：看完了，没有什么。

朴：哦，（沉吟，忽然）来人！

仆人由中门上。

朴：你告诉太太，叫她把鲁贵跟四凤的工钱算清楚，我已经把他们辞了。

仆人：是，老爷。

萍：怎么？他们两个怎么样了？

朴：你不知道刚才这个工人也姓鲁，他就是四凤的哥哥么？

萍：（惊）这个人就是四凤的哥哥？那么，爸爸——

朴：（向仆人）跟太太说，叫账房给鲁贵同四凤多算两个月的工钱，叫他们今天就走。去吧。

仆人由饭厅下。

萍：爸爸，不过四凤同鲁贵在家里都很好，很忠诚的。

朴：嗯，（呵欠）我很累了。我预备到书房歇一下。你叫他们送一碗浓一点的普洱茶来。

萍：是，爸爸。

周朴园由书房门下。

萍：（叹一口气）嗨！（急走向中门。）

周冲适由中门上。

ZHOU: Did your mother see the doctor?

PING: Yes, but he couldn't find anything wrong with her.

ZHOU: H'm. (*Lost in thought for a while, then, abruptly.*) Here, somebody!

(*A servant comes in through the centre door.*)

ZHOU: Tell the mistress I've dismissed Lu Gui and Sifeng, so she can make up their wages.

SERVANT: Very good, sir.

PING: But I say! What have they done wrong?

ZHOU: Aren't you aware that this fellow we had here just now is also a Lu Sifeng's brother, in fact?

PING (*taken aback*): That fellow Sifeng's brother? Why, Father —

ZHOU (*to the servant*): Tell the mistress that the office is to give Lu Gui and Sifeng two months' extra pay, but they must leave the house today. That's all.

(*The servant goes out through the dining-room.*)

PING: But, Father, Sifeng and Lu Gui have both been excellent servants, and very loyal.

ZHOU: H'm. (*Yawning.*) I'm tired. Think I'll go and have a rest in the study. Tell them to bring me a cup of Yunnan tea — strong.

PING: Very well, Father.

(*Zhou Puyuan goes into the study.*)

PING (*heaving a sigh*): Phew! (*He hurries towards the centre door.*)

(*Just at that moment Zhou Chong comes in through the same door.*)

雷雨

冲：(着急地)哥哥,四凤呢?

萍：我不知道。

冲：是父亲要辞退四凤么?

萍：嗯,还有鲁贵。

冲：即便是她的哥哥得罪了父亲,我们不是把人家打了么? 欺负这么一个女孩子干什么?

萍：你问父亲去。

冲：这太不讲理了。

萍：是啊。

冲：父亲在哪儿?

萍：在书房里。

　　周冲到书房去;周萍在屋里踱来踱去。四凤擦着眼泪由中门走进。

萍：(忙走至四凤前)四凤,对不起你,我实在不认识他。

　　四凤摇一摇手,满腹说不出的话。

萍：可是你哥哥也不应该那样乱说话。

四：不必提了。(即向饭厅去。)

萍：你干什么去?

四：我收拾我自己的东西去。再见吧,明天你走,我怕不能看你了。

萍：不,你不要去。(拦住她。)

四：不,放开我。你不知道我们已经叫你们辞了么?

萍：(难过)凤,你——你不怪我么?

CHONG (*anxiously*): Ping, where's Sifeng?

PING: I've no idea.

CHONG: Is it true that Father's dismissed her?

PING: Yes, and Lu Gui, too.

CHONG: Even if her brother did upset Father, he got a good hiding for it, didn't he? No point in taking it out on the girl, is there?

PING: Go and ask Father.

CHONG: But it's quite preposterous.

PING: Yes, isn't it?

CHONG: Where is Father?

PING: In the study.

(*Zhou Chong goes into the study, leaving Zhou Ping pacing up and down. Sifeng comes in through the centre door, drying her eyes.*)

PING (*hurrying across to her*): I'm sorry, Sifeng. I really had no idea who he was.

(*Sifeng gestures helplessly. Her heart is too full for words.*)

PING: Your brother shouldn't have said such wild things, though.

FENG: No use bringing it up again. (*She makes straight for the dining-room.*)

PING: Where are you off to now?

FENG: I'm going to pack my things. It's good-bye now. Since you'll be leaving tomorrow, I may never see you again.

PING: No, don't go. (*He stands in her way.*)

FENG: No, let me go. Don't you realize we've already got the sack from this place?

PING (*hurt*): Feng, you — you don't blame me, do

四:我知道早晚是有这么一天的,可今天晚上你千万不要来找我。

萍:可是,以后呢?

四:那——再说吧!

萍:不,四凤,我要见你;今天晚上,我一定要见你,我有许多话要同你说。四凤,你……

四:不,无论如何你不要来。

萍:那你想旁的法子来见我。

四:没有旁的法子。你难道看不出这是什么情形?

萍:我是一定要来的。

四:不,不,你不要胡闹。你千万不……

繁漪由饭厅上。

四:哦,太太。

繁:你们在这儿啊!(向四凤)等一会,你的父亲叫电灯匠就回来。你的东西,我可以交给他带回去,也许我派人给你送去。——你家住在什么地方?

四:杏花巷十号。

繁:你不要难过,没事可以常来找我。东西,我回头叫人送到你那里。是杏花巷十号吧?

四:是,谢谢太太。

鲁妈的声音:四凤!四凤!

you?

FENG: I knew it would end up like this sooner or later. Don't come to see me tonight whatever you do.

PING: But — what about the future?

FENG: Well — we'll just have to wait and see.

PING: Yes, Sifeng, I will see you this evening — I must. I've got so many things to talk over with you. Sifeng, you —

FENG: No. Whatever happens you mustn't come.

PING: Then you'll have to find some other way of seeing me.

FENG: There isn't any other way. Can't you see how things are?

PING: Whatever you say, I'm coming round.

FENG: No, you mustn't. Don't be a fool. I absolutely forbid you —

(*Zhou Fanyi enters from the dining-room.*)

FENG: Oh, madam.

FAN: Oh, I didn't know you two were here. (*To Sifeng.*) I'll have your things sent round in a short while. Either your father can take them, or else one of the servants can come. — Where do you live?

FENG: No. 10, Almond Blossom Lane.

FAN: Don't let it upset you. You can come and see me whenever you're free, as often as you like. Yes, I'll have one of the servants take your things along. No. 10, Almond Blossom Lane, you said?

FENG: Yes. Thank you, madam.

LU MA'S VOICE: Sifeng! Sifeng!

四：妈，我在这儿。

鲁妈由中门上。

鲁：四凤，收拾收拾零碎的东西，我们先走吧。快下大雨了。

风声，雷声渐起。

四：是，妈妈。

鲁：(向蘩漪)太太，我们走了。(向四凤)四凤，你跟太太谢谢。

四：(向蘩漪请安)太太，谢谢！(含着眼泪望周萍，周萍缓缓转过头去。)

鲁妈与四凤由中门下。

蘩：萍，你刚才同四凤说的什么？

萍：你没有权利问。

蘩：你不要以为她会了解你。

萍：你这是什么意思？

蘩：你不要再骗我，我问你，你说要到哪儿去？

萍：用不着你问。请你自己放尊重一点。

蘩：你说，你今天晚上预备上哪儿去？

萍：我——(突然)我找她。你怎么样？

蘩：(恫吓地)你知道她是谁，你是谁么？

FENG: Yes, Mother? I'm in here.
  (*Lu Ma comes in through the center door.*)
MA: Come on, Sifeng, pack up your odds and ends and let's go before it comes on to pour.
  (*Noise of wind, and distant thunder approaching.*)
FENG: All right, Mother.
MA (*to Fanyi*): I'll say good-bye to you now, madam. (*To her daughter.*) Thank your mistress for everything, Sifeng.
FENG (*dropping a curtsey to Fanyi*): Thank you, madam! (*She gazes tearfully at Zhou Ping, who slowly turns his head away.*)
  (*Lu Ma and Sifeng go out through the centre door.*)
FAN: Now, Ping, what were you and Sifeng talking about just now?
PING: You've no right to ask me that.
FAN: Don't imagine she could ever understand you.
PING: What do you mean?

FAN: Don't try and put me off with lies again. I want to know where you said you were going.
PING: It's none of your business. I should have thought you had more self-respect than ask a thing like that.
FAN: You must tell me: where is it you're proposing to go tonight?
PING: I — (*abruptly*) I'm going to see her. Now, what are you going to do about it?
FAN (*menacingly*): Do you realize who she is and who you are?

萍：我不知道。我只知道我现在真喜欢她,她也喜欢我。过去这些日子,我知道你早明白得很,现在你既然愿意说破,我当然不必瞒你。

繁：你受过这样高等教育的人同这么一个底下人的女儿,这么一个下等女人——

萍：(爆裂)你胡说！你不配说她下等,你不配！

繁：(冷笑)小心,小心！你不要把一个失望的女人逼得太狠了,她是什么事都做得出来的。

萍：我已经打算好了。

繁：好,你去吧！小心,现在(望窗外,自语)风暴就要起来了！

萍：(领悟)我知道。

周朴园由书房上。

朴：你们在这儿说什么？

萍：我正跟母亲说刚才的事情呢。

朴：他们走了么？

繁：走了。

朴：繁漪,冲儿又叫我说哭了。你叫他出来,安慰安慰他。

繁：(走到书房门口)冲儿,冲儿！(不听见里面答应的声音,便走进去。)

PING: No. All I know is that I'm really in love with her now, and that she loves me in return. I'm well aware that you've known all about it all the time. Since you now want to have it out in the open, there's no reason why I should conceal it from you any longer.

FAN: To think of a well-educated young man like you carrying on with such a low-class girl, a mere servant's daughter —

PING (*exploding*): How dare you! Who are you to call her low class, you of all people!

FAN (*with a sneer*): Take care. Take care. Don't drive a disappointed woman too hard. She's capable of anything.

PING: I'm prepared for the worst.

FAN: All right. Go, then! But be careful — (*looking out of the window, half to herself*) there's a storm coming!

PING (*understanding her*): I know.

(*Zhou Puyuan comes in from the study.*)

ZHOU: Hullo, what are you all talking about?

PING: I was just telling Mother what had happened.

ZHOU: Have they gone?

FAN: Yes.

ZHOU: Fanyi, I've gone and made Chong burst into tears again. Call him out and calm him down, would you?

FAN (*going across to the door of the study*): Chong! Chong!

(*Receiving no answer, she goes into the study.*)

雷雨

外面风雷大作。

朴：(走到窗前,风声甚烈,外面花盆落地打碎的声音)萍儿,花盆叫大风吹倒了,你叫下人快把百叶窗关上。大概是暴雨就要来了。

萍：是,爸爸！（由中门下。）

周朴园在窗前,望着外面的闪电。

——幕落

(*Outside, wind and thunder howl and roar together.*)

(*Zhou goes over to the window. A shrieking gust of wind sends flower-pots on the window-sill outside crashing to the ground.*)

ZHOU: Ping, the flower-pots are being blown down by the wind. Tell the servants to hurry up and close the shutters. I expect there's a storm coming.

PING: Very well, Father. (*He goes out through the centre door.*)

(*Zhou Puyuan stands in front of the window, watching the lightning outside.*)

(*Curtain*)

雷雨

第三幕

杏花巷十号,鲁贵家里。

下面是鲁家屋外的情形:

车站的钟打了十下,杏花巷的老少还沿着那白天蒸发着臭气,只有半夜才从租界区域吹来一阵好凉风的水塘边上乘凉。虽然方才落了一阵暴雨,天气还是郁热难堪。天空黑漆漆地布满了恶相的黑云,人们都像晒在太阳下的小草,虽然半夜里沾了点露水,心里还是热燥燥的,期望着再来一次雷雨。倒是躲在池塘芦苇根下的青蛙叫得起劲,一直不停。闲人谈话的声音有一阵没一阵的。无星的天空时而打着没有雷的闪电,蓝森森地一晃,闪露出来池塘边的垂柳在水面颤动着。闪光过去,还是黑黝黝的一片。

Act Three

Inside Lu Gui's house — at No. 10, Almond Blossom Lane. First let us look at the scene outside the bouse:

The station clock has struck ten, and the people of Almond Blossom Lane, old and young, are taking the air along the banks of a pond which, although it is the source of evil exhalations drawn up by the summer sun in the daytime, provides late at night an open space where one may catch the fresh, cool breezes that blow in from the less crowded area of the foreign concession. Despite a sharp downpour a moment ago, it is still unbearably hot and close, and the sky is dark with thunderclouds, black and ominous. It is the sort of weather that makes people feel like sun-scorched blades of grass, which, although they have been moistened by a light dew during the night, are still parched inside and thirsting for another thunderstorm. Yet the frogs that crouch among the reeds by the pond are as untiringly strident as ever. The sound of the strollers' voices comes in desultory snatches. From time to time a silent flash of lightning splashes the starless sky with a harsh blue glare and for one startled moment shows us the weeping willows by the pond, drooping and trembling over the water. Then, just as suddenly, it is dark again.

雷雨

渐渐乘凉的人散了，四周围静下来，雷又隐隐地响着，青蛙像是吓得不敢多叫，风又吹起来，柳叶沙沙地响。在深巷里，野狗寂寞地狂吠着。

以后闪电更亮得蓝森森地可怕，雷也更凶恶似地隆隆地滚着。四周却更沉闷地静下来，偶尔听见几声青蛙叫和更大的木梆声，野狗的吠声更稀少，暴雨就快要来了。

最后暴风暴雨，一直到闭幕。

不过观众看见的还是四凤的屋子（即鲁贵两间房的内屋）。前面的叙述，除了声音，只能由屋子中间一扇木窗户显出来。

在四凤的屋子里面：

鲁家现在才吃完晚饭，每个人的心绪都是烦恶的。各人有各人的心思，在一个屋角，大海一个人在擦什么东西。鲁妈同四凤一句话也不说，大家静默着。鲁妈低着头在屋子中间的圆桌旁收拾筷子碗，鲁贵坐在左边一张破靠椅上，喝得醉醺醺的，眼睛发了红丝，像个猴子，半身倚着靠背，

Then, one by one, the strollers drift away and silence closes in on all sides. A rumble of distant thunder seems to cow even the frogs into silence; a breeze springs up again and sifts through the rustling leaves of the willows. From some echoing alleyway comes the lonely, frantic barking of stray dogs.

Presently the lightning blazes again, stark and terrifying, then a jarring burst of thunder goes shuddering across the sky. In its wake comes a close, oppressive silence, broken only by the occasional croaking of a frog and, what is louder, the sharp clack of a night-watchman's bamboo "gong." A storm is about to break.

When the storm does come, it will last right through to the final curtain.

All the audience can see, however, is the interior of Sifeng's room. (It is, in fact, the back room of Lu Gui's two-roomed hut.) Of the scene just described, apart from the sounds, the audience can see only what is visible through the window in the middle of the back wall.

Now let us examine Sifeng's room:

The Lus have just finished their evening meal. All four of them are in an unpleasant mood, and each of them is occupied with his or her own thoughts. Dahai is sitting in a corner cleaning something. Lu Ma and Sifeng keep an uncomfortable silence. The former, her head bent, is clearing away the bowls and chopsticks from the round table in the centre of the room. A drink-fuddled Lu Gui sits slumped back in a rickety easy-chair on the left. Monkey-like, he

望着鲁妈打着噎。他的赤脚忽然放在椅子上,忽然又平拖在地上,两条腿像人字似地排开。他穿一件白汗衫,半臂已经汗透了,贴在身上,他不住地摇着芭蕉扇。

四凤在中间窗户前面站着:背朝着观众,面向窗外不安地望着。窗外池塘边有乘凉的人们说着闲话,有青蛙的叫声。她时而不安地像听见了什么似的,时而又转过头看了看鲁贵,又烦厌地迅速转过去。在她旁边靠左墙是一张搭好的木板床,上面铺着凉席,一床很干净的夹被,一个凉枕和一把蒲扇,很整齐地放在上面。

屋子很小,像一切穷人的房子,屋顶低低地压在头上。床头上挂着一张烟草公司的广告画,在左边的墙上贴着过年时粘上的旧画,已经破烂许多地方。靠着鲁贵坐的唯一的一张圆椅旁有一张小方桌,上面有镜子,梳子,女人用的几件平常的化装品,那大概就是四凤的梳装台了。在左墙有一条板凳,在中间圆桌旁边孤零零地立着一个圆凳子,在右边四凤的床下正排着

stares at his wife from bloodshot eyes and hiccups. He puts his bare feet now on the staves of the chair, now on the floor with his legs sprawled wide apart. He wears a white singlet, sweat-soaked and clinging. He fans himself incessantly with a palm-leaf fan.

Sifeng is standing in front of the window. Her back is towards the audience as she stares anxiously out. From outside the window comes the croaking of the frogs and the light-hearted voices of passers-by. She seems to be listening uneasily for something, and from time to time she looks round at her father and then looks swiftly away again in disgust. Beside her, standing against the left wall, is a plank-bed covered with a mat and a spotless double quilt. A mat pillow and a palm-leaf fan are neatly arranged on it.

The room is very small and, as is always the case in the houses of the poor, the ceiling comes oppressively low over one's head. On the wall over the head of the bed hangs an illustrated poster advertising a brand of cigarettes, while on the left-hand wall is pasted an old reproduction originally put up as a New Year decoration and now very tattered and torn. A small table stands by the only chair in the room — now occupied by Lu Gui — with a mirror, a comb and various cheap cosmetics on it: apparently Sifeng's dressing-table. Along the left-hand wall stands a bench, and by the table in the middle of the room there is a solitary stool. Under Sifeng's bed, there is a trunk draped with a white cloth and

雷雨

两三双很时髦的鞋。鞋的下头,有一只箱子,上面铺着一块白布,放着一个瓷壶同两三个粗碗。小圆桌上放着一盏洋油灯,上面罩一个鲜红的纸灯罩,还有几件零碎的小东西。在暗澹的灯影里,零碎的小东西虽看不清楚,却依然令人觉得这大概是一个女人的住房。

这屋子有两个门,在左边——就是有木床的一边——开着一个小门,外面挂着一幅色彩强烈的有花的红幔帐。里面存着煤,一两件旧家具;四凤为着自己换衣服用的。右边有一个破旧的木门,通着鲁家的外间,外面是鲁贵住的地方,是今晚鲁贵夫妇睡的处所。那外间屋的门就通着池塘边泥泞的小道。这里间与外间相通的木门,旁边斜放着一副铺板。

开幕时,正是鲁贵兴致淋漓地刚刚数落完半咒骂式的家庭训话。屋内是沉默而紧张的。沉闷中听得出池塘边唱着淫荡的春曲,参杂着乘凉人们的谈话。各人在想各人的心思,低着头不做声。鲁贵满身是汗,因为喝酒喝得太多,说话也过于卖了力气,嘴里流着涎水,脸红得吓人。他好像很

with several pairs of pashionable shoes, a teapot and several cheap bowls on it. An oil lamp with a bright red-paper lampshade stands on the round table. The light is not very strong, yet one sees enough of the articles on the table to know that it is a woman's bedroom.

The room has two doors, of which the one on the left — the side where the bed is — is no more than a gaudily patterned red curtain hanging over a recess which, besides providing storage-space for a heap of coal and bits of old furniture, also serves as Sifeng's dressing-room. The door on the right is of cracked and bat-tered planks and leads to the front room. This is Lu Gui's room, and it is in this front room that he and his wife will sleep tonight. From the front room a door opens on the muddy path leading to the edge of the pond. Just inside the door between the two rooms, leaning against the wall, are several long planks for making a bed with.

When the curtain rises, Lu Gui has just delivered a voluble and highly-coloured lecture to his family. In the tense silence which follows this spirited outburst one can hear the strains of some indelicate love-song coming from the direction of the pond, mingled with the murmur of conversation from the people outside relaxing in the cool of the evening. Inside the room, the four heads are bent in silent preoccupation. Hard drinking and the effort involved in the delivery of such a forceful lecture have bathed Lu Gui in perspiration from head to foot and now he sits with slobbering lips and his face an ugly red.

得意自己在家里面的位置同威风,拿着那把破芭蕉扇,挥着,舞着,指着。为汗水浸透了似的肥脑袋探向前面,眼睛迷腾腾的,在各个人的身上扫来扫去。

大海依旧擦他的手枪,两个女人都不做声,等着鲁贵继续嘶喊。这时青蛙同卖唱的叫声传了过来。

四凤立在窗户前,偶尔深深地叹着气。

贵:(咳嗽起来)他妈的!(兴奋地问着)你们想,你们哪一个对得起我?(向四凤同大海)你们不要不愿意听,你们哪一个不是我辛辛苦苦养到大?可是现在你们哪一件事做的对得起我?(对大海)你说?(对四凤)你说?(对着站在中间圆桌旁的鲁妈)你也说说,这都是你的好孩子啊?

静默。传来外面胡琴声,唱声。

大:(向四凤)这是谁?快十点半还在唱?

He is apparently revelling in his position of authority as head of the family judging by the gusto with which he brandishes his tattered palm-leaf fan and the way he points and gestures with it. His sweat-soaked, flesh-draped head is thrust forward and his glazed eyes swing from one member of his family to another.

Dahai is still busy cleaning the object in his hand, which the audience now sees to be a pistol. The two women wait in silence for Lu Gui to launch another shrill tirade against them. The croaking of the frogs and the voices of street-singers now drift in through the window.

Still standing in front of the window, Sifeng now and then heaves a deep sigh.

LU (*coughing*): God almighty! (*Heatedly.*) Just look at you. There's not one of you can look me in the face! (*Turning to Dahai and Sifeng.*) It's no good you pretending not to hear, either. I've worked my fingers to the bone to bring you two up, both of you, but what have either of you ever done to show your gratitude? (*To Dahia.*) Eh? (*To Sifeng.*) Answer me that! (*To Lu Ma, who is standing by the round table in the centre.*) Or perhaps you can tell me, seeing that they're your precious children?

(*Silence. From outside comes the sound of someone singing to the accompaniment of a Chinese fiddle.*)

HAI (*to Sifeng*): Who's that still singing at this time

四:(随意地)一个瞎子同他老婆,每天在这儿卖唱的。(挥着扇,微微叹一口气。)

贵:我是一辈子犯小人,不走运。刚在周家混了两年,孩子都安置好了,就叫你(指鲁妈)连累下去了。你回家一次就出一次事。刚才是怎么回事?我叫完电灯匠回公馆,凤儿的事没有了,连我的老根子也拔了。妈的,你不来,(指鲁妈)我能倒这样的楣?

大:(放下手枪)你要骂我就骂我。别指东说西,欺负妈好说话。

贵:我骂你?你是少爷!我骂你?你连人家有钱的人都当着面骂了,我敢骂你?

大:(不耐烦)你喝了不到两盅酒,就叨叨叨,叨叨叨,这半点钟你够不够?

贵:够?哼,我一肚子的冤屈,一肚子的火,我没个够!当初你爸爸也不是没叫人伺候过,吃

of night? It's almost half past ten.

FENG (*listlessly*): Oh, some blind man and his wife. They're round here every day. Street-singers. (*She heaves a faint sigh as she fans herself.*)

LU: All my life I've just had one patch of bad luck after another, and every time it's been because some miserable nobody has put a spoke in my wheel. Just when I've been with the Zhous two years and got my children fixed up with good jobs, you (*pointing at his wife*) have to come along and undo all that I've done. Every time you come home there's trouble. Look at what happened today: I go out to fetch an electrician and when I get back what do I find? Sifeng's lost her job and I'm out on my neck into the bargain. If you hadn't come home, damn you (*pointing at her again*), all this would never have happened!

HAI (*putting down the revolver*): If you want to swear at me, just get on with it. There's no need to take it out on Mother instead.

LU: Me swear at you? As if I'd dare swear at a young gentleman like you! You, who even swear at rich people to their face!

HAI (*losing patience with him*): You get two or three drinks inside you and you're off. You've been gabbling on and on for half an hour now. Can't you give it a rest?

LU: Give it a rest? Not on your life! I've just about had a bellyful of her, and I'm going to have my say. Oh no, I haven't finished yet! It's not as if your old dad had always been a servant: there

喝玩乐,我哪一样没讲究过!自从娶了你的妈,我是家败人亡,一天不如一天。一天不如一天,……

四:那不是你自己赌钱输光的!

大:你别理他。让他说。

贵:(只顾嘴头说得畅快,如同自己是唯一的牺牲者一样)我告诉你,我是家败人亡,一天不如一天。我受人家的气,受你们的气。现在好,连想受人家的气也不成了,我跟你们一块儿饿着肚子等死。你们想想,你们是哪一件事对得起我?(忽而觉得自己的腿没处放)侍萍,把那凳子拿过来。我放放大腿。

大:(看着鲁妈,叫她不要管)妈!

然而鲁妈还是拿了那唯一的圆凳子过来,放在鲁贵的脚下。他把腿放好。

贵:(望着大海)可是这怪谁?你把人家骂了,人家一气,当然就把我们辞了。谁叫我是你的爸爸呢?大海,你心里想想,我这么大年纪,

was a time when I had people waiting on me. I lived like a lord and had a good time — only the best was good enough. But from the day I married your mother, I started going to rack and ruin. Things have been going from bad to worse. Yes, from bad to worse....

FENG: You know very well it's gambling that's ruined you!

HAI: Take no notice of him. Let him ramble on.

LU (*carried away by his own eloquence, as if he has been the only one to suffer*): I tell you, I've been going to rack and ruin, from bad to worse. I've had to swallow insults from the people I've worked for, as well as insults from you lot. But now I haven't even got any employers to be insulted by! I've just got to stay here and starve to death with you! Now just ask yourselves: What have you ever done for me that you can be proud of? (*He suddenly finds that he has nothing to rest his legs on.*) Shiping, bring that stool over here for me to put my legs on.

HAI (*frowning discouragement at his mother*): No, Mother!

(*Nevertheless, Lu Ma brings the only stool in the room and places it at Lu Gui's feet. He puts his legs on it.*)

LU (*looking across at Dahai*): And who's to blame for it all? If you have to go and call people names and upset them, it's only natural that they're going to give us the sack. I can't help it if I'm your father, can I? Now just think, Dahai. Think of me,

要跟着你饿死。我要是饿死,你是哪一点对得起我?我问问你,我要是这样死了?

大:(忍不住,立起)你死就死了,你算老几!

贵:(吓醒了一点)妈的,这孩子!

鲁:大海!

四:(同时)哥哥!

贵:(看见大海那副魁梧的身体,同手里拿着的枪,心里有点怕,笑着)你看看,这孩子这点小脾气!——(又接着说)咳,说回来,这也不能就怪大海,周家的人从上到下就没有一个好东西。我伺候他们两年,他们那点出息我哪一样不知道?反正有钱的人顶方便,做了坏事,外面比做了好事装得还体面。文明词越用得多,心里头越男盗女娼,王八蛋!别看今天我走的时候,老爷太太装模做样地跟我尽打官话,好东西,明儿见!他们家里这点出息当我不知道?

四:得了吧,别扯了。

an old man, having to starve to death because of what you've done. If I did die, you'd have it on your conscience, now wouldn't you? Eh? If I did die like this?

HAI (*rising, unable to contain himself any longer*): Get on with it and die, then! Who do you think you are, anyway?

LU (*brought back to earth with a jolt*): Well, I'm damned!

MA
FENG (*together*): Dahai!

LU (*awed by Dahai's tall, muscular body and the gun in his hand, he smiles nervously*): Well, well! Proper temper the lad's got, hasn't he! (*After a pause.*) Though you know, on second thoughts, I don't think it's all Dahai's fault. There isn't a single decent Zhou in the whole of their family. I've been with them two years, and what I haven't found out about their little antics isn't worth knowing. Still, it's always the same for people with plenty of money — they can get away with anything. The worse they behave the more respectable they pretend to be. The more they give themselves airs, the nastier their minds, the dirty beasts! Look at the way they carried on when I left this afternoon. There they were, both of them, trying to smooth me down with their soft-soap. Well, just you wait and see, my hearties! They think I don't know about the little capers they cut!

FENG: That's enough. No scandal, now.

贵:(不觉骄傲起来)哼,明天,我把周家太太大少爷这点老底子给它一个宣布,就连老头这老王八蛋也得给我跪下磕头。忘恩负义的东西!(得意地咳嗽起来)他妈的!(向四凤)茶呢?

四:爸,你真是喝醉了么?刚才不给你放在桌子上了么?

贵:(端起杯子,对四凤)这是白水,小姐!(泼在地上。)

四:(冷冷地)本来是白水,没有茶。

贵:混账。我吃完饭总要喝杯好茶,你还不知道么?

大:哦,爸爸吃完饭还要喝茶的。(向四凤)四凤,你怎么不把那一两四块八的龙井沏上,尽叫爸爸生气。

四:龙井!家里连茶叶末也没有。

大:(向鲁贵)听见了没有?你就将就将就喝杯开水吧,别这样穷讲究啦。(拿一杯白开水,放在鲁贵身旁桌上,走开。)

贵:这是我的家。你要看着不顺眼,你可以滚开。

LU (*with unconscious complacency*): Ha! Wait until I start putting it all round — about the goings-on between the lady of the house and the eldest son; that ought to bring her old man himself round to see me on his bended knees, the old swine! Ungrateful lot they are! (*He coughs with satisfaction.*) I' ll show' em! (*To his daughter.*) Where's my tea?

FENG: I think you must be drunk, Dad. Didn't you see me put it on the table for you a minute ago?

LU (*picking up the cup, inspecting it and turning back to Sifeng*): What's this, my lady? Plain water? (*He empties the cup on the floor.*)

FENG (*coldly*): Of course it is. There isn't any tea.

LU: What the devil do you mean? You know very well I always have a nice cup of tea after my dinner!

HAI: Well, well, so Father would like tea after his dinner. (*To Sifeng.*) What do you mean by it, Sifeng? Upsetting Father like that! You should have made him a pot of best-quality Lungching — it's only four dollars eighty an ounce.

FENG: Lungching! Why, there isn't even a pinch of dust in the tea-caddy.

HAI (*to Lu Gui*): Hear that? You'll have to make do with boiled water and lump it, and stop being so damned fussy. (*He pours out a cup of boiled water, puts it on the table beside Lu Gui, then walks away.*)

LU: This is my house, and if you don't like it you can clear out.

247

大:(上前)你,你——

鲁:(阻大海)别,别,好孩子。看在妈的份上,别同他闹。

贵:你自己觉得挺不错,你到家不到两天,就闹这么大的乱子,我没有说你,你还要打我么?你给我滚!

大:(忍着)妈,他这样子我实在看不下去。妈,我走了。

鲁:胡说。就要下雨,你上哪儿去?

大:我有点事,办不好,也许到车厂拉车去。

鲁:大海,你——

贵:走,走,让他走。这孩子就是这点穷骨头。叫他滚,滚,滚!

大:你小心点。你少惹我。

贵:(赖皮)你妈在这儿。你敢把你的爹怎么样?你这杂种!

大:什么,你骂谁?

贵:我骂你。你这——

鲁:(向鲁贵)你别不要脸,你少说话!

贵:我不要脸?我没有在家养私孩子,还带着个(指大海)嫁人。

HAI (*advancing on him*): Now, you —

MA (*holding him back*): No, don't do anything, there's a good lad. Don't quarrel with him, for my sake.

LU: You really think you're somebody, don't you! You haven't been here two days before you manage to cause all this upset, and then before I've even breathed a word about it you're threatening to attack me! Go on, get out of my sight!

HAI (*keeping his temper*): I'm not staying here any longer if he's going to be like this, Mother. I'm going.

MA: Don't be silly. It'll come on to rain any minute. Where would you go, anyway?

HAI: I've got some business to attend to. If I don't pull it off I'll probably go rickshaw-pulling.

MA: Now look here, Dahai —

LU: Out he goes. Don't stop him. Cocky young whipper-snapper! He can get out. Right out. Go on!

HAI: You'd better watch it. Don't get me too riled.

LU (*brazening it out*): Don't forget your mother's here. You wouldn't dare do a thing to me with her here, you bastard!

HAI: What was that? Who do you think you're swearing at?

LU: At you, you bloody —

MA (*to Lu Gui*): Now shut up and stop making such an exhibition of yourself.

LU: Me make an exhibition of myself? Look who's talking! At least I didn't produce bastards — and take one of them — (*pointing at Dahai*) along with me when I got married.

雷雨

鲁：(又痛又恨)你！

大：(抽出手枪)我——我打死你这老东西！

贵：(站起，喊)枪，枪，枪！(僵立不动。)

四：(跑到大海的面前，抱着他的手)哥哥。

鲁：大海，你放下。

大：(对鲁贵)你跟妈说，说自己错了，以后永远不再乱说话，乱骂人。

贵：哦——

大：(进一步)说呀！

贵：(被胁)你，你——你先放下。

大：(气愤地)不，你先说。

贵：好。(向鲁妈)我错了，我以后永远不乱说，不骂人了。

大：(指那唯一的圆椅)还坐在那儿！

贵：(颓唐地坐在椅上，低着头咕噜着)这小杂种！

大：哼，你不值得我卖这么大的力气。

鲁：放下。大海，你把手枪放下。

大：(放下手枪，笑)妈，妈您别怕，我是吓唬吓唬他。

鲁：给我。你这手枪是哪儿弄来的？

大：从矿上带来的，警察打我们的时候掉的。

MA (*hurt and incensed*): Why, you — !

HAI (*drawing his pistol*): I'll — I'll kill you for that, you old swine!

LU (*leaping to his feet and shouting*): Help! Help! He'll shoot me! (*He stands petrified with fear.*)

FENG (*rushing across to Dahai and seizing his wrist*): Dahai!

MA: Put it away, Dahai

HAI (*to Lu Gui*): Now, tell Mother you're in the wrong, and promise that you'll never say such vile things to her again.

LU: Er —

HAI (*taking a step forward*): Say it!

LU (*intimidated*): If — if — if you put that gun down first.

HAI (*angrily*): No. You say it first.

LU: All right. (*To Lu Ma.*) It was wrong of me, and I'll never say such vile things to you again.

HAI (*pointing to the only chair in the room*): And sit over there again!

LU (*completely deflated, he sits down on the chair. He hangs his head and mutters to himself*): Bastard!

HAI: Humph! You're not worth me wasting my energy on!

MA: Put that gun down, Dahai.

HAI (*putting it down and smiling*): Don't worry, Mother. I only wanted to put the wind up him.

MA: Give it to me. Where did you get it from?

HAI: I brought it from the mine. Police dropped it in

鲁：你现在带在身上干什么？

大：不干什么。

鲁：不，你要说。

大：(狞笑)没有什么，周家逼得我没有路走，这就是一条路。

鲁：胡说，交给我。

大：(不肯)妈！

鲁：刚才吃饭的时候我跟你说过。周家的事算完了，我们姓鲁的永远不提他们了。

大：(低声，缓慢地)可是我们在矿上流的血呢？周家大少爷刚才打在我脸上的巴掌呢？就完了么？

鲁：嗯，完了。这一本账算不清楚，报复是完不了的。什么都是天定，妈愿意你多受点苦。

大：那是妈自己，我——

鲁：(高声)大海，你是我最疼的孩子，你听着，我从来不这样对你说过话。你要是伤害了周家的人，不管是那里的老爷或者少爷，你只要伤害了他们，我是一辈子也不认你的。

大：(恳求)可是妈——

鲁：(肯定地)你知道妈的脾气，你若要做了妈最怕你做的事情，妈就死在你的面前。(向大

the scuffle when they fired on us.

MA: What have you got it on you now for?

HAI: No particular reason.

MA: Oh yes, you have. Now tell me.

HAI (*smiling grimly*): It's nothing, really. If the Zhous drive me to the wall, this will be one way out.

MA: Nonsense. Give it to me.

HAI (*protesting*): Oh, Mother!

MA: I told you all about it at dinner. Our family's finished with the Zhous, and we'll never mention them again.

HAI (*quietly and slowly*): And what about the blood they spilt at the mine? What about the slap in the face I got from that young Mr. Zhou? You expect me to forget these things just like that?

MA: Yes, I do. These scores can never be properly settled. Once you start retaliating there'll be no end to it. What is to be will be. I only wish you don't have to suffer too much.

HAI: It's all right for you, Mother, but I —

MA (*raising her voice*): Now, listen to me, Dahai. You're my favourite child, and I've never talked to you like this before; but let me tell you this: if you hurt any of the Zhous — I don't care whether it's the master or the young gentlemen — if you so much as lay a hand on any of them, I'll have nothing more to do with you so long as I live.

HAI (*pleading*): But surely, Mother —

MA (*categorically*): You ought to know what I'm like by now. If you go and to the one thing I just

253

雷雨

海)把手枪给我。

大海不肯。

鲁：交给我！（走近大海，把手枪拿了过来。）

大：（痛苦）妈，您——

四：哥哥，你给妈！

大：那么您拿去吧。不过您搁的地方得告诉我。

鲁：好，我放在这个箱子里。（把手枪放在床头的木箱里）可是（对大海）明天一早我就报告警察，把枪交给他。

贵：对极了，这才是正理。

大：你少说话！

鲁：大海。不要这样同父亲说话。

大：（看鲁贵，又转头）好，妈，我走了。我要看车厂子里有熟人没有。

鲁：好，你去。不过，你可得准回来。一家人不许这样呕气。

大：嗯。就回来。（由左边与外间通的房门下。）传来大海关外房的大门的声音。

贵：（自言自语）这个小王八蛋。（问鲁妈）刚才我叫你买茶叶，你为什么不买？

couldn't bear you to do, I'll kill myself before your eyes. Give me that gun. (*Dahai refuses.*)

MA: Give it to me! (*She goes up to him and seizes hold of the pistol.*)

HAI (*hurt*): But Mother, you —

FENG: Let Mother have it, Dahai.

HAI: All right. You'd better have it, then. But you must tell me where you put it.

MA: Very well, I'll put it in this chest here. (*She puts it in the chest by the bed.*) But — (*looking at Dahai*) I'll take it round to the police and hand it in first thing tomorrow morning.

LU: Quite right. That's the most sensible thing you can do.

HAI: You shut up!

MA: Dahai, you mustn't speak to your father like that.

HAI (*looking at Lu Gui, then turning back to Lu Ma*): Well, Mother, I'm off now. I'll go down the rickshaw rank and see if I can find any of my old mates.

MA: Go on, then. But you must be sure to come back. We can't have all the family falling out with each other like this.

HAI: All right. I'll come straight back. (*He goes out through the outer room on the left.*)

(*The sound of Dahai closing the outer door is heard.*)

LU (*muttering to himself*): The bastard! (*Turning to Lu Ma.*) Why didn't you buy some tea? I told you to, didn't I?

鲁：没有闲钱。

贵：可是，四凤，我的钱呢？——刚才你们从公馆领来的工钱呢？

四：您说周公馆多给的两个月的工钱？

贵：对了，一共连新加旧六十块钱。

四：(知道早晚也要告诉他)嗯，是的，还给人啦。

贵：什么，你还给人啦？

四：刚才赵三又来堵门要你的赌账，妈就把那个钱都还给他了。

贵：(问鲁妈)六十块钱？都还了账啦？

鲁：嗯，把你这次的赌账算是还清了。

贵：(急了)妈的，我的家就是叫你们这样败了的，现在是还账的时候么？

鲁：(沉静地)都还清了好。这儿的家我预备不要了。

贵：这儿的家你不要么？

鲁：我想，大后天就回济南去。

贵：你回济南，我跟四凤在这儿，这个家也得要啊。

鲁：这次我带着四凤一块儿走，不叫她一个人在这儿了。

贵：(对四凤笑)四凤，你听你妈要带着你走。

MA: We can't afford it.

LU: But, Sifeng, where's my money? — The wages you brought from the Zhous' this afternoon?

FENG: You mean the two months' extra pay?

Lu: Yes. There should be sixty dollars altogether.

FENG (*realizing that he will have to be told the truth sooner or later*): It's all gone. To pay off your debts.

LU: What do you mean, "all gone"?

FENG: That fellow Chao was here again not long ago. Wouldn't go away till we'd paid off your gambling debts. So Mother gave him the money.

LU (*turning to Lu Ma for corroboration*): The whole sixty dollars? You gave him the lot?

MA: Yes. Which means that your latest gambling debts are as good as settled up.

LU (really anxious now): My God! No wonder you've ruined me, if that's the way you carry on. What's this — quarterday or something?

MA (*unemotionally*): It's better to have all your debts paid. I've decided to give up this house.

LU: You've what?

MA: I'm thinking of going back to Jinan in three days' time.

LU: But when you've gone there'll still be Sifeng and myself here. We'll still need the place even if you don't.

MA: I'm taking Sifeing with me this time. I'm not going to leave her here on her own any more.

LU (*smiling at Sifeng*): Hear that, Sifeng? Your mother wants to take you away with her.

雷雨

鲁：上次我走的时候，我不知道我的事情怎么样。外面人地生疏，在这儿四凤有邻居张大婶照应她，我自然不带她走。现在我那边的事已经定了。四凤在这儿又没有事，我为什么不带她走？

四：(惊)您，您真要带我走？

鲁：(沉痛地)嗯，妈以后说什么也不离开你了。

贵：不成，这我们得好好商量商量。

鲁：这有什么可商量的！你要愿意去，大后天一块儿走也可以。不过那儿是找不着你这一帮赌钱的朋友的。

贵：谁要到那儿去？可是你带四凤到那儿干什么？

鲁：女孩子当然随着妈走，从前那是没有法子。

贵：(滔滔地)四凤跟我有吃有穿，见的是场面人。你带着她，活受罪，干什么？

鲁：(对他没有办法)跟你也说不明白。你问问

MA: When I went away last time, I didn't know how this job of mine would turn out. I was going to a strange place and I hadn't got any friends there, and all the while she stayed here she'd at least have Mrs. Chang next door to look after her, so naturally I didn't take her with me. I know now that the job's a steady one, and she's lost her job here, so why shouldn't I take her with me?

FENG (*alarmed*): So you — you really want to take me with you?

MA (*in a pained voice*): Yes. Nothing will ever induce me to leave you on yoru own any more.

LU: Here, hold on. We'll have to talk all this over properly first.

MA: What is there to talk about? If you feel so inclined you can come with us, and we can all go together. Though it'll mean leaving all your cronies that you gamble with if you do.

LU: Jinan's the last place I want to go. Though I still don't see why you should want to take Sifeng with you.

MA: It's only natural that a girl should be with her mother. It's just that I had no choice but to leave her here last time.

LU (*glibly*): If Sifeng stays with me she won't have to worry about a thing. She'll live in comfort and she'll only mix with the best people. If she goes with you, her life won't be worth living. So what's the point?

MA (*giving him up as hopeless*): Oh, it's no good talking to you. You just won't understand. You'd

雷雨

她愿意跟我,还是愿意跟你?

贵:自然是愿意跟我。

鲁:你问她!

贵:(自信一定胜利)四凤,你过来,你听清楚了。你愿意怎么样?随你。跟你妈,还是跟我?

四凤转过身来,满脸的眼泪。

贵:咦,这孩子,你哭什么?

鲁:凤儿。

贵:说呀,这不是大姑娘上轿,说呀?

鲁:(安慰地)哦,凤儿,告诉我,刚才你答应得好好的,愿意跟着妈走,现在又怎么哪?告诉我,好孩子。老实告诉妈,妈还是喜欢你。

贵:你说你带她走,她心里不高兴。我知道,她舍不得这个地方。(笑。)

四:(向鲁贵)去!(向鲁妈)别问我,妈,我心里难过。妈,我的妈,我是跟您走的。妈呀!(抽咽,扑在鲁妈的怀里。)

鲁:孩子,我的孩子今天受了委屈了。

better ask her if she wants to come with me or to stay with you.

LU: She wants to stay with me, of course.

MA: Ask her!

LU (*confident of winning*): Come here, Sifeng. Now, you've heard what it's all about. Well, which do you want to do? Up to you entirely. Will you go with your mother, or stay here with me?

(*Sifeng turns round, her face streaming with tears.*)

LU: Well, I'll be — what are you crying for?

MA: Oh, Feng!

LU: Well, come on. It's not as if you were swearing your life away! Who's it to be?

MA (*comforting her*): That's all right, Feng, you can tell me. You promised to come with me a little while ago, but perhaps you've changed your mind now? Tell me, my dear, tell me truly. I'll still love you whichever way you choose.

LU: You see, you've upset her with all your talk about taking her with you. I happen to know that she can't tear herself away from this place. (*He smiles.*)

FENG (*to Lu Gui*): Oh, go away! (*To her mother.*) Don't ask me, Mother. I can't bear it. Oh, Mother, my dear, dear mother! I will go with you. Oh, Mother! (*She flings herself sobbing into her mother's arms.*)

MA: There, there, my dear. I know you've had a bad time of it today.

贵:你看看,这股子小姐脾气,她要跟你不是受罪么?

鲁:(向鲁贵)你少说话,(对四凤)妈对不起你,以后跟妈在一块儿,没有人会欺负你。我的心肝孩子。

大海由左边上。

大:妈,张大婶回来了。我刚才在路上碰见的。

鲁:你提到我们卖家具的事么?

大:嗯,提了。她说,她能想法子。

鲁:车厂上找着认识的人么?

大:有,我还要出去,找一个保人。

鲁:那么我们一同出去吧。四凤,你等着我,我就回来!

大:(对鲁贵)你酒醒点了么?(向鲁妈)今天晚上我不回家睡觉了。

大海,鲁妈同下。

贵:(目送他们出去)哼,这东西!(见四凤立在窗前,便向她)你妈走了,四凤。你说吧,你预备怎么样呢?

四凤不理他,叹一口气,听外面的青蛙声同雷声。

贵:(蔑视)你看,你这点心思还不浅。

LU: See what I mean? She's too much of a lady with her little scenes. She'll find it tough going if she goes with you.

MA (*to her husband*): Be quiet, you. (*To Sifeng.*) I'm sorry I didn't look after you properly. But from nw on you'll be with me, and no one will take advantage of you. My own dear child.

(*Lu Dahai enters from the right.*)

HAI: Mrs. Chang's back now, Mother. I ran into her on my way home.

MA: Did you say anything to her about selling our furniture?

HAI: Yes, I did mention it. She said she can help.

MA: Did you find anybody you knew down at the rickshaw rank?

HAI: Yes, but I'll have to go out again fo find a guarantor.

MA: We can go together, then. I won't be a minute, Sifeng, I'll be straight back.

HAI (*to Lu Gui*): Are you sobering up yet? (*To Sifeng.*) I won't be home tonight.

(*He and his mother go out together.*)

LU (*following them out with his eyes*): Blast him! (*Noticing that Sifeng has gone back to her place at the window, he turns to her.*) Well, that's your mother out of the way, Sifeng. Now, tell me, what are you going to do?

(*Sifeng sighs, but pays him no attention. She stands listening to the croaking of the frogs outside and the rumble of distant thunder.*)

LU (*scornfully*): All this business is a bigger head-

四:(掩饰)什么心思?天气热,闷得难受。

贵:你不要骗我,你吃完饭眼神直瞪瞪的,你在想什么?

四:我不想什么。

贵:凤儿,你是我的明白孩子。我就有你这一个亲女儿,你跟你妈一走,那就剩我一个人在这儿哪。

四:您别说了,我心里乱得很。(外面打闪)又打雷了。

贵:孩子,别打岔,你真预备跟妈回济南么?

四:嗯。(吐一口气。)

贵:(无聊地唱)"花开花谢年年有,人过了个青春不再来!……"(忽然地)四凤,人活着就是两三年好日子,好机会一错过就完了。

四:您去吧。我困了。

贵:周家的事你不要怕。有了我,明天我们还是得回去。你真走得开,你放得下这儿这样好的地方么?你放得下周家——

ache for you than you thought it would be, isn't it?

FENG (*with assumed indifference*): A headache for me? Nothing of the sort. It's just that I feel uncomfortable when the weather's as close as this.

LU: You can't fool me. Ever since supper-time you've been miles away, just staring into space. What's worrying you?

FENG: Nothing.

LU: Now be sensible about it, my dear. You're my only daughter — all I have got. If you go away with your mother, I'll be left here all on my own.

FENG: Please don't go on. I feel all mixed up inside as it is. (*There is a flicker of lightning outside.*) Listen, it's thundering now.

LU: Don't change the subject. Have you really made up your mind to go to Jinan with your mother?

FENG: Yes. (*She heaves a short sigh.*)

LU (*singing dispiritedly*):
Every springtime brings the flowers
Which died in last year's autumn rain;
The springtime of this life of ours,
Once past, can ne'er come back again....

(*Suddenly.*) You know, Sifeng, we're only young once, and we have to make the most of it. And opportunity only knocks once.

FENG: Oh, please go. I'm ready for bed.

LU: You haven't got to worry about your job at the Zhous'. Once I get going I'll have us back there overnight. Do you really believe you could tear yourself away from a nice place like this, though?

四：您还说什么，睡去吧！外边乘凉的人都散了。

贵：别胡思乱想。这世界上没有一个人靠得住，只有钱是真的。唉，偏偏你同你母亲不知道钱的好处。

四：听，我像是听见有人来敲门。

外面敲门声。

贵：快十一点了，这会有谁？

四：爸爸，让我去看。

贵：别，让我出去。（开门）谁？

周冲的声音：这儿姓鲁么？

贵：是啊，干什么？

周冲的声音：找人。

贵：你是谁？

周冲的声音：我姓周。

贵：（喜形于色）你看，来了不是？周家的人来了。

四：（惊骇）不，爸爸，您说我们都出去了。

贵：咦，（乖巧地看她一眼）这叫什么话？（下。）

四凤把屋子略微整理一下，不用的东西放在左边小屋里，等候着客进来。

Could you really bear to leave the Zhous'— ?

FENG: Oh, I wish you'd stop talking and go to bed! Look, everybody's gone home outside.

LU: Don't you be a little idiot. All these fancy notions about things. You can't rely on anybody in this life. Money's the only real thing. Though of course you and your mother haven't the sense to appreciate it.

FENG: Listen. I thought I heard a knock.

(*A knock is heard at the front door.*)

LU: Who can it be at this time of night? It's nearly eleven.

FENG: Let me go and see, Dad.

LU: No, I'll go. (*Opening the door leading to the outer room.*) Who is it?

CHONG'S VOICE: Hullo! Is this where the Lus live?

LU: Yes. What do you want?

CHONG'S VOICE: I've come to see someone.

LU: Who are you?

CHONG'S VOICE: My name's Zhou.

LU (*his face lighting up*): There you are! What did I say? Somebody from the Zhous.

FENG (*alarmed*): No, Dad. Tell him there's nobody at home.

LU: Eh? (*Throwing her a shrewd glance.*) What's the idea? (*He goes out.*)

(*Sifeng hurriedly straightens up the room as best she can. She tidies some of the things away into the curtained recess, then stands waiting for the visitor.*)

(*In the meantime, Zhou Chong can be heard in*

雷雨

这时,听见周冲同鲁贵说话的声音,移时鲁贵同周冲上。

冲:(见着四凤,高兴地)四凤!

四:二少爷!

贵:(谄笑)您别见笑,我们这儿穷地方。

冲:这地方真不好找。外边有一片水,(笑)很好的。

贵:二少爷。您先坐下。四凤,你把那张好椅子拿过来。

冲:(见四凤不说话)四凤,怎么,你不舒服么?

四:没有。——二少爷,你到这里来干什么?要是太太知道了,你——

冲:这是太太叫我来的。

贵:(明白了一半)太太要您来的?

冲:嗯,我自己也想来看看你们。(问四凤)你哥哥同母亲呢?

贵:他们出去了。

四:你怎么知道这个地方。

冲:(天真地)母亲告诉我的。没想到这地方还有一大片水。一下雨真滑,黑天要是不小心,真容易摔下去。

贵:二少爷,您没摔着么?

conversation with Lu Gui. After a moment they both come in.)

CHONG (*delighted to find Sifeng here*): Why, Sifeng!

FENG: Master Chong!

LU (*smiling obsequiously*): I hope you don't mind, sir. This isn't much of a place to welcome you to.

CHONG: It was the devil's own job to get to. You've got quite a stretch of water outside — (*smiling*) most attractive.

LU: You must take a seat, Master Chong. Sifeng, bring the good chair over here.

CHONG (*struck by Sifeng's silence*): What's the matter, Sifeng? Aren't you feeling well or something?

FENG: I'm all right. — Master Chong, why did you have to come here? If the mistress finds out, you'll —

CHONG: But it was Mother who sent me.

LU (*beginning to understand*): The mistress herself sent you?

CHUNG: Yes, but I wanted to see you all in any case. (*To Sifeng.*) Where are your brother and your mother?

LU: They've gone out.

FENG: How did you find out where we live?

CHONG (*naively*): Mother told me. I didn't expect to find such a lot of water outside. And it's so slippery after the rain. You have to be careful in the dark, otherwise you'd soon come a cropper.

LU: I hope you didn't do anything like that, Master

雷雨

冲：没有。我坐着家里的车,很有趣的。(四面望望这屋子的摆设,很高兴地笑着,望四凤)哦,你原来在这儿!

四：我看你赶快回家吧。

贵：什么?

冲：(忽然)对了,我忘了我为什么来的了。妈跟我说,你们离开我们家,她很不放心。她怕你们一时找不着事情,叫我送给你母亲一百块钱。(拿出钱。)

四：什么?

贵：(以为周家的人怕得罪他,得意地笑着,对四凤)你看人家多厚道,到底是人家有钱的人。

四：不,二少爷,你替我谢谢太太,我们还好过日子。拿回去吧。

贵：(向四凤)你看你,哪有你这么说话的?太太叫二少爷亲自送来,这点意思我们好意思不领下么?(收下钞票)你回头跟太太回一声,我们都挺好的。请太太放心,谢谢太太。

四：(固执地)爸爸,这不成。

贵：你小孩子知道什么?

Chong?

CHONG: Oh no. I came in our own rickshaw. Great fun. (*His eyes stray round the room and finally come to rest on Sifeng. He beams at her.*) So this is where you live!

FENG: I think you'd better hurry up and get back.

LU: What!

CHONG (*struck by a sudden thought*): Oh yes, I was almost forgetting what I came for. Mother says she's rather concerned about you all now that you've left. She was afraid you might not be able to find a job straight away, so she's sent a hundred dollars for your mother. (*He produces the money.*)

FENG: What!

LU (*taking this to be an act of appeasement on the part of the Zhou family, he smiles smugly at Sifeng*): You see how kind and considerate they are? After all, you know, they are rich people.

FENG: No, Master Chong. Please thank madam for us, but we can manage all right on our own. Please take it back.

LU (*turning to Sifeng*): Here, what do you think you're saying? It would be rude of us to refuse it after rmadam's been so kind as to send Master Chong along with it in person! (*He takes the money.*) Give madam our best regards and tell her we're quite all right, all of us. Tell her not to worry about us, and thank her for everything.

FENG (*obstinately*): You can't do this, Father.

LU: You're too young to understand.

四：您要收下，妈跟哥哥一定不答应。

贵：(不理她，向周冲)谢谢您老远跑一趟。我先给您买点鲜货吃，您同四凤在屋子里坐一坐，我失陪了。

四：爸，你别走！不成。

贵：别尽说话，你先给二少爷倒一碗茶。我就回来。(忙下。)

冲：让他走了也好。

四：(厌恶地)唉，真是下作！——(不愿意地)谁叫你送钱来了？

冲：你，你像是不愿意见我似的。为什么呢？

四：(找话说)老爷吃过饭了么？

冲：刚刚吃过。老爷在发脾气，母亲没吃完就跑到楼上生气。我劝了她半天，要不我还不会这样晚来。

四：(不在心地)大少爷呢？

冲：我没有见着他，我知道他很难过。他又在自己房里喝酒，大概是喝醉了。

四：哦！(叹一口气)——你为什么不叫底下人替你来？何必自己跑到这穷人住的地方来？

冲：(诚恳地)你现在怨了我们吧！——(羞愧)

FENG: Mother and Dahai would never let you keep the money if you did take it.

LU (*ignoring her and turning to Zhou Chong*): Thank you for coming all this way. I'll just dash out and buy you some fruit now, if you'll excuse me a moment. Sifeng will keep you company.

FENG: You mustn't go, Father! You can't do this!

LU: Stop arguing and pour Master Chong a cup of tea. I won't be long. (*He hurries out.*)

GHONG: There's no harm in letting him go.

FENG (*with loathing*): Ugh! It's sickening! — (*Displeased.*) What business is it of yours to come here with money?

CHONG: You — er — you don't seem particularly pleased to see me. What's the matter?

FENG (*making conversation*): Has the master had his dinner yet?

CHONG: Yes, he's just finished. He lost his temper again, and Mother rushed upstairs before she'd finished eating. She was in a tearing rage. I went up to her and spent a long time trying to cheer her up, otherwise I'd have got here a bit earlier.

FENG (*casually*): How's Master Ping?

CHONG: I haven't seem him, but I know he's pretty upset. He's been drinking in his room again, so he's probably durnk by now.

FENG: Oh! (*She heaves a sigh.*) — Why couldn't you send one of the servants round with the money? There was no need for you to come to this slum of ours yourself.

CHONG (*earnestly*): You've got a grudge against us

今天的事,我真觉得对不起你们,你千万不要以为哥哥是个坏人。他现在很后悔,你不知道他,他还很喜欢你。

四:二少爷,我现在已经不是周家的用人了。

冲:然而我们永远不可以算是顶好的朋友么?

四:我预备跟我妈回济南去。

冲:不,你先不要走。早晚你同你父亲还可以回去的。我们搬了新房子,我的父亲也许回到矿上去。那时你就回来,那时候我该多么高兴!

四:你的心真好。

冲:四凤,你不要为这一点小事来忧愁。世界大的很,你应当读书,你就知道世界上有过许多人跟我们一样地忍受着痛苦,慢慢地苦干,以后又得到快乐。

四:唉,女人究竟是女人!(忽然)你听!

蛙鸣声。

冲:不,你不是个平常的女人,你有力量,你能吃苦,我们都还年轻,我们将来一定在这世界

now, isn't that it? — (*Shamefaced*.) That was a bad business today. It made me feel ashamed to see you treated like that. You mustn't think Ping really meant any harm. He's terribly sorry now for what he did. He's still very fond of you, you know.

FENG: Master Chong. Please remember that I'm not one of your family's servants now.

CHONG: But can't we always remain good friends?

FENG: I'm going back with my mother. To Jinan.

CHONG: No, don't go yet. We can get you and your father back with us sooner or later. By the time we've moved into our new house, Father will probably have gone back to the mine. Then you can come back to us, and I'll be jolly glad to have you back, I can tell you!

FENG: You're very kind-hearted, really.

CHONG: Sifeng, you mustn't let a little thing like this upset you. The world is such a big place. You ought to go to school, and then you'd learn that there have been lots of people like us in the world — putting up with suffering, working hard and biding their time, and in the end enjoying the happiness they've won.

FENG: Ah, but a woman's only a woman after all! (*Suddenly*.) Listen!

(*The croaking of frogs is heard*.)

CHONG: No, you're no ordinary woman. You've got strength, and you can put up with hardship. We're both young yet and we've got all our lives ahead of us to work for the welfare of mankind. I hate

为着人类谋幸福。我恨这不平等的社会,我恨只讲强权的人,我讨厌我的父亲,我们都是被压迫的,我们是一样。——

四:二少爷,您渴了吧,我给您倒一杯水喝。(站起倒水。)

冲:不,不要。

四:不,让我再伺候伺候您。

冲:你不要这样说话,现在的世界是不该存在的。我从来没有把你当做我的底下人,你是我的姐姐,我的引路的人,我们的真世界不在这儿。

四:哦,你真会说话。

冲:有时我就忘了现在,(沉醉在梦想里)忘了家,忘了你,忘了母亲,并且忘了我自己。像是在一个冬天的早晨,非常明亮的天空,……在无边的海上,……有一只轻得像海燕似的小帆船。在海风吹得紧,海上的空气闻得出有点腥,有点咸的时候,白色的帆张得满满的,像一只鹰的翅膀,斜贴在海面上飞,飞,向着天边飞。那时天边上只淡淡地浮着两三片白云,我们坐在船头,望着前面,前面就是我们的世界。

四:我们?

冲:对了,我同你,我们可以飞,飞到一个真真干

this present society of ours — it's so unfair. I hate people whose only language is brute force. I loathe my father. You and I are in the same boat together — we're both victims of oppression.

FENG: You must be thirsty, Master Chong. I'll get you some water. (*She stands up and pours him a cup of water.*)

CHONG: No, it's all right.

FENG: Yes, let me wait on you once again.

CHONG: You mustn't say things like that. The world as it is now should never have come into existence. I've never thought of you as a servant: you've always been my elder sister, my guide. Our world, the real world, is not this one.

FENG: You certainly know how to talk!

CHONG: Sometimes I forget the present — (*with a rapt expression on his face*) I forget my home, I forget you, I forget my mother — I even forget myself. It seems like a winter morning, with a brilliant sky overhead... on a boundless sea... there's a little sailing-boat, light as a gull. When the sea-breeze gets stronger, and there's a salty tang in the air, the white sails billow out like the wings of a hawk and the boat skims over the sea, just kissing the waves, racing towards the horizon. The sky is empty except for a few patches of white cloud floating lazily on the horizon. We sit in the bows, gazing ahead, for ahead of us is our world.

FENG: Ours?

CHONG: Yes, yours and mine. We can fly — fly to a

净,快乐的地方。那里没有争执,没有虚伪,没有不平等的……没有……(仰着头,好像眼前就是那么一个所在,忽然)你说好么?

四:你想得真好。

冲:(亲切地)你愿意同我一块儿去么?就是带着他也可以的。

四:谁?

冲:你昨天告诉我的,你说你的心已经许给了他。那个人他一定也像你,他一定是个可爱的人。

大海进。

四:哥哥。

大:(冷冷地)这是怎么回事?

冲:鲁先生!

四:周家二少爷来看我们来了。

大:哦——我没想到你们现在在这儿。父亲呢?

四:出去买东西去啦。

大:(向冲)奇怪得很!这么晚!周少爷会到我们这个穷地方来——看我们。

冲:我正想见你呢。我觉得我对你很抱歉的。

大:什么事?

冲:(红脸)今天下午,你在我们家里——

大:(勃然)你少提那桩事。

place that is truly clean and happy, a place, where there is no conflict, no hypocrisy, no inequality, no — (*Lifting his head as though such a world were there before his eyes, then, abruptly.*) Do you like it?

FENG: You've got a wonderful imagination.

CHONG (*warmly*): Will you go there with me? You could even bring him too, if you wanted to.

FENG: Who?

CHONG: The one you told me about yesterday, when you said your heart already belonged to another. I'm sure he must be just like you — someone nice and friendly.

(*Dahai comes in.*)

FENG: Hullo, Dahai.

HAI (*coldly*): What's all this?

CHONG: Ah, Mr. Lu!

FENG: Master Chong from the Zhous has come round to see us.

HAI: Oh. I didn't expect to come in and find you two here. Where's Father?

FENG: He's gone out shopping.

HAI (*to Zhou Chong*): I can't for the life of me imagine why you should want to come down to this wretched slum at this time of night — to see us!

CHONG: It was you that I really came to see. I feel I owe you an apology.

HAI: What for?

CHONG (*blushing*): What happened at our place this afternoon, when you —

HAI (*flaring up*): Cut it out!

四:哥哥,你不要这样。人家是好心好意来安慰我们。

大:少爷,我们用不着你的安慰,我们生成一副穷骨头,用不着你半夜的时候到这儿来安慰我们。

冲:你大概是误会了我的意思。

大:(清楚地)我没有误会。(回头向四凤)出去。

四:哥哥!

大:你先出去,我有几句话要同他说。(见四凤不走)出去!

四凤慢慢地由左门出去。

大:我们谈过话,我知道你在你们家里还算是明白点的;不过你记着,以后你要再到这儿来,来——安慰我们,(突然)我就要不客气了。

冲:(笑)我想一个人无论怎样,总不会拒绝别人的同情吧。

大:同情不是你同我的事,也要看看地位才成。

冲:大海,我觉得你有时候有些偏见太重;有钱的人并不是罪人,难道说就不能同你们接近么?

大:你太年轻,多说你也不明白。告诉你吧,你

FENG: Don't be like that, Dahai. He's come with the best of intentions — to offer us his sympathy.

HAI: We've no use for your sympathy, Master Chong. We were born and bred in poverty and we're used to being treated like that. We don't need to have anybody coming here in the middle of the night to give us their sympathy.

CHONG: Oh, I think you've got me all wrong.

HAI (*distinctly*): I haven't, you know. (*Turning to Sifeng.*) Go on out.

FENG: But, Dahai!

HAI: Go and leave us on our own; I want to have a word with him. (*Sifeng makes no move.*) Go on!

(*Sifeng goes out slowly through the door on the right.*)

HAI: I've already had a chat with you, and I realize you're a little more enlightened than the rest of your family. But remember this: if you even come here again to — to be kind to us (*with a sudden ferocity*), I'll lose my temper with you.

CHONG (*with a smile*): But I don't see how anybody can be offended by an offer of sympathy.

HAI: There could never be any sympathy between you and me. Our stations in life are too far apart.

CHONG: I think your prejudices get the better of you sometimes, Dahai. It's no crime to be wealthy, so why should wealth stand in the way of our being friends?

HAI: You're too young to understand. I'd be wasting my breath if I tried to explain it any further. I'll

雷雨

就不应当到这儿来,这儿不是你来的地方。

冲:为什么?——你今早还说过,你愿意做我的朋友,我想四凤也愿意做我的朋友,那么我就不可以来帮点忙么?

大:少爷,你不要以为这样就是好心。我听说,你想叫四凤念书,是么?四凤是我的妹妹。她是个穷人的孩子,她的将来是给一个工人当老婆,洗衣服,做饭,捡煤渣。哼,念书,上学,那是小姐的梦!

冲:你的话固然有点道理,可是——

大:所以如果矿主的少爷真替四凤着想,那就请少爷从今以后不要同她往来。

冲:我认为你的偏见太多,你不能说我的父亲是个矿主,你就要——

大:(瞪起眼睛)现在我警告你,……

冲:警告?

大:如果什么时候我再看见你跑到我家里,再同我的妹妹在一起,我一定——(忽然态度和缓一些)好,时候不早了,我们要睡觉了。

冲:你,你那样说话,——是我想不到的,我没想到我的父亲的话还是对的。

just say this much: you should never have come here. This is no place for you.

CHONG: But why? — Only this morning you said you'd like to be friends with me, and I think Sifeng would like to be friends with me, too, so why won't you even let me come and offer my help?

HAI: Don't imagine you're doing us a good turn, Master Chong. They tell me you wanted to send Sifeng to school, that right? Well, she's my sister, the daughter of a poor man, and her lot in life will be to marry somebody from her own class — a life of washing, cooking and scrabbling among the cinders for scraps of coal. Schooling? Education? Humph! That's something for young *ladies* to dream about!

CHONG: There's something in what you say, of course, but —

HAI: So if you're really concerned about Sifeng, Sir Mine-owner's-son, you'll oblige by not having anything more to do with her.

CHONG: I think you're too prejudiced. Just because my father's a mine-owner, that's no reason why you should say that you —

HAI (*glaring at him*): Now I'm warning you —

CHONG: Warning me?

HAI: If I ever catch you here with my sister again, I'll — (*some of the tension suddenly goes out of him*) oh, well, it's getting late. Time for bed.

CHONG: I — I never expected that you'd be like that about it. I never expected that what Father said would turn out to be right after all.

大:(爆发)你的父亲是个老混蛋!

冲:什么?

大:你的哥哥是——

四凤由左门跑进。

四:你,你别说了!(指大海)我看你,你简直是怪物!

大:糊涂虫!

四:我不跟你说话了!(向周冲)你走吧,你走吧,不要同他说啦。

冲:(无奈地看看大海)好,我走。(向四凤)我觉得很对不起你,来到这儿,再叫你不快活。

四:不要提了,你走吧。

冲:好,我走!(向大海,温和地)我还是愿意做你的朋友。(伸出手来)你愿意同我拉一拉手么?

大海没有理他,把身子转过去。

四:哼!

周冲也不再说什么,即将走下。

鲁贵由左门上,捧着水果,酒瓶同酒菜。

贵:(见周冲要走)怎么?

大:让开点,他要走了。

贵:别,别,二少爷为什么刚来就走?

四:(愤愤)你问哥哥去!

HAI (*exploding*): Your father's an old swine!

CHONG: What!

HAI: And your brother's a —

(*Sifeng comes running back into the room.*)

FENG: Stop! Stop saying such things! (*Pointing at Dahai.*) I think you're — you're being utterly beastly!

HAI: Idiot!

FENG: I've nothing more to say to you! (*To Zhou Chong.*) Now go, go. Don't say another word to him.

CHONG (*looking helplessly at Dahai*): All right, then, I'll go. (*To Sifeng.*) I'm really terribly sorry. I didn't realize I'd only make things more unpleasant for you by coming here.

FENG: Forget it and please go.

CHONG: All right, I'm going. (*To Dahai, good-naturedly.*) I'd still like to be friends with you. (*Holding out his hand.*) Won't you shake hands with me?

(*Dahai ignores him and turns away.*)

FENG: Humph!

(*Having nothing more to say, Zhou Chong makes for the door. Just then, Lu Gui comes in with fruit, wine and various kinds of food.*)

LU (*seeing that Zhou Chong is leaving*): What's this?

HAI: Get out of the way. He's going.

LU: No, wait, wait. Why are you rushing off like this, Master Chong? You've only just got here.

FENG (*angrily*): Ask Dahai!

雷雨

贵：（笑着向周冲）别理他，您坐一会。

冲：不，我是要走了。

贵：那二少爷吃点什么再走，我老远地给您买的鲜货，吃点，喝两盅再走。

冲：不，不早了，我要回家了。

大：（向四凤）他从哪儿弄来的钱买这些东西？

贵：（转过头）我自己的，你爸爸赚的钱。

四：不，爸爸，这是周家的钱！你又胡花了！（回头向大海）刚才周太太送给妈一百块钱。妈不在，爸爸不听我的话收下了。

贵：（狠狠地看四凤一眼，向大海）人家二少爷亲自送来的。我不收还像话么？

大：（到周冲面前）什么，你刚才是给我们送钱来的？

四：（向大海）你现在才明白！

贵：你看，人家周家都是好人。

大：（掉过脸来）把钱给我！

贵：（疑惧地）干什么？

大：你给不给？（声色俱厉）不给，你可记得住放在箱子里的是什么东西。

贵：（恐惧地）我给，我给！（把钞票掏出来交给

LU (*with a smile, to Zhou Chong*): Don't mind him. Stay a little longer, won't you?

CHONG: No, I really am going.

LU: But you'll have something to eat first, won't you, sir? I've been a long way to get these things for you. You will have a bite and a glass of wine before you go, won't you?

CHONG: No, it's getting late now. I'll have to be getting along.

HAI (*to Sifeng*): Where did he get the money to buy all this stuff?

LU (*turning round*): It was my own money, that I'd earned myself.

FENG: No, it wasn't, Father: it was money from the Zhous. And you're squandering it. (*Turning to Dahai.*) Mrs. Zhou sent Mother a hundred dollars. Mother was out, and Dad would insist on taking it. He wouldn't listen to me.

LU (*looking daggers at Sifeng, then turning to Dahai*): Master Chong brought it in person, so I couldn't very well refuse it, now, could I?

HAI (*going up to Zhou Chong*): So! You came to bring us money, did you?

FENG (*to Dahai*): Now perhaps you'll understand!

LU: You see what kind-hearted people the Zhous are?

HAI (*turning to Lu Gui*): Give me the money!

LU (*apprehensively*): What for?

HAI: Are you going to give it to me or aren't you? (*With menacing voice and eyes.*) If you don't, well, just remember what's in the chest there.

LU (*terrified*): All right, you can have it! (*He fishes

大海)钱在这儿,一百块。

大:(数一遍)怎么少两块?

贵:(强笑着)我,我,我花了。

冲:(不愿再看鲁贵同大海)再见吧,我走了。

大:(拉住他)你别走,你以为我们能上你这样的当么?

冲:怎么?

大:我有钱,我有钱,我口袋里刚刚剩下两块钱。(拿出零票同现洋,放在一块)刚刚两块。拿走吧,我们不需要。

贵:这不像话!

冲:你这个人真有点儿不懂人情。

大:对了,我不懂人情,我不懂你们这种虚伪,这种假慈悲,我不懂……

四:哥哥!

大:拿走。你给我滚,给我滚蛋。

冲:(失望地立了一会,忽然拿起钱)好,我走,我错了。

大:我告诉你,以后你们周家无论哪一个再来,我就打死他,不管是谁!

冲:谢谢你。我想周家除了我不会再有人这么

the notes out of his pocket and hands them over to Dahai.) Here you are. A hundred dollars.

HAI (*after counting the notes*): Two dollars short. Well?

LU (*forcing a smile*): Well — er — I — I've spent it.

CHONG (*not wishing to see any more*): Well, cheerio. I'm off now.

HAI (*grasping his arm*): Oh no, you don't. Don't imagine we can be caught as easily as that.

CHONG: What do you mean?

HAI: Now I've got some money somewhere. Ah, yes. Just two dollars left in my pocket. (*He produces some silver and small notes, then counts them.*) Two dollars exactly. Here's your money back. We've no use for it.

LU: This is outrageous!

CHONG: You don't seem to be able to appreciate kindness.

HAI: You're quite right. I don't. And the same goes for your family's hypocrisy and crocodile tears, and for their —

FENG: Dahai!

HAI: Take it away. Now get out. Go on, out!

CHONG (*his illusions shattered, he stands there for a moment, then suddenly picks up the money*): All right. I'm going, I'm sorry.

HAI: Now I'm telling you: if any of you Zhous come here after this, I'll kill you, whoever you are!

CHONG: Well, thank you! Though I don't suppose for one moment that anyone else in the family would

糊涂的,再见吧!(向右门下。)

贵:大海。

大:(大声)叫他滚!

贵:好好好,我给您点灯,外屋黑!

冲:谢谢你。

鲁贵同周冲由右门下。

四:二少爷!(跑下。)

大:四凤,四凤!

鲁妈由左门上。

大:妈,您知道周家二少爷来了。

鲁:嗯,我看见一辆洋车在门口,我不知道是谁来了,我没敢进来。

大:您知道刚才我把他赶了么?

鲁:(点一点头)知道,我刚才在门口听了一会。

大:周家的太太送了您一百块钱。

鲁:(愤然)不用她给钱,我明天就带着四凤走。

大:明天?

鲁:我改主意了,明天。

大:好极啦!那我就不必说别的了。

鲁:什么?

大:没有什么,我回来的时候看见四凤跟这位二

be so foolish as to do what I've done. Good-bye!
(*He goes towards the door on the right.*)

LU: Dahai!

HAI (*shouting*): Get him out of here!

LU: All right, all right. I'll show you a light. It's dark in the front room.

CHONG: Thank you.
(*Lu Gui and Zhou Chong go out through the door on the right.*)

FENG: Master Chong! (*She runs out after them.*)
(*Lu Ma comes in through the door on the right.*)

HAI: Did you know that Master Chong from the Zhous was here?

MA: Well, I saw a rickshaw outside the door, but I didn't dare come in as I didn't know who it was that had come to see us.

HAI: You realize I've just thrown him out?

MA (*nodding*): Yes, I know. I've been listening at the door for a while.

HAI: Mrs. Zhou sent you round a hundred dollars.

MA (*indignantly*): I don't want any money from her. I'm leaving tomorrow and taking Sifeng with me.

HAI: Tomorrow?

MA: Yes, tomorrow, I've changed my mind.

HAI: Glad to hear it! Then there's no need for me to tell you the rest of it.

MA: What's that?

HAI: Nothing, really. Just that when I got back I found Ssufeng here passing the time of day with this

少爷谈天。

鲁:(不自主地)谈什么?

大:不知道。

鲁:(自语)这个糊涂孩子。

大:妈,我走了。

鲁:你上哪儿去?

大:钱完了,我也许拉一晚上车。

鲁:干什么?用不着,妈这儿有钱,你在家睡。

大:您留着自己用吧,我走了。(由右门下。)

鲁:(喊)大海,大海!

四凤上。

四:妈,(不安地)您回来了。

鲁:你忙着送周家的少爷,没有顾到看见我。

四:(解释地)二少爷是他母亲叫他来的。

鲁:我听见你哥哥说,你们谈了半天了。

四:您说我跟周家二少爷?

鲁:嗯,他说了些什么?

四:没有什么!——平平常常的话。

鲁:真的?

四:你听哥哥说了些什么话?

鲁:(严肃地)凤儿。(盯着四凤。)

四:妈,您怎么啦?

鲁:妈是不是顶疼你?

Master Chong.

MA (*anxiously, in spite of herself*): What were they talking about?

HAI: I don't know.

MA (*to herself*): Silly girl!

HAI: Well, I'll be off now, Mother.

MA: Where to?

HAI: The last of my money's gone, so I'm thinking of doing a night's rickshaw-pulling.

MA: What for? There's no need to do that. I've got some money here. You can stay here the night.

HAI: Keep it. You may need it yourself. I'm away, then. (*He goes out through the door on the right.*)

MA (*calling after him*): Dahai! Dahai!

(*Sifeng comes in.*)

FENG: Hullo, Mother. (*Uneasily.*) You're back, then.

MA: You were too busy seeing your young Mr. Zhou off to notice me.

FENG (*making an effort to explain*): It was his mother who told him to come.

MA: Dahai tells me you had a long chat together.

FENG: You mean me and Master Chong?

MA: Yes. What did he say to you?

FENG: Nothing much. Just the usual sort of thing.

MA: You're sure?

FENG: What's Dahai been telling you now?

MA (*sternly*): Feng! (*She looks her daughter full in the face.*)

FENG: What's the matter, Mother?

MA: Don't yo know that I love you more than anyone

293

四：您为什么说这些话？

鲁：那我求你一件事。

四：妈，您说。

鲁：你得告诉我，你跟周家的孩子是怎么回事？

四：哥总是瞎说八道的——他跟您说了什么？

鲁：不是，他没说什么，妈要问你！

远处的雷声。

四：妈，您为什么问这个？我不跟您说过么？一点也没什么。妈，没什么！

远处的雷声。

鲁：你听，外面打着雷。可怜你的妈，我的女儿在这些事上不能再骗我！

四：(顿)妈，我不骗您！我不是跟您说过，这两年——

鲁贵的声音：(在外屋)侍萍，快来睡觉吧，不早了。

鲁：别管我，你先睡你的。(对四凤)你说什么？

四：我不是跟你说过，这两年，我天天晚上——回家的？

鲁：孩子，你可要说实话，妈经不起再大的事啦。

四：妈，(抽咽)您为什么不信您自己的女儿呢？

else?

FENG: Why do you ask that?

MA: I want to ask a favour of you.

FENG: Of course. What is it?

MA: You've got to tell me what there is between you and that Zhou boy.

FENG: That's Dahai's silly nonsense again. What's he been telling you?

MA: No, it's not Dahai. He hasn't told me anything. It's just that I want to know.

(*The rumble of distant thunder is heard.*)

FENG: But what makes you ask these things, Mother? Haven't I told you there's nothing at all between us? There isn't, Mother.

(*The sound of thunder again.*)

MA: Listen. There's thunder. Now be fair with your poor mother. I can't have my own daughter continually deceiving me about such things!

FENG (*after a pause*): I'm not deceiving you, Mother! Haven't I told you that all the time you've been away —

LU'S VOICE (*from the front room*): Shiping. Come on in to bed. It's late.

MA: Don't worry about me. Get to bed yourself. (*To Sifeng.*) What were you saying?

FENG: Haven't I told you that all the time you're been away I've come home — every night?

MA: Now you must tell me the truth, child. I couldn't bear to have anything really serious happen to you.

FENG: Mother (*sobbing*), why can't you trust your

(扑在鲁妈怀里。)

鲁:(落眼泪)可怜的孩子,不是我不相信你,(沉痛地)我是太不相信这个世道上的人了。傻孩子,你不懂,妈的苦多少年是说不出来的,你妈就是在年轻的时候没有人来提醒,——可怜,妈就是一步走错,就步步走错了。孩子,我就生了你这么一个女儿,我的女儿不能再像她妈似的。孩子,你疼我!你要是再骗我,那就是杀了我了,我的苦命的孩子!

四:不,妈,不,我以后永远是妈的了。

鲁:(忽然)凤儿,我在这儿一天担心一天,我们明天一定走,离开这儿。

四:(立起)明天就走?

鲁:(果断地)嗯。我改主意了,我们明天就走。永远不回这儿来了。

四:永远?妈,不,为什么这么快就走?

鲁:你还要干什么?

四:(踌躇地)我,我——

鲁:不愿意早一点儿跟妈走?

own daughter? (*She flings herself into her mother's arms.*)

MA (*shedding tears*): My poor child, it's not that I don't trust you — (*with anguish in her voice*) but that I don't trust the world. You've no idea, you silly girl, all that I've been through all these years. I could never begin to describe it. I never had anyone to warn me when I was young. And that's the pity of it. One false step, and I lost my way completely. You're the only daughter I ever had, Feng, and I can't bear to see you go the way I did. You do love me, don't you, Feng? I just couldn't bear you to deceive me ever. Oh, my poor child!

FENG: No, Mother, I'll never deceive you. From now on I'll be yours — always.

MA (*abruptly changing the subject*): I shan't be able to set my mind at rest all the time I stay here, Feng. We must go tomorrow — get away from this place.

FENG (*rising*): Tomorrow? As soon as that?

MA (*with finality*): Yes. I've changed my mind. We'll go tomorrow and we'll never come back here again.

FENG: What, never? But Mother, why have we got to go rushing off like this?

MA: You've got nothing else to do here before you go, have you?

FENG (*hesitantly*): I — er —

MA: Don't you *want* to leave here with me as soon as we can?

四:(叹一口气,苦笑)也好,我们明天走吧。

鲁:(忽然疑心地)孩子,你还有什么事瞒着我。

四:(擦着眼泪)没有什么。

鲁:(慈祥地)好孩子,你记住妈刚才的话么?

四:记得住!

鲁:凤儿,我要你一辈子不见周家的人!

四:好,妈!

鲁:(沉重地)不,要起誓。

四凤畏怯地望着鲁妈的严厉的脸。

四:这何必呢?

鲁:(依然严肃地)不,你要说。

四:(跪下)妈,(扑在鲁妈身上)我——我说不了。

鲁:(眼泪流下来)你是要伤妈的心么?你忘记妈这一生为着你——(回头泣哭。)

四:妈,我说,我说。

鲁:(立起)你就这样跪下说。

四:妈,我答应您,以后我永远不见周家的人。

雷声滚过去。

鲁:天上在打着雷。你要是以后忘了妈的话,见了周家的人呢?

FENG (*with a sigh and a wry smile*): All right, then. Let's go tomorrow.
MA (*suddenly suspicious again*): Sifeng, I think there's still something your're keeping from me.
FENG (*wiping her eyes*): No, there isn't, Mother.
MA (*tenderly*): You'll remember what I was telling you just now, my dear?
FENG: Yes, Mother, I will!
MA: Feng, I want you never to see any of the Zhous again so long as you live!
FENG: All right, I won't.
MA (*gravely*): No, you must swear that you won't.
(*Sifeng looks fearfully at her mother's stern face.*)
FENG: Oh, must I?
MA (*as gravely as before*): Yes, you must.
FENG (*falling to her kness*): Mother — (*throwing herself against Lu Ma's knees*) I — I can't.
MA (*with tears streaming down her cheeks*): Do you want to break your mother's heart? You forget that for your sake — all my life I've — (*She turns her head aside and sobs.*)

FENG: All right, Mother. I'll swear.
MA (*risign*): Then do it on your knees, as you are now.
FENG: I promise, Mother, that I'll never see any of the Zhous again.
(*A peal of thunder rolls across the sky.*)
MA: Hear the thunder? Now, what if you should forget what I've told you and see any of the Zhous again?

四:(畏怯地)妈,我不会的,我不会的。

鲁:孩子,你要说,你要说。你要是忘了妈的话,——

外面的雷声。

四:(不顾一切地)那——那天上的雷劈了我。

(扑在鲁妈怀里)哦,我的妈呀!(哭出声。)

雷声轰轰。

鲁:(抱着女儿)孩子,我的孩子!

鲁贵由左门上。脱去短衫,只穿一件线坎肩。

贵:(向鲁妈)这么晚还不睡?你说点子什么?

鲁:你别管。

贵:什么?

四:不,妈,您去吧。让我一个人在这儿。

贵:凤儿这孩子难过一天了,你搅她干什么?

鲁:不要妈陪着?

四:妈,您让我一个人在屋子里歇着吧。

鲁贵下。

鲁:那你就好好地睡吧。

四:嗯,妈!

鲁妈下。

四凤把右边门关上,隔壁鲁贵又唱"花开花谢年年有,人过了个青春不再来"的小曲。

她到圆桌前面,把洋灯的火捻小了,这时听

FENG (*apprehensively*): But I won't, Mother, I won't.

MA: No, my child, you must swear that you won't. If you should ever forget what I've told you —

(*A peal of thunder.*)

FENG (*in desperation*): — Then may I be struck dead by lightning. (*Flinging herself into her mother's arms.*) Oh, Mother, Mother! (*She bursts into tears.*)

(*Crashes of thunder.*)

MA (*her arms round Sifeng*): Feng, my child!

(*Lu Gui comes in, shirtless and wearing only a singlet.*)

LU (*to his wife*): Aren't you ever coming to bed tonight? What's all the jaw about?

MA: None of your business.

LU: What!

FENG: Now go on, Mother. Please go to bed now and leave me to myself.

LU: The poor kid's had enough to put up with for one day. What have you got to keep on at her for?

MA: You sure you don't want me to keep you company?

FENG: No, Mother. I only want to be left on my own.

(*Lu Gui goes out.*)

MA: All right, go to bed like a good girl, then.

FENG: Yes, Mother.

(*Lu Ma goes out.*)

(*Sifeng closes the door behind her. In the next room Lu Gui is singing his song again: "Every springtime brings the flowers...." She goes over to the round table and turns the lamp down to a*

见外面的蛙声同狗叫。她解开几个扣子,走了两步,又回来坐在床边,深深地叹一口气倒在床上。屋外一声一声的梆子。四凤又由床上坐起,拿起蒲扇用力地挥着。闷极了,她把窗户打开,立在窗前。

鲁贵由左门上,赤足,拖着鞋。

贵:你怎么还不睡?

四:(望望他)嗯。

贵:(拿起酒瓶同酒菜)歇着吧。

四:(失神地)嗯。

贵:(走到门口)不早了。(下。)

四凤到右门口,把门关上,立在右门旁一会,听见鲁贵同鲁妈说话的声音。走到圆桌旁,长叹一声,低而重地捶着桌子,扑在桌上抽咽。外面有口哨声。四凤突然惊起,把桌上的灯捻亮,跑到窗前,探望一下,又关上。她倚着窗户,惶惑不安。口哨的

glimmer. From outside come the croaking of the frogs and the barking of dogs. She undoes two or three buttons as she paces restlessly up and down, then goes and sits on the edge of the bed. Finally, she heaves a deep sigh and throws herself down on the bed. The regular, hollow clop-clop-clop of a night-watchman's bamboo "gong" breaks the silence. Sifeng sits up again and fans herself vigorously with her palm-leaf fan. Finding the air too close and stifling, she opens the window and stands in front of it.)

(Lu Gui comes in, his bare feet in heelless slippers.)

LU: What, still up?

FENG *(throwing him a brief glance)*: Mm.

LU *(picking up the bottle of wine and the food he bought for Zhou Chong)*: Come on, now, get some sleep.

FENG *(absent-mindedly)*: Mm.

LU *(at the door)*: It's getting late. *(He goes out.)*

(Sifeng goes across to the door on the right and closes it. She stands by the door for a few moments, listening to her parents talking in the next room, then goes back to the round table with a long sigh and throws herself down across it, sobbing and quietly pounding the table-top. Suddenly, someone whistles outside. Sifeng starts up, turns up the lamp and runs across to the window. She puts her head out for a quick look round, then closes the window and stands leaning against the window-sill in a state of

声音更清楚,她把一张红纸罩着的灯,放在窗前。口哨愈近,远远一阵雷,窗外面有脚步的声音。

外面敲着窗户。

四:(颤声)哦!

周萍的声音:(低声)喂! 开开!

四:谁?

周萍的声音:(含糊地)你猜!

四:(颤声)你,你来干什么?

周萍的声音:你猜猜!

四:我现在不能见你,(急切地)妈在家里。

周萍的声音:不用骗我! 她睡着了。

四:(关心地)你小心,我哥哥恨透了你。

周萍的声音:(不在意地)他不在家,我知道。

四:你走!

周萍的声音:我不!

外面向里用力推窗门,四凤用力挡住。

四:(焦急地)不,不,你不要进来。

周萍的声音:(低声)四凤,我求你,你开开!

great agitation. The whistles become more distinct. She puts the lamp with the red-paper lampshade in the window. The whistles come nearer and nearer. There is a distant rumble of thunder, then the sound of footsteps outside the window.)

(There is a tap on the window.)

FENG *(gasping)*: Oh!

PING'S VOICE *(in an undertone)*: Hey! Open up!

FENG: Who is it?

PING'S VOICE *(disguised)*: Guess!

FENG *(her voice trembling)*: What — what are you doing here?

PING'S VOICE: Guess!

FENG: I can't see you now. *(Desperately.)* Mother's at home.

PING'S VOICE: You can't put me off with that: she's gone to bed.

FENG *(with a note of concern in her voice)*: You'd better be careful. My brother hates you like poison.

PING'S VOICE *(indifferently)*: I happen to know he's not at home.

FENG: You must go away!

PING'S VOICE: Not likely!

(He tries to force the window open by pushing it inwards but Sifeng holds it shut by pressing as hard as she can against it.)

FENG *(anxiously)*: No, don't. You can't come in.

PING'S VOICE *(in an undertone)*: Now, come on, Sifeng. Open up. Please!

四:不,不!已经到了半夜,我的衣服都脱了。

周萍的声音:(急迫地)什么?

四:我已经上床睡了!

周萍的声音:那……那……我就……(叹一口长气。)

四:(恳求地)那你走吧,好不好?

周萍的声音:(转了口气)好,也好,我就走,(又急切地)可是你先打开窗门,叫我……

四:不,不,你就走!

周萍的声音:(急切地)不,你只叫我……只叫我亲亲你。

四:(苦痛地)啊,大少爷,这不是你的公馆,你饶了我吧。

周萍的声音:(怨恨地)那么你忘了我了,你不再想……

四:(决心地)对了,我忘了你。你走吧。

周萍的声音:(忽然地)是不是刚才我的弟弟来了?

四:嗯,(踌躇地)他来了!

周萍的声音:(尖酸地)哦!(长长叹一口气)那就怪不得了。(狠毒地)哼,没有心肝,只要你变了心,——

四:谁变了心?

周萍的声音:(躁急地)那你为什么不打开门,让

FENG: No, I can't! It's the middle of the night, and I've already got undressed.

PING'S VOICE (*urgently*): What?

FENG: I've already gone to bed!

PING'S VOICE: In that case.... I'd — I'd better — (*He heaves a long sigh.*)

FENG (*pleading*): Then you will go away, won't you?

PINGS VOICE (*submissively*): All right, then. If I must. I'll be off, then. (*Suddenly becoming urgent once more.*) But first open the window a minute, so that I can —

FENG: No. You must go away at once!

PING'S VOICE (*urgently*): Now listen: all I want is — is to give you a kiss.

FENG (*as if it hurts her to say it*): Oh, Master Ping, you're not at home now. You must forgive me this time.

PING'S VOICE (*bitterly*): So you've forgotten me. You no longer want to —

FENG (*resolutely*): Yes, I've forgotten you. Now go away.

PING'S VOICE (*suddenly*): Wasn't my brother here a short while ago?

FENG: Yes. (*Hesitantly.*) He was.

PING'S VOICE (*acidly*): Oh! (*Heaving a deep sigh.*) That explains it. (*Viciously.*) If you *have* thrown me over, you heartless little —

FENG: What do you mean, "thrown you over"?

PING'S VOICE (*impatiently*): Then why won't you open the window and let me in? Don't you real-

我进来？你不知道我——爱你么？

四：你别再缠我好不好？今天一天你替我们闹出许多事，你还不够么？

周萍的声音：那我知道错了，不过，现在我要见你，要见你。

四：(叹一口气)好，那明天说吧！明天我依你，什么都成！

周萍的声音：(犹疑地)明天，真的？

四：嗯，真的，我不骗你。

周萍的声音：好吧，就这样吧，不要冤我。

　　足步声。

四：你走了？

周萍的声音：嗯，走了。

　　足步声渐远。

四：(心里一块石头落下来，自语)他走了！(把窗户打开，风吹进来)唉！

　　周萍忽然立在窗口。

四：哦，妈呀！(忙关窗门。)

萍：(已推开一点窗门，继续推着)这次你赶不走我了。

四：(用力关)你……你……你走！

　　周萍到底越过窗进来，他满身泥泞，脸上沾着血。

ize that I — love you?

FENG: Please don't pester me any more. All day you've been making trouble for us. Don't you think you've done enough?

PING'S VOICE: I know I did wrong. But now I want to see you — I must.

FENG (*with a sigh*): All right, we'll see about it tomorrow. I'll do what you like tomorrow.

PING'S VOICE (*suspiciously*): Tomorrow? You really mean that?

FENG: Yes, I do. I really mean it.

PING'S VOICE: All right, then, we'll leave it like that. You'd better not be having me on, though.

(*The sound of footsteps.*)

FENG: You going now?

PING'S VOICE: Yes, I'm off.

(*The footsteps fade into the distance.*)

FENG (*to herself, as if a weight has been lifted from her mind*): He's gone! (*She opens the window to let in the breeze.*) Oh!

(*Zhou Ping suddenly appears at the window.*)

FENG: Help! Mother! (*She quickly closes the window.*)

PING (*forcing the window ajar and continuing to press against it*): You won't get rid of me so easily this time!

FENG (*straining to hold the window shut*): No — no — go away!

(*Zhou Ping finally succeeds in forcing his way into the room. He is smothered in mud and his face is bloody.*)

萍：你看我还是进来了。

四：(退后)你又喝醉了。

萍：你为什么躲我？为什么害怕不敢见我？(转过脸。)

四：(怕)你的脸怎么啦？

萍：(摸脸，一手的血)为着找你，我路上摔的。(关窗户。)

四：你走吧，我求你，走吧。

萍：(奇怪地笑着)不，我得好好地看看你。

雷声。

四：(躲开)不，我怕。

萍：(挨近)你怕什么？

四：(颤声)我怕，(退后)你的脸满是血。……我简直不认识你……你……你……

萍：(怪样地笑)你以为我是谁？傻孩子。(拉她的手。)

雷声大作，一声霹雳。

四：哦，妈。(跑到周萍怀里)我怕！

雷声轰轰，大雨下，舞台渐暗。窗户推开了。外面黑黝黝的。忽然一片蓝森森的闪电，照见了繁漪的惨白的脸露在窗台上面，像个死

PING: You see? I've got in after all.
FENG (*recoiling from him*): You're drunk again!
PING: Why did you want to get rid of me? Why were you afraid to see me? (*He turns towards her.*)
FENG (*frightened*): What's happened to your face?
PING (*feeling his face with his hand, which comes away covered in blood*): That's where I fell over on my way here — just to see you. (*He closes the window.*)
FENG: You must go! Please, *please* —
PING (*with a strange laugh*): No. I want to have a good look at you first.
(*A peal of thunder.*)
FENG (*shrinking away from him*): No, I'm afraid.
PING (*closing in on her*): What are you afraid of?
FENG (*her voice trembling*): Because — (*still retreating*) there's blood all over your face... I just don't recognize you — you —
PING (*again with a strange laugh*): Who do you think I am? You silly girl! (*He takes her hand.*)
(*Against the background of a crescendo of thunder there is a deafening crash overhead.*)
FENG: Oh, Mother! (*Taking refuge in Zhou Ping's arms.*) I'm frightened!
(*As the thunder roars and the rain pours down in torrents, the lights are gradually dimmed. The window opens, pushed from outside. It is pitch-dark outside the window. A sudden blue flash of lightning lights up an eerie white face at the window. It is Fanyi. She looks like a corpse as she stands there, heedless of the rain that pelts*

尸,任着一条一条的雨水向散乱的头发上淋。

繁漪伸进手,将窗子关上。雷更隆隆地响着,屋子整个黑下来。

四:(听到雷声)你抱紧我,我怕!

舞台渐明。

听见屋外大海叫门的声音。

周萍坐在圆椅上,四凤神色紧张,立在门侧。

萍:(谛听)这是谁?

四:你别作声!

鲁妈的声音:怎么回来了,大海?

大海的声音:雨下得太大,车厂的房子塌了。

四:(低声,急促地)哥哥来了,你走,你赶快走。

周萍忙到窗前,推窗。

萍:(推不动)奇怪!

四:怎么?

萍:(急迫地)窗户外面有人关上了。

四:(怕)真的,那会是谁?

萍:(再推)不成,开不动。

四:你别作声,他们就在门口。

大海的声音:铺板呢?

鲁妈的声音:在四凤屋里。

四:他们要进来。你藏,藏起来。

down on her dishevelled hair. She reaches out
and pulls the window to again, then fastens it
on the outside. As the thunder crashes and roars
louder than ever, the stage is plunged into complete darkness.)

FENG (*at the sound of the thunder*): Hold me tight. I'm afraid.

(*The lights gradually come on again.*)

(*Lu Dahai's voice is heard outside shouting to be let in. Zhou Ping is sitting on the chair, while Sifeng stands by the door, her face tense.*)

PING (*listening*): Who's that?

FENG: Sh! Don't make a sound!

MA'S VOICE: What, back again, Dahai?

MA'S VOICE: It's been raining so hard that the sheds at the rickshaw rank have collapsed.

FENG (*in a low, urgent voice*): It's my brother. You'll have to get out. Fast.

(*Zhou Ping dashes to the window and tugs at it.*)

PING (*unable to make it budge*): That's funny!

FENG: What is?

PING (*anxiously*): Someone's fastened the window from the outside.

FENG (*frightened*): No! Who could have done that?

PING (*tugging at the window again*): It's no good, it won't budge.

FENG: Quiet! They're just outside the door.

HAI'S VOICE: Where are the bed-planks?

MA'S VOICE: In Sifeng's room.

FENG: They're coming in. Hide yourself in here, quick. (*Just as she is bundling Zhou Ping into*

313

雷雨

四凤正引周萍入右门,大海持灯推门进。

大:什么?(见四凤同周萍,二人僵立不动)妈,您快进来,我见了鬼!

鲁妈跑进。

鲁:(喑哑)天!

四:(夺门而出)啊!

鲁妈扶着门闩,几乎晕倒。

大:哦,原来是你!(拾起桌上菜刀,奔向周萍。)

鲁:(用力拉着大海的衣襟)大海,你别动,你动,妈就死在你的面前。

大:您放下我!您放下我!(顿脚。)

鲁:(见周萍惊立不动)糊涂东西,你还不跑?周萍由右门跑下。

大:(喊)抓住他!爸,抓住他!

鲁:(见周萍已跑远,才放开大海,坐在地上发呆)哦,天!

大:(顿脚)妈!妈!你好糊涂!

鲁贵上。

贵:他走了?咦,可是四凤呢?

the curtained recess, Dahai comes in with a lamp.)

HAI: What's this? (*He sees the pair of them standing petrified.*)Mother! Come in here, quick! I'm seeing things!

(*Lu Ma runs in.*)

MA (*gasping*): God!

FENG (*bursting out of the room*): Oh!

(*Lu Ma, clinging to the door, almost faints.*)

HAI: So it's you, is it! (*He snatches the kitchen knife from the table and rushes at Zhou Ping with it.*)

MA (*catching him by the sleeve and holding him back with all her strength*): Stop, Dahai, stop! Over my dead body!

HAI: Let me go! Leave go of me! (*He stamps his foot.*)

MA (*realizing that Zhou Ping is still standing there rooted to the spot*): Run, you fool! Don't just stand there!

(*Zhou Ping runs out through the door on the right.*)

HAI (*shouting*): Grab him, Dad! Grab him!

MA (*waits until she is satisfied that Zhou Ping has made good his escape before releasing Dahai, then sits down on the floor in a stupor*): My God!

HAI (*stamping his foot*): Mother, Mother! What an idiotic thing to do!

(*Lu Gui comes in.*)

LU: Has he gone? Whew! — Where's Sifeng?

雷雨

大：不要脸的东西,她跑了。

鲁：哦,我的孩子,外面的河涨了水！你别糊涂啊！孩子！(跑。)

大：(拉着她)你上哪儿?

鲁：不成,不成,要找她,要找她！

大：好,我也去。

鲁：快来吧！(喊)四凤！(追下。)

  鲁贵忽然也戴上帽子跑出。大海走到箱子那里,取出手枪,揣在怀里,快步走出。

  外面暴风雨声。

——幕急落

HAI: She's bolted, the little bitch.
MA: Oh, my child! The river's in flood out there! You mustn't do it! Sifeng! (*She goes to run out.*)
HAI (*holding her back*): Where are you going?
MA: No, no! I've got to find her! I've got to find her!
HAI: All right. I'm coming with you.
MA: Quick, then! (*Shouting.*) Sifeng! (*She runs out.*)

(*Suddenly, Lu Gui puts on his hat and follows them out.*

Dahai goes across to the chest and takes out the pistol.

Thrusting it inside his coat, he hurries out.)

(*Noise of raging storm outside.*)

(*Quick Curtain*)

雷雨

第四幕

周宅客厅内。半夜两点钟的光景。

开幕时,周朴园一人坐在沙发上读报,旁边燃着一个立灯,四周是暗暗的。

外面雨声淅沥可闻,窗前帷幕垂下来了。中间的门紧紧地掩起,由门上玻璃望出去,花园的景物都掩埋在黑暗里。

朴:(放下报,疲倦地伸一伸腰)来人啦!来人!(擦着眼镜,走到左边饭厅门口)这儿有人么?(外面闪电。他走到右边柜前,按铃。)

仆人上。

仆人:老爷!

朴:我叫了你半天。

仆人:外面下雨,听不见。

朴:(指钟)钟怎么停了?

仆人:(解释地)每次总是四凤上的,今天她走了,这件事就忘了。

Act Four

In the Zhous' drawing-room. About two o'clock in the morning.

When the curtain rises, Zhou Puyuan is sitting on a sofa, reading a newspaper by the light of a floor-lamp beside him. The rest of the room is in darkness.

The hiss of the rain is loud even in the room, though the curtains are drawn and the centre door closed. Beyond the glass-panelled door the garden is shrouded in utter darkness.

ZHOU (*putting down his paper and stretching wearily*): Hullo, there! Here, somebody! (*He walks across to the dining-room door, polishing his spectacles as he goes.*) Anybody there?
(*Flashes of lightning outside. He goes over to the bureau and rings.*)
(*A servant appears.*)
SERVANT: You rang, sir?
ZHOU: I've been calling you long enough.
SERVANT: Job to hear anything with this rain, sir.
ZHOU (*indicating the clock*): What's happened to the clock? It's stopped.
SERVANT: Well, you see, sir, it was always Sifeng's job to wind it, but as she's gone today, it's been overlooked.

朴：什么时候了？

仆人：嗯，——大概有两点钟了。

朴：刚才我叫账房汇一笔钱到济南去，他们弄清楚了没有？

仆人：您说寄给济南一个，一个姓鲁的，是么？

朴：嗯。

仆人：预备好了。

　　外面闪电，周朴园回头望花园。

朴：藤萝架那边的电线，太太叫人来修理了么？

仆人：叫了，电灯匠说下着大雨不好修理，明天再来。

朴：哦。——什么，现在几点了？

仆人：快两点了。老爷要睡觉么？

朴：你请太太下来。

仆人：太太睡觉了。

朴：(无意地)二少爷呢？

仆人：早睡了。

朴：那么，你看看大少爷。

仆人：大少爷吃完饭出去，还没有回来。

　　半晌。

朴：(走回沙发前坐下，寂寞地)怎么这屋子一个人也没有？

仆人：是，老爷，都睡了。

ZHOU: What's the time now?

SERVANT: Er — must be about two.

ZHOU: I told the office to have some money sent to Jinan. Are they clear what they've got to do?

SERVANT: The money that was to go to somebody in Jinan by the name of — er — Lu, you mean, sir?

ZHOU: Yes.

SERVANT: It's been attended to.

(*Flashes of lightning outside. Zhou Puyuan turns and looks out at the garden.*)

ZHOU: The electric cable down by the wistaria-trellis — did your mistress send for someone to mend it?

SERVANT: Yes, but the electrician said he couldn't work in this heavy rain and that he'd have to come back tomorrow.

ZHOU: I see. — Er, what did you say the time was?

SERVANT: Nearly two o'clock. Will you be retiring now, sir?

ZHOU: You can ask your mistress to come down here.

SERVANT: She's retired for the night.

ZHOU (*casually*): What about Master Chong?

SERVANT: He went up some time ago.

ZHOU: Well, see if Master Ping's still up, them.

SERVANT: Master Ping went out after dinner and isn't back yet.

(*A pause.*)

ZHOU (*going back to his seat on the sofa and speaking in a mournful voice*): So there's no one else in the house still up, then?

SERVANT: No, sir. They've all gone to bed.

雷雨

朴：好，你去吧。

仆人：您不要什么东西么？

朴：我不要什么。

　　仆人由中门下。周朴园站起来，在厅中来回沉闷地踱着，又停在右边柜前，开了中间的灯，沉思地望着侍萍的相片。

　　周冲由饭厅上。

冲：（没想到父亲在这儿）爸！

朴：（露喜色）你——你没有睡？

冲：嗯。

朴：找我么？

冲：不，我以为母亲在这儿。

朴：（失望）哦——你母亲在楼上。

冲：没有吧，我在她的门上敲了半天，她的门锁着。——是的，也许在屋里。——爸，我走了。

朴：冲儿。

　　周冲站住。

朴：不要走。

冲：爸，您有事？

朴：没有。（慈爱地）你现在怎么还不睡？

冲：（服贴地）是，爸，我睡晚了，我就睡。

朴：你今天吃完饭把克大夫给的药吃了么？

ZHOU: All right. That'll be all.

SERVANT: Nothing more you require, sir?

ZHOU: No.

  (*The servant goes out through the centre door. Zhou Puyuan gets up again and paces moodily up and down. Presently he stops in front of the bureau, switches on the main light, and gazes abstractedly at Shiping's photograph.*)

  (*Zhou Chong comes in from the dining-room.*)

CHONG (*not expecting to find his father here*): Father!

ZHOU (*obviously glad of the interruption*): Haven't — haven't you gone to bed yet?

CHONG: No.

ZHOU: Did you want to see me?

CHONG: No, I thought I'd find Mother here.

ZHOU (*disappointed*): Oh — er — your mother's upstairs.

CHONG: I don't think she is, though. I knocked at her door a long time, until I found it was locked. — Though of course she may have been there all the time. — Well, I'll be going now, Father.

ZHOU: Chong.

  (*Zhou Chong stops.*)

ZHOU: Don't go yet.

CHONG: Is there anything I can do for you?

ZHOU: No. (*Affectionately.*) How is it you're still up?

CHONG (*submissively*): Sorry, Father. I am up rather late. I'll turn in straight away.

ZHOU: Did you take the medicine Dr. Kramer gave you?

雷雨

冲：吃了。

朴：打了球没有？

冲：嗯。

朴：快活么？

冲：嗯。

朴：(立起,拉起周冲的手)为什么,怕我么？

冲：是,爸爸。

朴：(干涩地)你像是有点不满意,是么？

冲：(窘迫)我,我说不出来,爸。

半响。

周朴园走回沙发,坐下叹一口气。招周冲来,周冲走近。

朴：(寂寞地)今天——呃,爸爸有一点觉得自己老了。(停)你知道么？

冲：(冷淡)不,不知道。

朴：(忽然)如果爸爸有一天死了,没有人照拂你,你不怕么？

冲：(无表情地)嗯,怕。

朴：(想让儿子亲近自己,可亲地)你今天早上说要拿你的学费帮一个人,你说说看,能答应的总是要答应的。

冲：那是我糊涂,以后我不会这样说话了。

CHONG: Yes, I did.
ZHOU: Have a game of tennis today?
CHONG: Yes.
ZHOU: Happy?
CHONG: Mm.
ZHOU (*getting up and taking Zhou Chong by the hand*): What's the matter? Afraid of me?
CHONG: Yes, I am, Father.
ZHOU (*drily*): You seem to be dissatisfied about something. Is that it?
CHONG (*ill at ease*): I — I hardly know how to put it, Father.
(*A pause. Zhou Puyuan goes back to the sofa and sits down with a sigh. He beckons Zhou Chong across to him.*)
ZHOU (*mournfully*): Today I — er, well, I somehow feel I'm getting old. (*Pauses.*) Know what I mean?
CHONG (*indifferently*): No, I don't.
ZHOU (*abruptly*): If I should die one of these days and leave you alone, with no one to look after you, wouldn't you be worried?
CHONG (*without any trace of emotion*): I expect I would.
ZHOU (*affectionately, in an attempt to put his son at his ease*): You said this morning you'd like to share your school allowance with someone. — Well, let's hear all about it. I'm open to any suggestions within reason.
CHONG: I was just being silly. I promise I won't say anything like that again.

半响。

朴：(责备地望着周冲)你对我说话很少。

冲：我——我说不出,您平时总像不愿意见我们。(嗫嚅地)今天您就有点——有点特别,您——

朴：(不愿他向下说)嗯,你去吧!

冲：是,爸爸。(由饭厅下。)

周朴园失望地看着他儿子走出,又拿起侍萍的相片。

蘩漪由中门不做声地走进来,雨衣上的水还在往下滴,颜色惨白,鬓发湿漉漉的。

蘩：(看见周朴园惊愕地望着她,冷漠地)还没有睡?(立在门前。)

朴：你?(走近她)你上哪儿去了?冲儿找你一晚上。

蘩：(平常地)我出去走走。

朴：这样大的雨,你出去走?

蘩：嗯,——(忽然报复地)我有神经病。

朴：我问你,你刚才在哪儿?

蘩：(厌恶地)你不用管。

朴：(打量地)你的衣服都湿了,还不脱了它?

(*A long pause.*)

ZHOU (*gazing reproachfully into Zhou Chong's face*): You don't seem to have much to say to me.

CHONG: I — I don't know what to say. As a rule, you don't seem particularly willing to see us. (*Falteringly.*) But — but today you seem rather — rather different, somehow. You —

ZHOU (*who has heard enough*): All right. You may go now.

CHONG: Very well, Father. (*He goes out through the dining-room.*)

(*Zhou Puyuan looks disappointed as he watches his son out of the room. When he is alone, he picks up Shiping's photograph again.*)

(*Zhou Fanyi comes in quietly through the centre door. Her raincoat is still dripping wet. Her face is pale and haggard, and her hair drenched.*)

FAN (*assuming an air of unconcern when she sees the startled look that her husband gives her*): Still up? (She remains standing by the door.)

ZHOU: Well, I'm damned! (*Going across to her.*) Where have you been? Chong's been looking for you all the evening.

FAN (*simply*): I've been for a walk.

ZHOU: What, when it's pouring like this?

FAN: Mm. — (*Suddenly vindictive.*) I'm neurotic, remember?

ZHOU: And now perhaps you'll tell me where you've been?

FAN (*crossly*): None of your business.

ZHOU (*looking her up and down*): You're wet

繁：我心里发热，我要在外面冰一冰。

朴：(不耐烦地)不要胡言乱语的，你刚才究竟上哪儿去了？

繁：(望着他，一字一字地)在你的家里！

朴：(烦恶地)在我的家里？

繁：(微笑)嗯，在花园里赏雨。

朴：一夜晚？

繁：(快意地)嗯，淋了一夜晚。

半晌。周朴园惊疑地望着繁漪，她像一座石像，仍然站在门前。

朴：繁漪，我看你上楼去歇一歇吧。

繁：(硬生生地)不。(忽然)你拿的什么？(轻蔑)哼，又是那个女人的照片！(伸手去拿。)

朴：你可以不看，萍儿母亲的。

繁：(抢过来，就灯下看)萍儿的母亲很好看。

周朴园没有理繁漪，自己在沙发上坐下。

繁：我问你，是不是？

朴：嗯。

繁：样子很温存的。

周朴园不理她。

through. You'd best hurry up and get those wet things off.

FAN: I felt feverish in my mind, so I went out to cool off in the rain.

ZHOU (*impatiently*): Don't talk such utter nonsense. Where exactly have you been?

FAN (*looking him full in the face, a syllable at a time*): I've been at your place!

ZHOU (*annoyed*): At my place?

FAN (*with a faint smile*): Mm. Enjoying the rain in the garden!

ZHOU: What, all this time?

FAN (*cheerfully*): Yes, I've had a nice long soak.

(*A pause. Puyuan stares at her in startled bewilderment. She just stands where she is by the door, impassive as a statue.*)

ZHOU: Fanyi, I think you'd best go upstairs and get some rest.

FAN (*stubbornly*): No. (*Suddenly.*) What's that you've got in your hand? (*Scornfully.*) Humph! That woman's photograph again! (*She reaches out for it.*)

ZHOU: You needn't look at it. It's Ping's mother, you know.

FAN (*snatching it from him and looking at it under the light*): Ping's mother was very good-looking.

(*Puyuan ignores her, and goes and sits down on the sofa.*)

FAN: Mm? Don't you think so?

ZHOU: I suppose so.

FAN: She looks very good-natured.

(*Puyuan ignores her.*)

繁：她很聪明。

朴：(冥想)嗯。

繁：(欣赏地)真年轻。

朴：(不自觉地)嗯,年轻。

繁：(放下相片)奇怪,我像是在哪儿见过似的。

朴：(抬起头,疑惑地)不会吧。——你在哪儿见过她？好,我看你睡去吧。(立起,把相片拿起来。)

繁：拿这个做什么？

周朴园望望繁漪,没有理她。

繁：(从周朴园手中取过来)放在这儿！(怪样地笑)不会掉的,我替你守着她。(放在桌上。)

朴：不要装疯！你现在有点胡闹！

繁：我是疯了。请你不用管我。

朴：(愠怒)好,你上楼去吧。我要一个人在这儿歇一歇。

繁：不,我要一个人在这儿歇一歇,你给我出去。

朴：(严肃)繁漪,我叫你上楼去！

繁：(轻蔑)我不愿意,告诉你,我不愿意。

半晌。

朴：(低声)你要注意(指头)这儿,记着克大夫的

FAN: Intelligent, too.

ZHOU (*absorbed in his own thoughts*): Mm.

FAN (*appreciatively*): And so young!

ZHOU (*unconsciously echoing her*): Yes, so young.

FAN (*putting the photograph down*): It's funny, I seem to have seen her somewhere.

ZHOU (*looking up suspiciously*): Impossible! Where could you have seen her? Now, come on, time for bed. (*He gets up and takes the photograph from her.*)

FAN: Well, don't just stand there holding it.

(*Puyuan gazes through her but makes no reply.*)

FAN (*taking the photograph from him*): Put it over here! (*With an unnatural laugh.*) You won't lose it. I'll look after it for you. (*She puts it on the table.*)

ZHOU: Don't pretend you're mad! You're playing the fool with me!

FAN: But I *am* mad. And I'd rather you left me alone.

ZHOU (*annoyed*): All right. Now go on up to bed. I want to be left on my own here to have a rest.

FAN: Oh no. I want to be left here on my own to have a rest. You'll have to get out.

ZHOU (*glowering at her*): Fanyi, I'm telling you to go up stairs!

FAN (contemptuously): I don't wish to. You hear? I don't wish to.

(*A pause.*)

ZHOU (*in a low voice*): What you've got to be careful of — (*tapping his own head*) is this. Remember what Dr. Kramer said. He wants you to be qui-

话，他要你静静的，少说话。明天克大夫还来，我已经替你请好了。

繁：(望着前面)明天？哼！

周萍低头由饭厅走出，神色忧郁，走向书房。

朴：萍儿。

萍：(抬头，惊讶)爸！您还没有睡。

朴：(责备地)怎么，现在才回来？

萍：不，爸，我早回来了。我出去买东西去了。

朴：你来做什么？

萍：我到书房，看看爸写的介绍信在那儿没有。

朴：你不是明天早车走么？

萍：我忽然想起今天夜晚两点半有一趟车，我预备现在就走。

繁：(忽然地)现在？

萍：嗯。

繁：就这样急么？

萍：是，母亲。

朴：(和蔼地)外面下着大雨，半夜走不大方便吧？

萍：这时走，明天一早到，找人方便些。

et and not talk so much. He'll be here again tomorrow. I've made an appointment for you.

FAN (*looking straight in front of her*): Here again tomorrow? Humph!

(*A chap-fallen Zhou Ping comes in from the dining-room and walks with bent head towards the study.*)

ZHOU: Ping.

PING (looking up with a start): Why, Father! You're still up.

ZHOU (*censoriously*): Only just got back home, I suppose?

PING: Oh no, Father. I've been back some time now. I only went out to do some shopping.

ZHOU: What do you want here?

PING: I was going to the study to see if your letter of introduction was ready.

ZHOU: But you're not leaving until tomorrow morning, are you?

PING: I suddenly remembered there was a train leaving at half past two tonight, so I've decided to go straight away.

FAN (*suddenly*): Straight away?

PING: Mm.

FAN: You're in a tearing hurry, aren't you?

PING: Yes, Mother.

ZHOU (*pleasantly*): But it's raining hard just now. Not much of weather to go out in at this time of night.

PING: If I go on this train I'll get there first thing in the morning, which will give me more time to look up all the people I've got to see.

朴：信就在书房书桌上，你要现在走也好。

周萍点头，走向书房。

朴：你不用去！（向蘩漪）你到书房把信替他拿来。

蘩：（看周朴园，不信任地）嗯！（走进书房下。）

朴：（望蘩漪出，谨慎地）她不愿意上楼，回头你先陪她到楼上去，叫底下人好好地伺候她睡觉。

萍：是，爸爸。

朴：（更小心）你过来！

周萍走近。

朴：（低声）告诉底下人，叫他们小心点，（烦恶地）我看她的病更重了，刚才她忽然一个人出去了。

萍：出去了？

朴：嗯。（严重地）在外面淋了一夜晚的雨，说话也非常奇怪，我怕这不是好现象。——我老了，我愿家里平平安安的……

萍：（不安地）我想爸爸只要把事不看得太严重了，事情就会过去的。

朴：（畏缩地）不，不，有些事简直是想不到的。人间的事很——有点古怪。今天一天叫我忽然悟到作人不容易，太不容易。（疲倦地）

ZHOU: The letter's on the desk in the study. I suppose you'd better go now, if you think you must.
(*Zhou Ping nods and turns to go into the study.*)
ZHOU: Wait. You needn't fetch it yourself. (*To Fanyi.*) Go and get the letter for him, will you?
FAN (*looking distrustfully at her husband*): All right. (*She goes into the study.*)
ZHOU (*waiting until she has gone out and then, cautiously*): She refuses to go upstairs. I want you to take her up to her room and tell one of the maids to see her into bed all right.
PING: Very well, Father.
ZHOU (*even more cautiously*): Come here!
(*Zhou Ping comes closer.*)
ZHOU (*in an undertone*): And tell the servants to keep their wits about them. (*With annoyance.*) I think her nerves are getting worse than ever. A short while ago she suddenly went off on her own.
PING: Went off?
ZHOU: Yes. (*Gravely.*) She'd been standing out in the rain all the evening. And she says such funny things! I don't like the look of it at all. — I'm getting on in years, and I want everything to go smoothly in the family —
PING (*uneasily*): I think, Father, if only you don't attach too much importance to these things, you'll find they'll straighten themselves out.
ZHOU (*as though overawed by something*): No, no. Sometimes things turn out in a way you'd never have imagined. The world's a — a funny place. What's happened today has made me suddenly re-

你肯到矿上去磨炼一下,我很高兴。有一样东西,你可以带去。(领周萍到方桌前,拉开抽屉给他看)但是,只为着保护自己,不要拿它来闯祸。(把抽屉锁上)拿着钥匙!走的时候,不要忘了带着。(把抽屉的钥匙交给周萍。)

繁漪持信上。

繁:(嫌恶地)信在这儿!

朴:(如梦初醒,向周萍)好,你走吧,我也想睡了。繁漪,你也好好休息一下。

繁:(盼望他走)嗯,好。

周朴园由书房下。

繁:(见周朴园走出,阴沉地)这么说你是一定要走了。

萍:嗯。

繁:(忽然)刚才你父亲对你说什么?

萍:(闪避)他说要我陪你上楼去,请你睡觉。

繁:(冷笑)他应当叫几个人把我拉上去,关起来。

萍:(故意装做不明白)你这是什么意思?

繁:(迸发)你不用瞒我。我知道,我知道,(辛酸

alize just how difficult, how terribly difficult life can be. (*Wearily*.) I'm glad you want to go to the mine for a bit of real hard work. I've got something here for you to take with you. (*He takes Zhou Ping over to a square table and opens a drawer for him to look into.*) But it's strictly for self-defence. Don't go getting into mischief with it. (*He locks the drawer.*) Here's the key. Don't forget to take it with you when you go. (*He gives Zhou Ping the key.*)

(*Fanyi comes back in with the letter.*)

FAN (*resentfully*): Here's your letter!

ZHOU (*coming back to earth with a start and turning again to Zhou Ping*): All right, off you go, then. I'm going to bed. You'd better get some rest, too, Fanyi.

FAN (*eager to get rid of him*): Yes, all right.

(*Zhou Puyuan goes out through the study.*)

FAN (*as soon as Zhou Puyuan is gone, despondently*): So you've really made up your mind to go, then.

PING: Yes.

FAN (*suddenly*): What was your father saying to you just now?

PING (*evasively*): He said I was to see you up to your room and ask you to go to bed.

FAN (*with a sardonic smile*): I should have thought he'd have had me dragged upstairs by the servants and locked in!

PING (*pretending not to understand*): What on earth do you mean?

FAN (*letting fly*): Don't think you can pull the wool

地)他说我是神经病,疯子,我知道他要你这样看我,他要什么人都这样看我。

萍:(心悸)不,你不要这样想。

繁:(奇怪的神色)你?你也骗我?(阴郁地)我从你们的眼神看出来,你们父子都愿我快成疯子!你们——父亲同儿子——偷偷在我背后说冷话,笑我,在我背后计算着我。

萍:(镇静)你不要神经过敏,我送你上楼去。

繁:(突然地)我不要你送,走开!(低声)我还用不着你父亲偷偷地背着我,叫你小心,送一个疯子上楼。

萍:(抑制着自己的烦嫌)那么,你把信给我,让我自己走吧。

繁:(不明白地)你上哪儿?

萍:(不得已)我要走,我要收拾收拾我的东西。

繁:(冷静地)我问你,你今天晚上上哪儿去了?

萍:(敌对地)你不用问,你自己知道。

繁:(恐吓地)到底你还是到她那儿去了。半晌,繁漪望周萍,周萍低头。

over my eyes! I know all about it. (*Bitterly*.) He's been telling you I'm neurotic — mad. I know quite well he's trying to convince you that I am. He's trying to convince everybody that I am.

PING (*nervously*): Oh no, you mustn't go getting ideas like that.

FAN (*making a wry face*): You, too? Even you trying to deceive me? (*Morosely*.) I can see it in your eyes, both of you. You and your father are both the same — you want me to go mad! You and your father, you sneer about me behind my back, and laugh at me, and plot against me!

PING (*calmly*): You're imagining things. I'll see you up to your room.

FAN (*sharply*): I don't want your help! Get away from me! (*Faintly*.) I haven't got to the stage yet where your father needs to go behind my back and tell you to be careful and see the lunatic up to her room!

PING (*suppressing his distaste and annoyance*): If that's the case, perhaps you'll give me the letter, so that I can get out of your way.

FAN (*puzzled*): Where are you going, then?

PING (*helplessly*): I'm going away. I've got some packing to do.

FAN (*suddenly cold and calm*): Might I inquire where you went tonight?

PING (*with animosity*): You don't need to ask. You know very well.

FAN (*menacingly*): So you went to see her after all. (*A pause. Fanyi stares at Zhou Ping until he drops his eyes to the floor.*)

萍：(断然)嗯,我去了,我去了,(挑战地)你要怎么样?

繁：(软下来)不怎么样。(强笑)今天下午的话我说错了,你不要怪我。我只问你走了以后,你预备把她怎么样?

萍：以后？——(冒然)我娶她!

繁：娶她?

萍：嗯。

繁：父亲呢?

萍：(淡然)以后再说。

繁：(神秘地)萍,我现在给你一个机会。

萍：(不明白)什么?

繁：(劝诱地)如果今天你不走,你父亲那儿我可以替你想法子。

萍：不必,这件事我认为光明正大,我可以跟任何人谈。

繁：(忧郁地)萍!

萍：干什么?

繁：(阴郁地)你知道你走了以后,我会怎么样?

萍：不知道。

繁：(恐惧地)你看看你的父亲,你难道想像不出?

萍：我不明白你的话。

繁：(指着头)就在这儿;你不知道么?

萍：(似懂非懂地)怎么讲?

PING (*with an air of finality*): Yes. I did. (*Challenging her.*) What are you going to do about it?

FAN (*crumpling*): Nothing. (*Forcing a smile.*) It was wrong of me to say what I did this afternoon. You mustn't think too badly of me because of that. There's just one thing I want to know: what are you going to do about her after you've gone?

PING: After I've gone? — (*Impulsively.*) I'll marry her!

FAN: Marry her?

PING: Yes.

FAN: What about your father?

PING (*nonchalantly*): Plenty of time to think about that.

FAN (*mysteriously*): Ping, I'll give you a chance.

PING (*blankly*): Eh?

FAN (*persuasively*): If you don't leave today, I think I can get round your father for you.

PING: Thanks, but there's no need to. This business is quite square and aboveboard so far as I'm concerned. I don't care who knows.

FAN (*miserably*): Oh, Ping!

PING: Well?

FAN (*moodily*): You realize what will become of me after you've gone?

PING: I've no idea.

FAN (*trembling at the prospect*): Can't you imagine what it will be like? You've only got to look at the way your father goes on.

PING: I don't understand what you mean.

FAN (*tapping her head*): This. Know what I mean?

PING (*not sure whether he understands or not*):

繁：(好像在叙述别人的事情)第一,那位专家,克大夫免不了会天天来的,要我吃药,逼我吃药。吃药,吃药,吃药!渐渐伺候着我的人一定多,守着我,像个怪物似地守着我。他们——

萍：(烦)我劝你,不要这样胡想,好不好?

繁：他们渐渐学会了你父亲的话："小心,小心点,她有点疯病!"到处都偷偷地在我背后低着声音说话,叽咕着。慢慢地无论谁都要小心点,不敢见我,最后铁链子锁着我,那我真就成了疯子了。

萍：(无办法)唉!(看表)不早了,给我信吧,我还要收拾东西呢。

繁：(恳求地)萍,这不是不可能的。萍,你想一想,你就一点——就一点无动于衷么?

萍：你——(故意恶狠地)你自己要走这一条路,我有什么办法?

繁：(愤怒)什么,你忘记你自己的母亲也是被你父亲气死的么?

What exactly *do* you mean?

FAN (*with an air of detachment, as though she were speaking about someone else*): Well, first of all, this specialist, Dr. Kramer, is bound to come here every day, giving me medicine and forcing me to take it. And so it'll go on: medicine, medicine, medicine, day in and day out! Gradually there'll be more and more people to wait on me, to look after me, to keep watch over me, as if I were something peculiar — a freak. They'll —

PING (*becomes impatient with her*): Now listen to me: you're just imagining things.

FAN: They'll gradually start talking the way your father does: Be careful, watch your step, she's got a touch of insanity. Wherever I go, I'll hear people whispering behind my back, gossiping about me. Gradually everyone will become wary of me, and no one will dare come and see me. Finally I'll be put in chains, and by that time I really shall have gone mad.

PING (*at a complete loss*): Well! (*Glancing at his watch.*) It's getting late. Give me the letter, then: I've still got some packing to do.

FAN (*pleading*): Ping, don't think that that can't happen. Think it over, Ping. Haven't you even a — even a spark of feeling?

PING: If you — (*with deliberate venom*) if you're so set on taking that road, what can I do about it?

FAN (*indignantly*): What! Have you forgotten that your own mother was also hounded to her death by this father of yours?

343

萍：(一了百了)我母亲不像你,她懂得爱!她爱她自己的儿子,她没有对不起我父亲。

繁：(眼睛射出疯狂的火)你有权利说这种话么?你忘了就在这屋子,三年前的你么?你忘了你自己才是个罪人;你忘了,我们——(突停,压制自己)哦,这是过去的事,我不提了。

周萍低头,坐沙发上。

繁：(转向周萍)哦,萍,好了。这一次我求你,最后一次求你。我从来不肯对人这样低声下气说话,现在我求你可怜可怜我,这家我再也忍受不住了。(哀婉地诉说)今天这一天我受的罪过你都看见了,这样子以后不是一天,是整月,整年地,以至到我死,才算完。他厌恶我,你的父亲;他知道我明白他的底细,他怕我。他愿意人人看我是怪物,是疯子,萍!——

萍：(心乱)你,你别说了。

繁：(急迫地)萍,我没有亲戚,没有朋友,没有一个可信的人,我现在求你,你先不要走——

萍：(躲闪地)不,不成。

PING (*abandoning all reserve*): My mother wasn't like you. She knew what love meant. She loved her son, and she was at least faithful to my father.

FAN (*her eyes ablaze with the light of madness*): What right have you to say a thing like that? Have you forgotten what you did three years ago, in this every room? You forget that it's you yourself that's the guilty one. You forget we — (*checking herself abruptly*) but what's the use of bringing all that up again? It's over and done with.

(*Zhou Ping, his head bowed, drops into a sofa.*)

FAN (*turning to Zhou Ping*): All right, Ping. This time I'm begging you — begging you for the last time. I've never gone down on my hands and knees like this to anyone else, and now I'm begging you to have pity on me. I can't stand this house any longer. (*Plaintively.*) You saw with your own eyes what I went through today, and it isn't only going to be today: it'll go on for days, months, years at a time, and it won't stop until I'm dead. He hates the sight of me, your father. And he's afraid of me, because I can see through him, and know all about him. He wants everybody to think I'm a freak, a lunatic! Oh, Ping! —

PING (*profoundly disturbed*): Don't — don't talk like that.

FAN (*insistently*): I've got no relatives, Ping, no friends, nobody I can trust. I beg you, Ping, stay a little longer —

PING (*trying to put her off*): Oh, no, I couldn't do that.

繁：（恳求地）即使你要走，你带我也离开这儿——

萍：（恐惧地）什么？你简直胡说！

繁：（恳求地）不，不，你带我走，——带我离开这儿，（不顾一切地）日后，甚至于你要把四凤接来——块儿住，我都可以，只要，只要（热烈地）只要你不离开我。

萍：（惊惧地望着她）我——我怕你真疯了！

繁：不，你不要这样说话。只有我明白你，我知道你的弱点，你也知道我的。你什么我都清楚。（忽然那样诱惑地笑起来）你过来，你——你怕什么？

萍：（望着她，忍不住喊出）你不要笑！（更重）你不要这样对我笑！（苦恼地打着自己的头）哦，我恨我自己，我恨，我恨我为什么要活着。

繁：（酸楚地）我这样累你么？然而你知道我活不到几年了。

萍：（痛苦地）你难道不知道这种关系谁听着都厌恶么？

繁：（冷冷地）我跟你说过多少遍，我不这样看，我的良心不是这样做的。（郑重地）萍，今天

FAN (*imploring him*): Well, if you must go, take me with you. Anything to get away from this —
PING (*horrified*): What! You're off your head!
FAN (*still imploring him*): I'm not, I'm not. Take me with you, away from this place! (*Becoming desperate.*) And afterwards, if you wanted to have Sifeng come and — and live with you, I'd agree to that, even, if only — if only — (*frantically*) if only you don't leave me!
PING (*looking at her in horror and astonishment*): I'm — I'm beginning to think you really are mad!
FAN: No, you mustn't say things like that. I'm the only person that really understands you. I know your failings — and you know mine. I know you inside out. (*Suddenly putting on a seductive smile.*) Come here. What — what are you afraid of?
PING (*gazing at her and shouting in spite of himself*): Stop smiling like that! (*More emphatically still.*) Don't smile at me like that! (*Beating his head in distress.*) Oh, I hate myself. I wish I were dead!

FAN (*bitterly*): Am I such a burden to you? But you know I haven't got many more years to live.
PING (*in an anguished voice*): But surely you realize that such a relationship must seem revolting to anyone else?
FAN (*coldly*): How many times have I told you that I don't look at it like that? My conscience isn't made that way. (*Solemnly.*) Ping, I was wrong in

雷雨

我做错了,如果你现在听我的话,不离开家,我可以再叫四凤回来。

萍:什么?

繁:(清清楚楚地)叫她回来还来得及。

萍:(走到她面前,沉重地)你给我滚开!

繁:什么?

萍:你现在不像明白人,你上楼睡觉去吧。

繁:(明白自己的命运)那么,完了。

萍:(趁机把信夺过来)嗯,你去吧。

繁:(绝望地)刚才我在鲁家看见你同四凤。

萍:(惊)什么,你刚才是到鲁家去了。

繁:(坐下)嗯,我在他们家附近站了半天。

萍:(恐惧)什么时候你在那里?

繁:(低头)我看着你从窗户进去。

萍:(急切)你?

繁:(失神地望着前面)我就走到窗户前面站着。

萍:你什么时候走的?

繁:(清朗地)一直等到你也走了。

萍:(走到她身旁)那窗户是你关上的。

繁:(阴沉地)嗯,我。

what I did this afternoon. If you'll follow my advice now and not go away, I can get Sifeng to come back here.

PING: What!

FAN (*distinctly*): It's still not too late to get her back.

PING (*going up to her and speaking in a low, level voice*): Get out of my sight!

FAN: What!

PING: You sound as if you'd taken leave of your senses. Get upstairs to bed.

FAN (*resigning herself to the inevitable*): That's that, then.

PING (*seizing this opportunity to snatch the letter from her*): Yes. Now off you go.

FAN (*despairingly*): I saw you with Sifeng at the Lus' tonight.

PING (*astounded*): Eh? Is that where you went, then?

FAN (*sitting down*): Yes. I spent quite a long time standing about near their place.

PING (*disturbed*): What time were you there?

FAN (*hanging her head*): I watched you get in through the window.

PING (*anxiously*): Then what?

FAN (*looking straight ahead with lifeless eyes*): Then I went over to the window and stood there.

PING: How long were you there?

FAN (*distinctly*): Right up until the time you left.

PING (*going across to her*): So it was you that closed the window!

FAN (*gloomily*): Yes, it was me.

萍:(恨极)你是我想不到的一个怪物!

蘩:(抬起头)什么?

萍:你真是一个疯子!

蘩:(无表情地望着他)你要怎么样?

萍:(狠恶地)我要你死!(由饭厅下,门猝然关上。)

蘩:(呆呆地坐着,望着饭厅的门。瞥见侍萍的相片,拿起来看看又放下。她沉静地立起来,踱了两步)奇怪,我要干什么?

中门轻轻推开,蘩漪回头,鲁贵悄悄走进来。

贵:(弯了弯腰)太太,您好。

蘩:(略惊)你来做什么?

贵:(假笑)给您请安来了。我在门口等了半天。

蘩:(镇静)哦,你刚才在门口?

贵:对了。(秘密地)我看见大少爷正跟您打架,我——(假笑)我就没敢进来。

蘩:(沉静地,不为所迫)你来要做什么?

贵:(有把握地)我倒是想报告给太太,说大少爷今天晚上喝醉了,跑到我们家里去。现在太

PING (*revolted*): Why, you're more of a monster than I ever imagined!

FAN (*looking up*): What?

PING: You *are* a lunatic after all!

FAN (*looking at him without any expression on her face*): Well, what are you going to do about it?

PING (*ferociously*): Oh, go to hell! (*He goes out through the dining-room, slamming the door behind him.*)

(*Fan sits there in a daze, staring at the dining-room door. Catching sight of the photograph, she picks it up and puts it down again after a glance at it. Then, calm and poised, she stands up and begins pacing up and down.*)

FAN: What *is* it that I want to do? I wonder.

(*The centre door opens quietly. Fanyi turns to find Lu Gui stealing in.*)

LU (*with a slight bow*): Good evening, madam.

FAN (*somewhat taken aback*): What are you doing here?

LU (*with an oily smile*): I've come to see how you're getting on, madam. I've been waiting outside the door for some time.

FAN (*calmly*): I see, outside the door, were you?

LU: That's right. (*Mysteriously.*) When I saw that Master Ping was quarrelling with you, I — (*with a mirthless smile*) I didn't like to come in.

FAN (*still poised and unruffled*): What do you want?

LU (*with complete assurance*): Well, I really came to tell you that Master Ping got drunk again tonight and came round to our place. But now, seeing that

太既然是也去了,那我就不必多说了。

繁:(嫌恶地)你现在想怎么样?

贵:(倨傲地)我想见见老爷。

繁:老爷睡觉了,你要见他什么事?

贵:没有什么,要是太太愿意办,不找老爷也可以。——(有意义地)都看太太要怎么样。

繁:(半晌,忍下来)你说吧,我也许可以帮你的忙。

贵:(重复一遍,狡黠地)要是太太愿意做主,不叫我见老爷,多麻烦。那就大家都省事了。我们只是求太太还赏饭吃。

繁:(不高兴地)你,你以为我——(转缓和)好,那也没有什么。

贵:(得意地)谢谢太太。(伶俐地)那么就请太太赏个准日子吧。

繁:(爽快地)那就后天来吧。

贵:(行礼)谢谢太太恩典!(忽然)我忘了,太太,您没见着二少爷么?

繁:没有。

贵:你刚才不是叫二少爷赏给我们一百块钱么?

繁:(烦厌地)嗯?

贵:可是,可是都叫我们少爷回了。

you were there yourself, madam, there's nothing more for me to say.

FAN (*with disgust*): What are you after now?

LU (*haughtily*): I'd like to see the master.

FAN: The master's gone to bed. What do you want to see him about?

LU: Oh, nothing important. If you'd like to see to it yourself, madam, then we needn't trouble the master. — (*With a meaningful look.*) It all depends on you, madam.

FAN (*deciding, after a pause, to put up with him*): Very well, then; tell me what it is. Perhaps I can help you.

LU (*craftily*): If you would like to handle the matter and save me seeing the master, everybody will be spared a lot of unnecessary trouble. All we want is to ask you to give us our jobs back, madam.

FAN (*crossly*): Do you suppose I — (*suddenly unbending*) very well, I think we can manage that.

LU (*pleased with himself*): Thank you, madam. (*Shrewdly.*) Then perhaps you'd fix a definite date for us to come back, madam?

FAN (*simply*): Make it the day after tomorrow, then.

LU (*bowing*): Thank you for your kindness, madam. (*Suddenly.*) Oh, I almost forgot. Have you seen Master Chong, madam?

FAN: No.

LU: Didn't you send him round to our place with a present of a hundred dollars?

FAN (*irritated*): Well?

LU: Well, you see, the money was sent back by our

雷雨

繁：你们少爷？

贵：（解释）就是大海——我那个狗食的儿子。

繁：怎么样？

贵：（很文雅地）我们的侍萍，实在还不知道呢。

繁：侍萍？（沉下脸）谁是侍萍？

中门推开。

贵：（回头）谁？

大海由中门进，衣服俱湿，脸色阴沉。繁漪惊讶地望着他。

大：（向鲁贵）你在这儿！

贵：你怎么进来的？

大：（冰冷地）铁门关着，叫不开，我爬墙进来的。

贵：你来干什么？四凤怎么样了？

大：（用一块湿手巾擦着脸上的雨水）四凤没找着，妈在门外等着呢。

贵：（觉得大海小题大做，烦恶地皱着眉毛）你别管啦，四凤一会儿就会回家。你跟我回去。周家的事情也妥了，都好了！走吧！

大：别走，——你先给我把这儿大少爷叫出来，我找不着他。

贵：（疑惧地）你又要怎么样？

大：（冷静）没什么，跟他谈谈。

own young gentleman.

FAN: Your young gentleman?

LU (*explaining*): That's to say Dahai — that wretched son of mine.

FAN: Well, what about it?

LU (*smoothly*): Well, Shiping — our Shiping, still knows nothing about it.

FAN: Shiping? (*With a look of alarm.*) Who's Shiping?

(*The centre door opens.*)

LU (*looking round*): Who is it?

(*Lu Dahai comes in, his clothes drenched and his face glum. Fanyi looks at him in astonishment.*)

HAI (*to Lu Gui*): So here you are!

LU: How did you get in?

HAI (*coldly*): The gates were shut and I couldn't make anybody hear, so I climbed over the wall.

LU: What are you doing here? What's happened to Sifeng?

HAI (*wiping the rain off his face with a wet handkerchief*): Can't find her. Mother's waiting outside.

LU (*frowning with annoyance at what he regards as a lot of fuss about nothing*): Oh, give it up. Sifeng will be back home any minute. Now you come home with me. I've fixed everything up with the Zhous here. Everything's all right now. Let's be off, then.

HAI: Not yet — not until you've got me the young gentleman here. I can't find him.

LU (*apprehensively*): What are you up to now?

HAI (*calmly*): Nothing. I just want to have a little

雷雨

贵:(不信地)不对,你大概又要——

大:(盯视)你找不找?

贵:(怯弱地)可你就跟他说两句话。

大:我告诉你,我不是打架来的。

繁:(镇静地)鲁贵,叫他来吧,我在这儿,不要紧的。

大:你去吧,可你要是不找他出来就一人跑了,你可小心!——你叫他们把门打开,让妈进来。

贵:好,好,好,完了我可就这么走了。——(低声,自语)这个小王八蛋!(走进饭厅下。)

繁:(立起)你是谁?

大:四凤的哥哥。

繁:你要见我们大少爷么?

大:嗯。

繁:(缓缓地)听说他现在就要上车。

大:(回头)什么!

繁:他现在就要走。

大:他要跑了?

繁:嗯,他!

周萍由饭厅上,一眼就看见大海。

萍:(极力镇静)哦!

大:好。你还在这儿。(回头)你叫这位太太走

chat with him.

LU (*disbelieving him*): Oh no, you don't. I know what your little game is —

HAI (*glowering at him*): Will you find him for me or won't you?

LU (*cowed*): Only if you don't do more than talk.

HAI: You can take it from me that I haven't come here to quarrel with him.

FAN (*calmly*): Go and fetch him, Lu Gui. It'll be all right with me here.

HAI: Go on, then, but if you sneak away without fetching him, you'd better look out! — And tell them to open the gate and let Mother in.

LU: All right, all right. But as soon as I've finished I'm off — (*In an undertone, to himself.*) The young bastard! (*He goes out through the dining-room.*)

FAN (getting up): Who are you?

HAI: Sifeng's brother.

FAN: You want to see Master Ping, you say?

HAI: Yes.

FAN (*easily*): I think he's just off to the station to catch a train.

HAI (*looking round*): Eh?

FAN: In fact, he's leaving immediately.

HAI: Running away, eh?

FAN: He certainly is!

(*Zhou Ping comes in from the dining-room. He catches sight of Dahai at once.*)

PING (*steadying himself with an effort*): Oh!

HAI: Ah, good, you're still here. (*Looking round.*)

开,我有话要跟你一个人说。

萍:(望着蘩漪,她不动,再走到她面前)请您上楼去吧。

蘩:好。(由饭厅下。)

半晌。大海愤恨地望着周萍。

萍:(耐不住)没想到你现在就来了。

大:(阴沉沉)听说你要走。

萍:(强笑)不过现在也赶得上,你来得还是时候。你预备怎么样?我已经准备好了。

大:(狠恶地)你准备好了?

萍:(望着大海)嗯。

大:(走到周萍面前)你!(用力打周萍的脸。)

萍:(脸上的血流下来,握着拳抑制自己)你,你,——(由袋内抽出手绢,擦脸上的血。)

大:(切齿地)哼!现在你要跑了!

半晌。

萍:(压下自己的怒气,辩白地)我早有这个计划。

大:(恶狠地笑)早有这个计划?

萍:(平静下来)我以为我们中间误会太多。

大:误会!(看自己手上的血,擦在身上)我对你没有误会,你就是一个没有血性,只顾自己

Ask the lady to leave us. I want to have a word with you alone.

PING (*looks at Fanyi, and when she does not move he goes across to her*): Please go upstairs.

FAN: All right. (*She goes out through the dining-room.*)

(*A pause. Dahai glares angrily at Zhou Ping.*)

PING (unable to bear the suspense any longer): I didn't expect to see you again so soon.

HAI (*ominously*): I hear you're going away.

PING (*forcing a smile*): It's still not too late, though. You got here in plenty of time. What is it you want? I'm ready.

HAI (*ferociously*): Ready, you say?

PING (*looking him full in the face*): Yes.

HAI (*going up to him*): Take that! (*He strikes Zhou Ping hard in the face.*)

PING (*his face bleeding, his fists clenched in an effort to control himself*): Why, you — (*He takes a handkerchief out of his pocket and wipes the blood off his face with it.*)

HAI (*grinding his teeth*): Humph! So you were going to run away!

(*A pause.*)

PING (*suppressing his anger and explaining*): I'd arranged to go away some time ago.

HAI (*with a malignant laugh*): You had, eh?

PING (*becoming calmer*): I think there are too many misunderstandings between us.

HAI: Misunderstandings! (*Notices the blood on his hand and wipes it off on his clothes.*) There isn't much I misunderstand about you! All you care

萍:(柔和地)我们两次见面,都是我性子最坏的时候,叫你得着一个最坏的印象。

大:(轻蔑地)不用推托,你是个少爷,你心地混账!你们都是吃饭太容易,有劲儿不知道怎样使,就拿着穷人家的女儿开开心,完了事可以不负一点儿责任。

萍:现在我想辩白是没有用的。我知道你是有目的而来的。(平静地)你把你的枪或者刀拿出来吧。随你收拾我。

大:你这样大方!——在你家里!你很聪明。哼,可是你不值得我这样,我现在还不愿意拿我这条有用的命换你这半死的东西。

萍:(直视大海)我想你以为我现在是怕你。你错了,与其说我怕你,不如说我怕我自己;我错了一步,不愿再错第二步。

大:(嘲笑地)我看像你这种人,活着就错了。刚才要不是我的母亲,我当时就宰了你!现在你的命还在我的手心里。

萍:我死了,那是我的福气。你以为我怕死,我不,我不,我欢迎你来。我够了,我是活厌了

about is yourself, you spineless thing!

PING (*in a soft, even voice*): We've met twice, but on both occasions I've been in a filthy temper. I'm afraid you must have got a rather bad impression of me.

HAI (*contemptuously*): Keep your excuses. You may be a young gentleman, but you act like a rat. Life's too easy for people like you. You've got plenty of surplus energy and nothing to do with it, so you pick up a poor man's daughter to amuse yourself with, then, when you've finished with her, off you go and responsibility be damned.

PING: I can see it's no use explaining anything to you now. I know you're here for something. (*Calmly.*) Well, out with your gun or your knife or whatever it is. Dispose of me as you think fit.

HAI: Very generous of you! — And in your own house, too! You're very clever. But you're not worth it. You won't catch me risking my own useful life for the sake of putting a dead-and-alive thing like you out of its misery.

PING (*looking him full in the face*): I suppose you think I'm afraid of you. Well, you're wrong. I'm more afraid of myself than I am of you. I've made one mistake, and I don't want to make another.

HAI (*scornfully*): So far as I can see, your biggest mistake was to be born. If it hadn't been for my mother, I'd have slaughtered you there and then! I hold your life in my hand even now.

PING: Death would be a welcome release for me. You imagine I'm afraid of death? Well, I'm not. Far from it — I'm glad to see you. I've had enough of

的人。

大：(厌恶地)哦,你——活厌了,可你还拉着我的妹妹陪着你,陪着你。

萍：(强笑)你说我自私么?你以为我是真没有心肝,跟她开开心就完了么?你问问你的妹妹,她知道我是真爱她。现在我活着就是为着她。

大：你倒说得很好!(突然)那你为什么——不正正当当地讲出来?

萍：(略顿)那就是我最恨的事情。我的环境太坏。你想想我这样的家庭怎么允许有这样的事。

大：(辛辣地)哦,所以你就可以一面表示你是真心爱她,跟她做出什么事都可以,一面你还得想着你的家庭,你的董事长爸爸。他们叫你随便就丢掉她,再娶一个门当户对的阔小姐来配你,对不对?

萍：我要你问问四凤,她知道我这次出去,是离开了家庭,设法脱离了父亲,有机会好跟她结婚的。

大：(嘲弄)你推得很好。那么像你深更半夜的,

life; I'm fed up with it.

HAI (*disgustedly*): Oh, so you're fed up with life, are you? — But not too much to make my sister share it with you, eh?

PING (*with a wry smile*): You mean I'm selfish? You really think I'm a heartless creature who only wants her for the amusement he can get out of her? Just ask your sister, will you? She knows I'm really in love with her. She's all I live for now.

HAI: You've got a smooth tongue, haven't you! (*Suddenly.*) Then why don't you — why don't you come out into the open with it all?

PING (*after a slight pause*): That's just what I hate myself most for. My position is an extremely difficult one. Can you imagine a family like mine approving of a thing like that?

HAI (*with pungent scorn*): So you think you can say you really do love her, and make that an excuse for doing whatever you like with her, while at the same time you say you've got to consider your family and your father's position as chairman of the board, eh? Then in the end they'll let you throw her over as and when you like so that you can marry some rich young lady who'll be a social asset to your family — is that it?

PING: I wish you'd go and ask Sifeng. She can tell you why I'm going away: it's to get away from my family and try to shake myself free of my father, so that I'll have a chance to marry her.

HAI (*mocking him*): You talked your way out of that pretty well! But how do you account for this busi-

刚才跑到我家里,你怎样说呢?

萍:(激昂地)我所说的话不是推托,我也用不着跟你推托。我现在看你是四凤的哥哥,我才这样说。我爱四凤,她也爱我。我们都年轻,我们都是人。两个人天天在一起,结果免不了有点荒唐。然而我相信我以后会对得起她,我会娶她做我的太太,我没有一点亏心的地方。

大:这么,你反而很有理了。可是,董事长大少爷,谁相信你会爱上一个工人的妹妹,一个当老妈子的穷女儿?

萍:(想了想)那,那——那我也可以告诉你。有一个女人逼着我,激成我这样的。

大:什么,还有一个女人?

萍:嗯,就是你刚才见过的那位太太。

大:她?

萍:(苦恼地)她是我的后母!——哦,我压在心里多少年,我当谁也不敢说。——她念过书,她受了很好的教育。她——她看见我就跟我发生感情,她要我——(突停)——那自然我也要负一部分责任。

ness of coming round to our place in the middle of the night?

PING (*roused*): I'm not talking my way out of anything, and I don't need to make excuses to you. I'm only telling you all this because you're Sifeng's brother. I love her. And she loves me. We're both young, and we're both human. When two young people are in each other's company day after day, something's bound to happen. But I'm sure I'll be able to do the right thing by her one day and marry her. My conscience is perfectly clear.

HAI: You'd have us believe your intentions were strictly honourable, then? And who do you imagine's going to believe that you, the boss' son and heir, had fallen in love with a poor girl whose brother's a miner and whose mother's a servant?

PING (*after some deliberation*): Well, I — er — I may as well tell you: my hand was forced by a woman who left me no alternative.

HAI: What? You mean there's another woman involved?

PING: Yes. The lady that was here just now.

HAI: Her?

PING (*distraught*): Yes, my stepmother! — All these years I've kept this secret bottled up inside me. I've never dared tell anyone. — She's had a good education and all that, but — the moment she set eyes on me she developed a passion for me and wanted me to — (*breaking off abruptly*) though of course I can't disclaim all responsibility for what happened.

大：四凤知道么？

萍：她知道,我知道她知道。(含着眼泪)那时我太糊涂,以后我越过越怕,越恨,越厌恶。我恨这种不自然的关系,你懂么？我要离开她,然而她不放松我。她拉着我,不放我。她是个鬼,她什么都不顾忌。我真活厌了,你明白么？我只要离开她,我死都愿意。过后我见着四凤,四凤叫我明白,叫我又活了一年。

大：哦。

萍：这些话多少年我对谁也说不出的,然而——(缓慢地)奇怪,我忽然跟你说了。

大：(阴沉地)这是你父亲的报应。

萍：(没想到,厌恶地)你,你——我告诉你,因为我认你是四凤的哥哥,我要你相信我的诚心,我没有一点骗她。

大：(略露善意)那么你真预备要四凤？你知道四凤是个傻孩子,她不会再嫁第二个人。

萍：(立刻)嗯,我今天走了,过了一两个月,我就来接她。

大：可是董事长少爷,这样的话叫人相信么？

HAI: Does Sifeng know about this?

PING: Yes, I'm sure of it. (*With tears in his eyes*.) I was a fool ever to have started: as time went on I became more and more afraid, and the whole business became more distasteful and hateful to me. I hated this unnatural relationship. Can you understand? I wanted to leave her, but she tightened her grip on me. She wouldn't let me go. She's a monster, capable of anything. My life was a burden to me. In the end I got so mad that I was prepared to do anything — anything to be free of her. Even death seemed preferable. And then Sifeng came along. She gave me hope — and another year of life.

HAI: I see.

PING: All this — I've never been able to bring myself to tell anybody about it, and yet — (*slowly*) the funny thing is, I've suddenly told it all to you!

HAI (*grimly*): This is a judgement on your father.

PING (*rather put out by Dahai's unexpected remark*): Why, you — ! The reason I'm telling you all this is because you're Sifeng's brother. I want you to believe that I'm sincere. I've never had the slightest intention of deceiving her.

HAI (*unbending a little*): Then you really intend to marry Sifeng? You know she's a silly girl. She'd never marry anybody else after this.

PING (*quickly*): I realize that. I'm leaving today, but in a month or two I'll be back to fetch her.

HAI: Now look here, you son-of-the-boss you, you don't expect me to swallow that, do you?

萍:(由衣袋取出一封信)你可以看这封信,这是我刚才写给她的,就说的这件事。

大:用不着给我看,我——没有工夫!

萍:(半晌,抬头)那我现在再没有什么旁的保证,你口袋里那件杀人的家伙是我的担保。你再不相信我,我现在人还是在你手里。

大:(辛酸地)周大少爷,你想想这样我就完了么?(恶狠地)你觉得我真愿意么?(忽然拿出手枪。)

萍:(惊慌)你要怎么样?

大:(狠恶地)我要杀了你。(对准周萍)你这个半死的东西!

萍:好,你来吧!(骇惧地闭上目。)

半晌。

大:(嘘出一口气,放下枪,厌恶地)你睁开眼吧!

萍:(莫名其妙)怎么?

大:(苦闷地)没有什么。我知道我的妈。我妹妹是她的命,你能够叫四凤好好地活着,我就先放过你。

周萍还想说话,大海挥手,叫他不必再说。

大:(命令地)你把我的妹妹叫出来吧。

萍:(奇怪)什么?

大:四凤——她自然在你这儿。

PING (*taking a letter out of his pocket*): You can read this letter that I've just written to her. It's all explained here.

HAI: I don't want to see it. I — I haven't got time now.

PING (*looking up after a moment's silence*): Then I'm afraid there's no other way of proving my good faith. Though that lethal weapon you've got there in your pocket should be guarantee enough. If you still don't believe me, I'm still at your mercy, you know.

HAI (*acidly*): You think I'm going to let you get away with it as easily as that? (*With a sudden ferocity.*) You really think I am? (*He suddenly whips out his pistol.*)

PING (*panic-stricken*): What are you going to do?

HAI (*fiercely*): I'm going to kill you! (*Taking aim at Zhou Ping.*) You spineless thing!

PING: All right, go on, then! (*He shuts his eyes in terror.*)

(*A pause.*)

HAI (*he exhales sharply, lowers the gun and speaks with distaste*): Open your eyes!

PING (*puzzled*): What's the matter?

HAI (*miserably*): Nothing. Only my mother. My sister is all she lives for. If you can give Sifeng a decent life, I'll let you go this once. (*Zhou Ping opens his mouth to speak, but Dahai stops him with a wave of the hand.*)

HAI (*peremptorily*): And now fetch my sister in.

PING (*bewildered*): What?

HAI: Sifeng. I take it she's here.

雷雨

萍：没有，没有。我以为她在你们家里呢。

大：（疑惑地）那奇怪，我同我妈在雨里找了她两个钟头，不见她。我想自然在这儿。

萍：（担心）她在雨里走了两个钟头，她——她没有到旁的地方去么？

大：（肯定地）半夜里她会到哪儿去？

萍：（突然恐惧）啊，她不会——

大：你以为——不，她不会。（轻蔑地）不，我想她没有这个胆量。

萍：（颤抖）不，她会的。你不知道她。她爱脸，她性子强，她——不过她应当先见我，她不该这样冒失。

半晌。

大：（忽然）哼，你装得好，你想骗过我，你？——她在你这儿！她在你这儿！

外面口哨声。

萍：（以手止之）不，你不要嚷。（哨声渐近）她，她来了！我听见她！

大：什么？

萍：这是她。我们每次见面，是这样的。

370

PING: No, no, she's not here. I thought she was at home.

HAI (*uncertainly*): Well, that's queer. Mother and I spent two hours looking for her in the rain, but there wasn't a sign of her. I naturally assumed she must be here.

PING (*anxiously*): You mean she's been out wandering around in the rain for two hours? Isn't there — anywhere else she could have gone to?

HAI (*positively*): No, where could she have gone in the middle of the night?

PING (*as a terrible suspicion crosses his mind*): No! Don't say she's gone and —

HAI: You think she's — no, she wouldn't do that. (*contemptuously*.) No, I don't think she'd have the guts.

PING (*his voice trembling*): Yes, she would. You don't know her. She's proud, and strong-willed, and she — but she should have seen me first. She shouldn't have been so rash. (*A pause*.)

HAI (*suddenly*): Humph! A fine bit of play-acting that was! Think you can put me off with tricks like that? Don't kid yourself. — She's here! She must be here!

(*A whistle is heard outside the window*.)

PING (*raising his hand for silence*): Sh! Stop shouting. (*The whistling comes nearer and nearer*.) That's her! Here she is! I can hear her!

HAI: Eh?

PING: That's her. When we meet, we always whistle first.

雷雨

大：她在哪儿？

萍：大概就在花园里。

周萍开窗吹哨。

半晌。

萍：（回头）她来了！

中门敲门声。

萍：（向大海）你先暂时在旁边屋子躲一躲。她没想到你在这儿。我想她再受不得惊了。

周萍引大海至饭厅门，大海下。

四凤的声音：萍！

萍：（跑至中门）凤儿！（开门）进来！

四凤由中门进，头发散乱，眼泪同雨水流在脸上，眼角粘着水淋淋的鬓发，呆呆地望着周萍。

四：萍！——（胆怯地）没有人吧。

萍：（难过）没有。（拉着她的手。）

四：萍！（抱着他抽咽。）

萍：你怎么，你怎么会这样？你怎么会找着我？（止不住地）你怎么进来的？

四：我从小门偷进来的。

萍：你的手冰凉，你先换一换衣服。

四：不，（抽咽）让我先看看你。

HAI: Where is she, then?

PING: Probably out in the garden.

(*He opens the window and whistles back.*)

(*A pause.*)

PING (*over his shoulder*): Here she comes!

(*There is a knock on the centre door.*)

PING (*to Dahai*): I think you'd better keep out of sight in the next room for the time being. She wouldn't be expecting to find you here. I don't think she could stand many more shocks. (*He shows Dahai into the dining-room.*)

SIFENG'S VOICE: Ping!

PING (*hurrying across to the centre door*): Feng! (*Opening the door.*) Come in!

(*Sifeng comes in, her face wet with tears and rain, and her tangled, dripping hair hanging in her eyes. She stares at Zhou Ping as if in a trance.*)

FENG: Ping! — (*Timidly.*) Anyone about?

PING (*perturbed*): No, it's all right. (*He grasps her hands.*)

FENG: Oh, Ping! (*She flings her arms round him and sobs convulsively.*)

PING: How — how did you get into such a state? How did you know I was here? (*Babbling with relief.*) How did you get in?

FENG: I slipped in through the back way.

PING: Your hands are like ice. You'd better hurry up and get those wet things off.

FENG: No — (*with a sob*) let me have a look at you first.

萍:(引她到沙发,坐在自己一旁)你,你上哪儿去了?

四:(看着周萍,含着眼泪)萍,你还在这儿,我好像隔了多年一样。

萍:我的可怜的,你怎么这样傻,你上哪儿去了?我的傻孩子!

四:我一个人在雨里跑,不知道自己在哪儿。天上打着雷,我什么都忘了,我像是听见妈在喊我,可是我怕,我拼命地跑,我想找着我们门口那一条河跳。

萍:(恐惧地)凤!

四:——可是不知怎么绕来绕去没找着。

萍:哦,凤,我对不起你,原谅我。你原谅我,不要怨我。

四:我真想死了。可是,我糊糊涂涂又碰到这儿,我忽然看见你窗户的灯,我想到你在房子里。我突然觉得,我不能死,我丢不了你。我想我们还是可以走,只要一块儿离开这儿。

萍:(沉重地)嗯,一块儿离开这儿。

四:(急切地)就是这一条路,萍,我现在已经没有家。(辛酸地)哥哥恨死我,母亲我是没有脸见的。我现在什么都没有,我没有亲戚,

PING (*taking her over to a sofa and sitting her down beside him*): But — but where have you been?

FENG (*looking at Zhou Ping with her eyes full of tears*): Here you are at last, Ping. It seems ages since I last saw you.

PING: My poor darling, how can you be so silly? But where have you been, my silly girl?

FENG: I just ran on and on in the rain until I didn't know where I was. The noise of the thunder seemed to drive everything out of my mind. I thought I heard Mother calling after me, but I was afraid, and I ran as fast as I could. I was looking for the river out in front of our place. I was going to throw myself in.

PING (*aghast*): Feng!

FENG: — But somehow I couldn't find it, though I went round and round in circles looking for it.

PING: Oh, Feng, it's all my fault. Please forgive me. Don't hold it against me.

FENG: Somehow I stumbled here in a daze. Suddenly I saw there was a light in your window and I realized you were in. All of a sudden I felt that I couldn't just die: I couldn't bear to be parted from you. I think we can still go away — only we must go away together.

PING (*solemnly*): Yes, we must go away together.

FENG (*earnestly*): It's the only way out, Ping. I've got no home to go to now. (*With feeling.*) Dahai hates me, and I just couldn't face Mother now. I've got nothing now — no family, no friends. I've got

没有朋友。我只有你,萍,你明天带我去吧。半晌。

萍:(顿)不,不。

四:(失望地)萍。

萍:(沉重地)我们现在就走。

四:(不相信地)现在就走?

萍:(怜惜地)嗯,我原来打算一个人走,以后再来接你,不过现在不必了。

四:(不信地)真的,一块儿走么?

萍:嗯,真的。

四:(狂喜地不住亲周萍的手,一面流着眼泪)真的,真的,萍,你是我的好人,你是天底下顶好顶好的人,你,你把我救了。

萍:(感动地)以后我们永远在一块儿了。

四:嗯,离开这儿了,不分开了。

萍:(立起)好,凤,走以前我们先见一个人。见完他,我们就走。

四:一个人?

萍:你哥哥。

四:哥哥?

萍:他找你,他就在饭厅里头。

四:(恐惧地)不,不,不要见他。他恨你,他会害

only you, Ping. Take me away with you tomorrow. (*A pause.*)

PING (*after a pause*): No., no.

FENG (*in despair*): Ping!

PING (*gravely*): We must go right now.

FENG (*incredulous*): What, this minute?

PING (*tenderly*): Yes. I was intending to go alone and then come back for you later, but there's no need to wait now.

FENG (*still incredulous*): You really mean it? We'll go together?

PING: Yes, I really do mean it.

FENG (*delirious with joy, she seizes Zhou Ping's hands and kisses them wildly, while the tears stream down her cheeks*): So it's true! It's true, then! Oh, Ping! You darling, you! You're the dearest darling in the whole world. You — you've saved my life!

PING (*fervently*): From now on we'll always be together.

FENG: Yes, once we get away from this place, we'll never be parted from each other.

PING (*getting up*): All right, Feng, but before we go there's someone we must see. As soon as we've done that, we'll be away.

FENG: Who do you mean?

PING: Your brother.

FENG: Dahai?

PING: He's been looking for you. He's in the dining-room there.

FENG (*frightened*): No, no, don't see him. He hates you. He'll hurt you. Let's go — let's get out —

你的。走吧,我们就走吧。

萍:我已经见过他。——我们现在一定要见他一面,(不可挽回地)不然,我们也走不了的。

四:(胆怯)可是,萍,你——

周萍走到饭厅门口,开门。

萍:(叫)鲁大海!鲁大海!——咦,他不在这儿,奇怪,也许他从饭厅的门出去了。(望着四凤。)

四:(走到周萍面前,哀告地)萍,我们走吧。(拉他向中门走)我们就这样走吧。

四凤拉周萍至中门,中门开,鲁妈与大海进。

鲁妈的样子仿佛另变了一个人,声音因为在雨里叫喊哭号已经喑哑,她似乎老了许多。

四:(惊惧)妈!

略顿。

鲁:(伸出手向四凤,哀痛地)凤儿。

四凤跑至母亲面前。

四:妈!

鲁:(抚摸四凤的头顶)孩子,我的可怜的孩子。

四:(泣不成声地)妈,饶了我吧,饶了我吧。

鲁:你为什么早不告诉我?

四:(低头)我怕,我怕您生气,看不起我,不要

quick.

PING: I've already seen him. — And now we must see him once more — (*with an air of finality*) otherwise we just won't be able to go.

FENG (*timorously*): But, Ping, you —

(*Zhou Ping goes across to the dining-room door and opens it.*)

PING (*calling*): Lu Dahai! Lu Dahai! — I say! He's gone! That's funny. He must have gone out through the other door. (*He looks at Sifeng.*)

FENG (*going up to Zhou Ping and pleading with him*): Come on, Ping, let's go. (*Dragging him towards the centre door.*) Let's go just as we are.

(*As Sifeng gets Zhou Ping to the door, it opens. Lu Ma and Lu Dahai come in.*)

(*Lu Ma looks a changed woman. She has cried and shouted herself hoarse in the rain. She seems to have aged considerably.*)

FENG (*in alarm*): Mother!

(*A slight pause.*)

MA (*in an agonized voice, her arms held out towards Sifeng*): Feng.

(*Sifeng rushes towards her mother.*)

FENG: Oh, Mother!

MA (*stroking Sifeng's head*): My child, my poor, poor child.

FENG (*sobbing quietly*): Oh, Mother, forgive me, forgive me.

MA: Why didn't you tell me earlier?

FENG (*hanging her head*): I was afraid. I was afraid you might be angry with me, and despise me, and

我，我不敢告诉您。

鲁：(沉痛地)这还是你的妈太糊涂了，我早该想到的。(酸苦地)可是这谁料得到，就会有这种事，偏偏又叫我的孩子碰着呢？妈的命苦，可你们——

大：(冷淡地)我们走吧，四凤先跟您回去。——我跟他(指周萍)商量好了，他先走，以后他再接四凤。

鲁：(迷惑)谁说的？谁说的？

大：(冷冷地望着鲁妈)妈，我知道您的意思，自然只有这么办。所以，——(顿)就让他们去吧。

鲁：什么？让他们去？

萍：(嗫嚅)鲁奶奶，您相信我，我一定好好地待她，我跟她现在就走。

鲁：(颤抖地)凤，你要跟他走？

四：(紧握着鲁妈的手)妈，我只好先离开您了。

鲁：你们不能够在一块儿！

大：(诧异)妈，您怎么？

鲁：(坚决地)不，不成！

四：妈！

鲁：四凤，我们走吧。(向大海)你出去叫一辆洋

turn me out. I just didn't dare tell you.

MA (*sorrowfully*): It's my own fault for being so stupid. I should have thought of it before. (*Bitterly*.) But who could have expected anything like this? And to think that it should have happened to my own child of all people! My own fate's been hard enough, but you —

HAI (*unemotionally*): Let's get going, then. Sifeng will be going home with you for the time being. — I've arranged everything with him — (*pointing to Zhou Ping*) he can go on in advance and come back for Sifeng later.

MA (*bewildered*): What are you saying? What are you saying?

HAI (*looking at his mother, unperturbed*): I know what's worrying you, Mother, but there's no other way out. So — (*after a pause*) we may as well let them go.

MA: What! Let them go?

PING (*hesitantly*): You can trust me, Mrs. Lu. I'll be good to her. I'm taking her with me and leaving at once.

MA (*her voice trembling*): Do you want to go with him, Feng?

FENG (*tightly gripping her mother's hands*): Mother, I'm afraid I'll have to leave you for a while.

MA: You can't live together!

HAI (*surprised*): What's the matter, Mother?

MA (*firmly*): No! It wouldn't do!

FENG: Mother!

MA: Sifeng, we're going home. (*To Dahai*.) Go and

车，四凤大概走不动了。我们走，赶快走。

四：(死命地退缩)妈，您不能这样做。

鲁：不，不成！(呆板地)走，走。

四：(哀求)妈，您愿您的女儿急得要死在您的眼前么？

萍：(走向鲁妈前)鲁奶奶，我知道我对不起你。不过我能尽我的力量补我的错，现在事情已经做到这一步，你——

大：妈，(不懂)您是怎么啦。

鲁：(严厉地)你先雇车去！(向四凤)凤儿，你听着，我情愿没有你，我不能叫你跟他在一块儿。——走吧！

大海刚至门口；四凤喊一声。

四：啊，妈妈！(晕倒在母亲怀里。)

鲁：(抱着四凤)我的孩子，你——

萍：(急)她晕过去了。

鲁：(按着四凤的前额，低声唤)四凤。

周萍向饭厅跑。

大：不要紧，一点凉水就好。她小时就这样。

周萍拿凉水灌在四凤面上，四凤渐醒。

call a rickshaw. I don't suppose Sifeng can do any more walking. We must go — as fast as we can!

FENG (*recoiling from her in desperation*): You can't do this to me, Mother!

MA: It wouldn't do, I say. (*Woodenly.*) Come on, we must go.

FENG (*imploring her*): Do you want to drive your daughter to distraction and see her die of worry before your very eyes?

PING (*going up to Lu Ma*): Mrs. Lu, I know I've done you wrong, but I'll do my best to make up for it. Now that things have come to such a pass, you —

HAI (*at a loss to understand his mother's behaviour*): What's the matter with you, Mother?

MA (*sternly*): You go and get a rickshaw! (*To Sifeng.*) Now listen to me, Feng: I'd rather lose you than see you living with him! — Come on, then.
(*Just as Dahai gets to the door, Sifeng screams.*)

FENG: A — a — ah! Mother! (*She faints into her mother's arms.*)

MA (*holding her in her arms*): My child! You —

PING (*agitated*): She's fainted.

MA (*feeling Sifeng's forehead and softly calling her name*): Sifeng.
(*Zhou Ping runs towards the dining-room.*)

HAI: Don't panic: a drop of cold water and she'll be all right. She was like that when she was little.
(*Zhou Ping gets some cold water and sprinkles it on Sifeng's face. She gradually comes to.*)

鲁:(拿凉水灌四凤)好孩子,你回来,回来。

四:(喘出一口气)啊,妈!

鲁:(安慰她)孩子,你不要怪妈心狠,妈的苦说不出。

四:(叹出一口气)妈!

鲁:什么?

四:(向周萍)我,我不能不告诉你。

萍:凤,你好点了?

四:我,我总是瞒着你,对您(乞怜地望着鲁妈)也不能讲。

鲁:什么,孩子。

四:(抽咽)我,——我跟他现在已经……(大哭。)

鲁:怎么,你说你——(讲不下去。)

萍:(拉起四凤的手)四凤!真的,你——

四:(哭)嗯。

萍:什么时候?什么时候?

四:(低头)大概已经三个月。

萍:哦,四凤,你为什么不告诉我,我,我的——

鲁:(低声)天哪。

萍:(走向鲁妈)鲁奶奶,你无论如何不要再固执哪,都是我错了。我求你!我求你放了她吧。我敢保我以后对得起她,对得起你。

MA (*splashing more cold water on her face*): Wake up, wake up, Sifeng.
FENG (*drawing a deep breath*): Ah, Mother.
MA (*trying to comfort her*): Don't be hard on me, child. I'm not being hard-hearted. I just can't tell you what I'm going through.
FENG (*sighing deeply*): Mother.
MA: What is it?
FENG (*to Zhou Ping*): I — there's something I've got to tell you.
PING: Feel better now, Feng?
FENG: I — I've been keeping it from you all the time. (*Looking piteously at her mother.*) I couldn't even bring myself to tell you, Mother.
MA: What is it, child?
FENG (*sobbing*): I — we're going to have a — (*She breaks down in a flood of tears.*)
MA: What? You mean you — (*Words fail her.*)
PING (*seizing Sifeng's hand*): Sifeng! You mean it? You —
FENG (*weeping*): Yes.
PING: But when? How long?
FENG (*hanging her head*): About three months now.
PING: But, Sifeng, why didn't you tell me? I — oh, my —
MA (*hoarsely*): My God!
PING (*going over to Lu Ma*): You just can't stand in our way now, Mrs. Lu. It's all my fault. Now, please, *please* let her go. I give you my word I'll be worthy of her, and a credit to you.

四:(走到鲁妈面前跪下)妈,您可怜可怜我们,答应我们,让我们走吧。

鲁:(不做声,坐着,发痴)我是在做梦。我的儿女,我自己生的儿女,三十年工夫——哦,天哪,(掩面哭,挥手)你们走吧,我不认得你们。(转过头去。)

萍:那么,(立起)我们走吧。

四凤起。

鲁:(不自主地)不,不能够!

四:(又跪下,哀求)妈,您是怎么?我的心定了。不管他是谁,我是他的了。我心里第一个许了他,我看得见的只有他,妈,我现在到了这一步:他到哪儿,我也到哪儿;他是什么,我也跟他是什么。妈,您难道不明白,我——

鲁:(叫四凤不要往下说,苦痛地)孩子。

大:现在既然是这样,让她去了也好。

萍:鲁奶奶,您要是一定不放她,我们只好不顺从您,自己走了。——凤!

四:(摇头)不,(还望着鲁妈)妈!

鲁:(低声)啊,天知道谁犯了罪,谁造的这种孽!——他们都是可怜的孩子,不知道自己做的是什么。天哪,如果要罚,也罚在我一

FENG (*going down on her knees at her mother's feet*): Have pity on us, Mother. Say "yes" and let us go.

MA (*sitting there in a daze, unable to speak for a moment*): I must be dreaming. My children, my own children, after thirty years — oh, my God! (*She buries her face in her hands and bursts into tears, then waves them away.*) Go away! I don't know you! (*She turns her face away.*)

PING: In that case — (*rising*) we'd better go.

(*Sifeng gets to her feet again.*)

MA (*unable to control herself*): No, you can't do it!

FENG (*falling on her knees again and pleading with her*): What's the matter with you, Mother? My mind's made up. Whoever he is, I belong to him now. My heart was promised to him from the very first, and there can never be anybody else for me but him. I've got now so that wherever he goes I'll go with him and whatever he does I'll do too. Can't you understand, Mother, that I —

MA (*stopping her with a gesture, distressed*): Child!

HAI: Well, things being as they are, I don't see why we shouldn't let her go.

PING: Mrs. Lu, if you refuse to let her go, we'll have no alternative but to disobey you and just go. — Feng!

FENG (*shaking her head*): No — (*still looking up at Lu Ma*) Mother!

MA (*in a low voice*): Oh, God knows what this is a punishment for — what have I ever done to bring such a calamity down on our heads? — My poor

个人身上；我一个人有罪，我先走错了一步。（伤心地）他们是我的干净孩子，他们应当好好地活着。冤孽是在我心里头，苦也应当我一个人尝。（立起，望着天）今天晚上，是我让他们一块儿走的。这罪过我知道，可是罪过我现在替他们担戴了；所有的罪孽都是我一个人惹的，我的儿女们都是好孩子，心地干净的，那么，要是真有了什么，也就让我一个人担戴吧。（回过头）凤儿，——

四：（不安地）妈，您怎么，您说的是什么？

鲁：（回转头）没有什么。（和缓地）你起来，你们一块儿走吧。

四：（立起，抱着她的母亲）妈！

萍：走，（看表）不早了，只有二十五分钟，叫他们把车子开出来，走吧。

鲁：（沉静地）不，凤儿，你们这次走，是偷偷地走，在黑地里走，不要惊动人。（向大海）大海，你去叫车去，我要回去了，你送他们到车站。

大：嗯。（由中门下。）

children, they didn't know what they were doing. Oh, God, if anyone has to be punished, why can't it just be me? It's my fault and no one else's: it all began when I took the first false step. (*Heart-broken.*) They're my innocent children; they deserve a chance in life. The guilt is here in my heart, and I should be the one to suffer for it. (*She rises to her feet and looks heavenwards.*) And tonight, here I am letting them go away together. I know I'm doing wrong, but this way the responsibility will all be mine; all this trouble was caused by me in the first place. My children haven't done anything wrong: they're too good and innocent to do anything wrong. If there must be a punishment, let me bear it — alone. (*Looking away.*) Feng —

FENG (*uneasily*): What's the matter with you, Mother? What are you talking about?

MA (*turning her face away*): It doesn't matter. (*Gently.*) Now get up. And go. Both of you.

FENG (*getting up and embracing her mother*): Oh, Mother!

PING: Come on, then. (*Looking at his watch.*) We haven't got much time. Only twenty-five minutes before the train goes. Tell them to get the car out. Come on.

MA (*calmly*): No, don't do that, Feng. If you're going away secretly like this in the middle of the night, it would be best not to attract too much attention. (*To Dahai.*) Dahai, you can go and get a rickshaw. I'm going home now. You can see them off at the station.

HAI: All right. (*He goes out through the centre*

雷雨

鲁:(向四凤,哀婉地)过来,我的孩子,让我好好地亲一亲。

四凤过来抱母亲。

鲁:(向周萍)你也来,让我也看你一下。

周萍至前,低头。

鲁:(望周萍,擦眼泪)好,你们走吧!——我要你们两个在走以前答应我一件事。

萍:您说吧。

鲁:你们不答应,我还是不要四凤走的。

四:妈,你说吧,我答应。

鲁:(看他们两人)你们这次走,最好越走越远,不要回头。今天离开,他们无论生死,就永远不要见我了。

四:(难过)妈,不——

萍:(使眼色,低声)她现在难过,——过后,就好了。

四:嗯,好,——妈,那我们走吧。(跪下,向鲁妈叩头;落泪。)

鲁妈竭力忍着。

鲁:(挥手)走吧!

萍:我们从饭厅里出去吧,饭厅里还放着我几件东西。

door.)

MA (*to Sifeng, with a sad tenderness*): Come here, my child. Let me kiss you good-bye.

(*Sifeng goes up to her mother and embraces her.*)

MA (*to Zhou Ping*): You come here, too. Let me have a look at you.

(*Zhou Ping goes and stands in front of Lu Ma, his head bent.*)

MA (*looking at him and wiping her eyes*): Go on, then. Off you go. — I want you both to promise me one thing before you go, though.

PING: What is it?

MA: If you don't promise, then I won't let Sifeng go after all.

FENG: Tell us what it is, Mother. I'll promise.

MA (*looking from one to the other*): When you go, you'd best go as far as you can and never come back. Once you've left tonight, you must never see me again as long as you live.

FENG (*in distress*): Oh, Mother, don't —

PING (*tipping her a wink and whispering*): She's overwrought just now — will be all right later on.

FENG: Yes, all right, then. — We'll be off now, then, Mother.

(*Her eyes fill with tears as she kneels for a farewell kowtow to her mother.*)

(*Lu Ma is controlling her own emotions with an effort.*)

MA (*waving them away*): Off you go, then.

PING: Let's go out through the dining-room. I've still got some of my things in there.

周萍，四凤，鲁妈走到饭厅门口。饭厅门开，繁漪走出。

四：(失声)太太！

繁：(沉稳地)咦，你们到哪儿去？外面还打着雷呢！

萍：(向繁漪)怎么你一个人在外面偷听！

繁：嗯，不只我，还有人呢。(向饭厅走)出来呀，你！

周冲由饭厅上，畏缩的。

四：(惊愕)二少爷！

冲：(不安地)四凤！

萍：(不高兴)弟弟，你怎么这样不懂事？

冲：(莫名其妙)妈叫我来的，我不知道你们这是干什么。

繁：(冷冷地)现在你就明白了。

萍：(焦燥，向繁漪)你这是干什么？

繁：(嘲弄地)我叫你弟弟来给你们送行。

萍：(气愤)你真卑鄙。——

冲：哥哥！

萍：(向周冲)对不起！——(突向繁漪)不过世界上没有像你这样的母亲！

冲：(迷惑地)妈，这是怎么回事？

繁：你看哪！(向四凤)四凤，你预备上哪儿去？

(*Just as the three of them get to the dining-room door, it opens and Fanyi comes in.*)

FENG (*involuntarily*): Madam!

FAN (*with composure*): Why, where are you all going? There's still a thunderstorm on outside, you know!

PING (*to Fanyi*): So you've been eavesdropping at the door, have you?

FAN: Yes, and I'm not the only one. There's someone else here. (*Turning back to the dining-room.*) Come out, you! (*A sheepish Zhou Chong emerges from the dining-room.*)

FENG (*startled*): Master Chong!

CHONG (*disconcerted*): Hullo, Sifeng!

PING (*annoyed*): I didn't expect such behaviour from you, Chong.

CHONG (*still at sea*): It was Mother who told me to come here. I'd no idea what was going on.

FAN (*coldly*): You'll know soon enough.

PING (*to Fanyi, fuming*): Now what's the meaning of all this?

FAN (mockingly): I just wanted your brother to come and give you a send-off.

PING (*furiously*): What a dirty, mean trick! —

CHONG: Now, Ping!

PING (*to Zhou Chong*): I'm sorry! (*Rounding abruptly on Fanyi again.*) But there isn't another mother like you on earth!

CHONG (*bewildered*): What's going on, then, Mother?

FAN: See for yourself! (*To Sifeng.*) Where are you going, Sifeng?

四:(嗫嚅)我……我?……

萍:不要说一句瞎话。告诉他们,说我们预备一块儿走。

冲:(明白)什么,四凤,你预备跟他一块儿走?

四:嗯,二少爷,我,我是——

冲:(半质问地)你为什么早不告诉我?

四:我不是不告诉你,我跟你说过,叫你不要找我,因为我——我已经不是个——

萍:(向四凤)不,你告诉他们!(指繁漪)讲,说你就要嫁我!

冲:(略惊)四凤,你——

繁:(向周冲)现在你明白了。

周冲低头。

萍:(突向繁漪,刻毒地)你真没有一点心肝!你以为他会替——会破坏么?冲弟弟,你说,你现在有什么意思,你说,你预备对我怎么样?你说吧。

周冲望繁漪,又望四凤,自己低头。

繁:冲儿,说呀!(半晌,急促)冲儿,你为什么不说话呀?你为什么不问?为什么不问你哥哥?(又顿。)

众人俱看周冲,周冲不语。

繁:冲儿,你说呀,怎么,难道你是个死人?哑

FENG (*falteringly*): I — er – I —

PING: Nothing silly, now. Tell them we're going away together.

CHONG (*now that the light has dawned*): What's this, Sifeng? You're going away with him?

FENG: Yes, Master Chong. I — I'm —

CHONG (*somewhat reproachfully*): Then why didn't you tell me so before?

FENG: But I did: I told you to leave me alone because I — I was no longer a —

PING (*to Sifeng*): Go on, tell them all about it! (*Pointing to Fanyi.*) Tell her that you're going to marry me!

CHONG (*rather taken aback*): Sifeng, you —

FAN (*to Zhou Chong*): Now you know what it's all about.

(*Zhou Chong hangs his head.*)

PING (*rounding on Fanyi with a sudden viciousness*): You spiteful creature! You think he'll spoil everything to help you? Well, Chong? What ideas have you got on the subject? Eh? What are you going to do about it? Eh?

(*Zhou Chong looks from his mother to Sifeng, then hangs his head in silence.*)

FAN: Come on, Chong! (*After a pause, more insistently.*) Why don't you say something, Chong? Why don't you ask him? Why don't you ask your brother something?

(*Another pause. Everybody looks at Zhou Chong, who stands mute.*)

FAN: Say something, Chong! You're not dead, are

巴？是个糊涂孩子？你难道看见这样的事情还不会吭一声么？

冲：（抬头，羔羊似地）不，妈！（又望四凤，低头）只要四凤愿意，我没有什么。

萍：（走到周冲面前）弟弟，我的明白弟弟！

冲：（疑惑地）不，我忽然发现……我觉得……我好像我并不是真爱四凤。（渺渺茫茫地）以前——我——大概是糊闹。（望着周萍热烈的神色，退缩地）不，你把她带走吧，只要你好好地待她！

繁：（幻灭）哦，你呀！（忽然气愤）你不是我的儿子，（昏乱地）你真没有点男人气，我要是你，（对四凤）我就打了她，烧了她，杀了她。你真是糊涂虫，一点生气也没有。我看错你了——你不是我的，不是我的儿子。

冲：（难过地）您怎么啦？

繁：（向周冲，半疯狂地）你不要以为我是你的母亲，（高声）你的母亲早死了，早叫你父亲压死了，闷死了。（揩眼泪，哀痛地）我忍了多少年了，我在这个死地方，监狱似的周公馆，

you? Or dumb? Or are you just a stupid child? Surely you're not just going to stand there with all this going on and not make a murmur?

CHONG (*lifting his head and replying with a lamb-like bleat*): No, Mother. (*He looks at Sifeng again, then hangs his head.*) So long as Sifeng is willing, I've no objection.

PING (*going up to Zhou Chong*): Spoken like a sensible fellow, Chong!

CHONG (*with a puzzled frown*): No. I've suddenly realized — it's just come to me — that I wasn't really in love with Sifeng after all. (*Staring abstractedly into space.*) What I felt about her was — probable only a silly infatuation. (*Shrinking back from the triumphant Zhou Ping.*) Yes. take her away with you — only be good to her.

FAN (*all her hopes dashed*): Ugh, you! (*With a sudden fury.*) You're no son of mine! (*Incoherently.*) You're no man at all! If I were you — (*turning on Sifeng*) I'd smash her, burn her, kill her! You're just a poor, feeble idiot — not a spark of life in you! I should have known better — you're none of mine — no son of mine!

CHONG (*pained*): What's the matter with you, Mother?

FAN (*to Zhou Chong, hysterically*): Don't think I'm your mother. (*Raising her voice.*) Your mother died long ago. She was crushed and smothered by your father. (*Wiping her eyes, in an anguished voice.*) After all these eighteen years of misery in this soul-destroying place, this "residence of the

陪着一个阎王十八年了,我的心并没有死;你的父亲只叫我生了冲儿,然而我的心,我这个人还是我的。(指周萍)就只有他才要了我整个的人,可是他现在不要我,又不要我了。

冲:(痛极)妈,我最爱的妈,您这是怎么回事?

萍:你先不要管她,她在发疯!

繁:(激烈地)你现在也学会你的父亲了,你这虚伪的东西! 没有疯——我一点也没有疯! 我要你说,我要你告诉他们——这是我最后的一口气!

萍:(狠狠地)你叫我说什么? 我看你上楼睡去吧。

繁:(冷笑)你不要装! 你告诉他们,我并不是你的后母。

大家俱惊,略顿。

冲:(无可奈何地)妈!

繁:(不顾地)告诉他们,告诉四凤,告诉她!

四:(忍不住)妈呀! (投入鲁妈怀。)

繁:你记着,是你才欺骗了你的弟弟,是你欺骗了我,是你才欺骗了你的父亲! (冷笑。)

Zhou family" that's more like a prison, married to a hateful tyrant — after all these years my spirit is still not dead. Your father may have made me have you, Chong, but my heart — my soul is still my own. (*Pointing to Zhou Ping.*) *He's* the only one that's ever possessed me body and soul. But now he doesn't want me, he doesn't want me any more.

CHONG (*considerably distressed*): Mother, my dearest mother, what *is* all this about?

PING: Take no notice of her. She's going off her head!

FAN (*heatedly*): Copying your father now, are you? You hypocrite, you! No, I'm not mad — not in the least! And now it's your turn to speak, and tell them all about it — it's my last chance to get even with you!

PING (*embarrassed*): What is there for me to tell? I think you'd better go up to bed.

FAN (*sneering*): Stop pretending! Tell them that I'm not your stepmother at all.

(*General astonishment. A short pause.*)

CHONG (*at his wit's end*): Mother!

FAN (*recklessly*): Go on, tell them. Tell Sifeng. Go on, tell her!

FENG (overcome): Oh, Mother! (She throws herself into her mother's arms.

FAN: Remember: it was you, and you alone, that deceived your brother, and deceived me, and deceived your father!

(*She looks at him with a contemptuous sneer.*)

萍：(向四凤)不要理她,我们走吧。

繁：不用走,大门锁了。你父亲就下来,我派人叫他来的。

鲁：天!

萍：你这是干什么?

繁：(冷冷地)我要你父亲见见他将来的好媳妇你们再走。(喊)朴园,朴园!……

冲：妈,您不要!

萍：(走到蘩漪面前)疯子,你敢再喊!

蘩漪跑到书房门口,喊。

鲁：(慌)四凤,我们出去。

繁：不,他来了!

周朴园由书房进,大家俱不动,静寂若死。

朴：(在门口)你叫什么?你还不上楼去睡?

繁：(倨傲地)我请你见见你的好亲戚。

朴：(见鲁妈,四凤在一起,惊)啊,你,你——你们这是做什么?

繁：(拉四凤向周朴园)这是你的媳妇,你见见。(指着周朴园向四凤)叫他爸爸!(指着鲁妈向周朴园)你也认识认识这位老太太。

鲁：太太!

繁：萍,过来!当着你的父亲,过来,给这个妈叩

PING (*to Sifeng*): Take no notice of her. Let's get out of here.

FAN: You wouldn't get far. The gate's locked. Your father will be down any minute. I've sent for him.

MA: God!

PING: What are you trying to do?

FAN (*with icy calm*): I want your father to meet his dear future daughter-in-law before you leave. (*Calling her husband.*) Puyuan! Puyuan! —

CHONG: Mother, please!

PING (*advancing on Fanyi*): Don't you dare shout again, you lunatic!

(*Fanyi runs to the door of the study and shouts again.*)

MA (*in great agitation*): Let's get out of here, Sifeng.

FAN: No. He's coming!

(*Zhou Puyuan comes in from the study. There is a deathly hush, and no one moves an inch.*)

ZHOU (*in the doorway*): What's all the shouting for? You ought to be in bed by now.

FAN (*haughtily*): I want you to meet some relatives of yours.

ZHOU (*amazed to find Lu Ma and Sifeng here*): Why, what the — what are you two doing here?

FAN (*taking Sifeng's hand and turning to Puyuan*): Let me introduce your daughter-in-law. (*To Sifeng, indicating Puyuan.*) Say hullo to your father! (*Then to Puyuan, indicating Lu Ma.*) And I'd like you to meet this lady here, too!

MA: Oh, madam!

FAN: Come here, Ping! You can pay your respects to

雷雨

　　头。

萍：(难堪)爸爸,我,我——

朴：(明白地)怎么——(向鲁妈)侍萍,你到底还是回来了。

繁：(惊)什么?

鲁：(慌)不,不,您弄错了。

朴：(悔恨地)侍萍,我想你也会回来的。

鲁：不,不！(低头)啊！天！

繁：(惊愕地)侍萍！什么,她是侍萍?

朴：(烦厌地)你不必再故意地问我。她就是萍儿的母亲,三十年前死了的。

繁：天哪！

　　半晌。四凤苦闷地叫了一声,望着她的母亲,鲁妈苦痛地低着头。周萍迷惑地望着父亲同鲁妈。这时繁漪渐渐移到周冲身边,她逐渐感受到另外一些人的更不幸的命运。

朴：(沉痛地)萍儿,你过来。你的生母并没有死,她还在世上。

萍：(半狂地)不是她！爸,不是她！

朴：(严厉地)混账！不许胡说。她没有什么好身世,也是你的母亲。

萍：(痛苦万分)哦,爸！

朴：(尊重地)不要以为你跟四凤同母,觉得脸上

your new mother now that your father's here.
PING (*embarrassed*): Father, I — I —
ZHOU (*taking in the situation*): Why — (*To Lu Ma.*) So you've come back again after all, Shiping.
FAN (*startled*): What?
MA (*desperately*): No, no, you're mistaken.
ZHOU (*remorsefully*): Yes, Shiping, I thought you'd be back.
MA: No! No! (*Hanging her head.*) Oh, God!
FAN (*stupefied*): Shiping? You mean she's Shiping?
ZHOU (*irritated*): Don't start pretending you didn't konw, and asking silly questions. She's Ping's mother, the one that died thirty years ago.
FAN: In Heaven's name!
(*A long silence, broken only by a cry of anguish from Sifeng as she stares at her mother, who sits there with her head bent, as if in pain. Dazedly, Zhou Ping's eyes travel from his father to Lu Ma, while Fanyi steals round to Zhou Chong. She is gradually becoming aware that a far greater tragedy than her own is unfolding before her eyes.*)

ZHOU (*with a heavy heart*): Ping, come here. Your own mother never died at all. She's here, alive.
PING (*beside himself*): No, it can't be her! Father, say it's not her!
ZHOU (*severely*): Idiot! Don't talk such utter nonsense! She may not be from a good family but she's your mother just the same.
PING (*in utter despair*): Oh, Father!
ZHOU (*seriously*): Don't forget that you owe her something for bringing you into the world, even if

不好看,你就忘了人伦天性。

四:(痛苦地)哦,妈!

朴:(沉重地)萍儿,你原谅我。我一生就做错了这一件事。我万没有想到她今天还在,今天找到这儿。我想这只能说是天命。(向鲁妈叹口气)我老了,刚才我叫你走,我很后悔,我预备寄给你两万块钱。现在你既然来了,我想萍儿是个孝顺孩子,他会好好地侍奉你。我对不起你的地方,他会补上的。

萍:(向鲁妈)您——您是我的——

鲁:(不自主地)萍——(回头抽咽。)

朴:跪下,萍儿!不要以为自己是在做梦,这是你的生母。

四:(昏乱地)妈,这不会是真的。

鲁妈不语。

繁:(向周萍,悔恨地)萍,我,我万想不到是——是这样,萍——

萍:(向周朴园)爸爸!(向鲁妈)母亲!

四:(与周萍互相望着,忽然忍不住)啊,天!(由中门跑下。)

周萍扑在沙发上,鲁妈死气沉沉地立着。

it is a bit of a blow to find that Sifeng's your half-sister.

FENG (*overcome with grief*): Oh, Mother!

ZHOU (*despondently*): Forgive me, Ping. This was the only real mistake I ever made. I never imagined for one moment that she was still alive and that one day she'd find us here. I can only put it down to divine justice. (*Turning to Lu Ma with a sigh.*) I'm getting old now. I felt very sorry after I told you to go this afternoon, and I've arranged to have twenty thousand dollars sent to you. Now that you've come back again, I think Ping will be a good son to you and look after you. He'll help to make amends for the wrong I did you.

PING (*to Lu Ma*): So you — you're my —

MA (*unable to control herself any longer*): Oh, Ping! — (*She turns her head away and sobs.*)

ZHOU: Down on your knees to her, Ping! You're not dreaming. She's your mother.

FENG (*in utter bewilderment*): This can't be true, Mother.

(*Lu Ma makes no reply.*)

FAN (*to Zhou Ping, repentantly*): I never expected it to — to turn out like this, Ping! —

PING (*to Puyuan*): Father! (*To Lu Ma.*) Mother!

FENG (*she and Zhou Ping stare at one another until, suddenly, she can bear it no longer*): Oh, my God! (*She rushes out through the centre door.*)
(*Zhou Ping throws himself down on the sofa and buries his head in his arms. Lu Ma stands motionless, lifeless.*)

繁：(急喊)四凤！四凤！(转向周冲)冲儿，她的样子不大对，你赶快出去看看她。

周冲由中门跑下，喊四凤。

朴：(至周萍前)萍儿，这是怎么回事？

萍：(突然)你不该生我！(由饭厅跑下。)

远处听见四凤的惨叫声，周冲狂呼四凤，过后周冲也发出惨叫。

鲁：(叫)四凤，你怎么啦！

繁：(同时叫)我的孩子，我的冲儿！

鲁妈同繁漪由中门跑出。

朴：(急走至窗前拉开窗幕，颤声)怎么？怎么？

仆人由中门跑上。

仆人：(喘)老爷！

朴：快说，怎么啦？

仆人：(急不成声)四凤……死了……

朴：(急)二少爷呢？

仆人：也……也死了。

朴：(颤声)不，不，怎……么？

仆人：四凤碰着那条走电的电线。二少爷不知

FAN (*calling anxiously*): Sifeng! Sifeng! (*Turning to Zhou Chong.*) I don't like the look of this, Chong. You'd better hurry out and find her.

(*Zhou Chong runs out through the centre door, calling after Sifeng.*)

ZHOU (*going up to Zhou Ping*): Now, Ping, what's all this about?

PING (*bursting out*): You should never have fathered me!

(*He runs out through the dining-room.*)

(*Suddenly, a scream is heard from Sifeng in the distance, followed by Zhou Chong's frantic shouting of "Sifeng! Sifeng!" Then comes a scream from Zhou Chong.*)

MA (*shouting*): Sifeng, what's happened?

FAN (*simultaneously*): Chong! My boy!

(*They both run out through the centre door.*)

ZHOU (*hurries to the window, pulls aside the curtain, and quavers*): What's happened? What's happened?

(*A servant comes running in through the centre door.*)

SERVANT (*gasping*): Sir!

ZHOU: Quick! What's happened?

SERVANT (*in a panic-stricken gabble*): Sifeng — she's — she's dead!

ZHOU (*aghast*): What about Chong?

SERVANT: He's — he's dead, too.

ZHOU (*in a trembling voice*): No! .... No! What — what happened?

SERVANT: Sifeng ran into the electric cable. It's live.

道,赶紧拉了一把,两个人一块儿中电死了。

朴:这不会。这,这,——这不能够,不能够!

周朴园与仆人跑下。

周萍由饭厅出,颜色惨白,但神气是沉静的。他走到方桌前打开抽屉,取出手枪,走进右边书房。外面人声嘈乱,哭声,叫声,混成一片。鲁妈由中门上。老年仆人跟在后面,拿着电筒。

鲁妈一声不响地立在台中。

老仆人:(安慰地)老太太,您别发呆! 这不成,您得哭,你得好好哭一场。

鲁:(无神地)我哭不出来!

老仆人:这是没有法子的事,——可是您得哭哭。

鲁:不,我,我——(呆立)。

中门大开,许多仆人围着蘩漪,蘩漪不知是在哭在笑。

仆人:(在外面)进去吧,太太,别看哪。

蘩漪为人拥至中门,倚门怪笑。

Master Chong didn't know about it, and he caught hold of her. They were both electrocuted.

ZHOU: No, it can't be true! It's — it's impossible! Just impossible! (*He hurries out with the servant.*)

(*Zhou Ping comes in from the dining-room. He is deathly pale, yet his manner is perfectly calm. He goes over to the square table, opens the drawer and takes out a pistol. Then he goes into the study.*)

(*There is a hubbub of voices outside — a babel of weeping, shouting, and altercation. Lu Ma comes in through the centre door, followed by an old servant with a torch.*)

(*Lu Ma stands silent in the centre of the stage.*)

OLD SERVANT (*trying to comfort her*): Now come on, my dear, don't stand there dumb. What you want is a good cry. You'll feel better when you've had a good cry.

MA (*expressionless*): I can't cry!

OLD SERVANT: Well, there's nothing else you can do now — now come on, you must have a cry.

MA: No, I — I — (*She stands there in a daze.*)

(*The centre door is flung wide open and Fanyi appears in the doorway, supported by a number of servants. It is difficult to decide whether she is laughing or crying.*)

SERVANT (*behind her in the doorway*): You'd best go in, madam, and not look.

(*The servants shepherd her into the room, but she stops just inside the door. She leans against the*

雷雨

繁：冲儿，你这么张着嘴？你的样子怎么直对我笑？——冲儿，你这个糊涂孩子。

周朴园走进中门。

朴：蘩漪，进来！我的手发木，你也别看了。

老仆人：太太，进来吧。人已经叫电火烧焦了，没有法子办了。

繁：(进来干哭)冲儿，我的好孩子。刚才还是好好的，你怎么会死，你怎么会死得这样惨？

朴：你要静一静。(擦眼泪。)

繁：(狂笑)冲儿，你该死，该死！你有了这样的母亲，你该死！

外面仆人与大海打架声。

朴：这是谁？谁在这时候打架。

老仆下问，立时另一仆人上。

朴：外面是怎么回事？

仆人：今天早上那个鲁大海，他这时又来了，跟我们打架。

朴：叫他进来！

仆人：老爷，他连踢带打地伤了我们好几个，他

door-post in a fit of hysterical laughter.)

FAN: Why are you gaping at me like that, Chong? Why are you smiling at me like that? — Oh, Chong, my silly boy!

(*Zhou Puyuan comes in through the centre door.*)

ZHOU: Come on in, Fanyi! My hands feel numb. You mustn't look at them any more.

OLD SERVANT: Come on in, madam. They're burned to a cinder, and there's nothing anybody can do about it now.

FAN (*coming forward into the room, convulsed with sobs*): Chong, my boy, my boy! You were alive and well a moment ago. How can you be dead — so horribly dead?

ZHOU: Steady, now. Steady. (*He wipes his eyes.*)

FAN (*laughing hysterically*): You deserve to die, Chong, you deserve to die! With a mother like me you deserve to die!

(*From outside comes the noise of a scuffle between Lu Dahai and the servants.*)

ZHOU: Who's that? Who's that making a disturbance at a time like this?

(*The old servant goes out to find out. Another servant comes in immediately.*)

ZHOU: What's going on out there?

SERVANT: It's that Lu Dahai again, the one who was here this morning. He's back again now, and starting a fight with us.

ZHOU: Tell him to come in.

SERVANT: He's gone now, sir. Got out the back way. — After he'd done quite a bit of damage to some

已经从小门跑了。

朴：跑了？

仆人：是，老爷。

朴：(忽然)追他去，给我追他去。

仆人：是，老爷。

　　仆人一齐下。屋中只有周朴园，鲁妈，蘩漪三人。

朴：(哀伤地)我丢了一个儿子，不能再丢第二个了。

　　周朴园，鲁妈，蘩漪都坐下来。

鲁：都去吧！让他去了也好，我知道这孩子。他恨极了，我知道，他不会回来的。

朴：(寂静，自己觉得奇怪)年轻的反而走在我们前头了，现在就剩下我们这些老——(忽然)萍儿呢？大少爷呢？萍儿，(无人应)来人呀！来人！(无人应)你们给我找呀，我的大儿子呢？

　　书房枪声，屋内死一般的静默。

蘩：(忽然)啊！(跑下书房，周朴园呆立不动，立时蘩漪狂喊跑出)他……他……

朴：他……他……

　　周朴园与蘩漪一同跑下，进书房。

——剧终

一九三三年

of us with his fists and his feet.

ZHOU: Got away, you say?

SERVANT: Yes, sir.

ZHOU (*suddenly*): Go after him, then, and bring him back here.

SERVANT: Very good, sir.

(*All the servants go out, leaving only Puyuan, his wife and Lu Ma in the room.*)

ZHOU (*broken-hearted*): I've lost one son. I can't afford to lose another.

(*They all sit down.*)

MA: Let them all go! Perhaps it's best that he has gone. I know what the boy's like. He's bursting with hatred. He won't come back.

ZHOU (*as if bewildered by the sudden quiet*): It doesn't seem true that the youngsters have gone first and left us old — (*Suddenly.*) Ping! Where's Ping? Ping! Ping! (*No reply.*) Come here, somebody! Where are you all? (*Still no reply.*) Go and find him for me! Where's my eldest son? (*The sound of a pistol shot from the study is followed by a deathly silence in the room.*)

FAN (*suddenly*): Oh! (*she runs into the study. Puyuan stands motionless, like a man in a trance. Fanyi returns at once, wailing dementedly.*) He — he —

ZHOU: He — he —

(*They both run into the study.*)

(*Curtain*)

of us with his fists and his feet.

ZHOU: Get away, you savage.

SERVANT: Yes, sir.

ZHOU (angrily): Go after him, then, and bring him
     back here.

SERVANT: Very good, sir.

All except PU SHIH go out, leaving only PU-YUAN. FAN
     I-P'ING and LU SSU on the stage.)

ZHOU (broken-hearted): We love one son. (Looks at
     LU SSU in turn.)

(They do not move.)

MA: Let them all go! Perhaps it's best that he has
     gone. I know what the boy's like. He's bursting
     with hatred. He won't come back.

ZHOU (one of resignation): In the sudden silence, I
     doesn't seem fine, that the policemen have got
     him and let he out — (Suddenly shouts) Where's
     P'ing, P'ing! (No reply.) (Come here,
     somebody! Where are you all?) (Still no reply.)
     Go and find him for me! There's my eldest son.
     (He screams of a violent spot from the stage, as if
     a wooden by a door.) (Silence on the stage.)

FAN (suddenly): Oh! (She cries, and then shudders.)
     Peiyuan, Peiyuan, (soliloquizes.) He is mad. He's
     mad. I keep telling it about, without meaning
     to. (Weeps.) He — the —

ZHOU: He — he —

(Goes hesitant into the study.)

(Curtain.)